THE SYSTEM

JACK KREIGE

THE SYSTEM

THE L.E.N.A. PROJECT IS CONTROLLING THEIR MINDS

VISION HOUSE
PUBLISHING, INC.

THE SYSTEM
© 1995 by Jack W. Kriege

Published by Vision House Publishing, Inc.
1217 NE Burnside, Suite 403
Gresham, Oregon 97030

Printed in the United States of America.

International Standard Book Number: 1-885305-23-0

95 96 97 98 99 00 01 02 03 04 - 10 9 8 7 6 5 4 3 2 1

1

Spots of white light moved slowly across the dark walls and ceiling of the gymnasium as the loud, monotonous beat of the music droned on. Tom Kerzig looked to the raised platform at one end of the gym, his eyes tracing the outline of the massive black speakers. A solitary person stood behind the huge amplifying system. His body moved slowly to the beat as his fingers ran across a set of stacked tapes, in search of the next twenty-minute segment. On his head was a sound-retarding device that resembled a set of heavy ear-phones. Tom wished he were wearing those. On the floor, the bodies of several hundred students bobbed up and down in rhythm with the music, their arms and heads swaying errati-cally from side to side. Another hundred or so sat on the bleachers, some nodding in time with the beat, some talking among themselves, and others quietly watching.

Tom slowly circled the dance area. In an hour and a half, he had been around eleven times. This time he met Joe Carter, the vice principal, walking slowly in the opposite direction. He raised his hand as they approached one another. Joe said something, but Tom couldn't hear over the blare of the music, so he cupped his hand to his ear.

Joe stepped up to him and spoke loudly into his ear. "I said, are you having fun yet?"

"Are we supposed to be having fun?" yelled Tom.

Joe motioned for Tom to follow him. They walked to the corner of the gymnasium opposite the sound system and stepped into a partially sheltered alcove near the entrance.

"Am I just getting older, or do these get louder every year?" asked Tom.

Joe laughed. "Both."

"Didn't I see you take out some boys out a few minutes ago?"

"Yeah, three of them," said Joe. "They keep pushing. They come in high and think they can con me."

"Alcohol?" asked Tom.

Joe shook his head. "No. They know that's too easy to detect. These guys had been smoking pot. But they should know by now I can pick that out from all the way across the gym, too."

"What'd you do with them?"

"Kicked them out for tonight and told them to be in my office Monday morning. I may be called on the carpet for that."

"Why?"

Joe brushed his hand across his close-cropped hair and shook his head. "I've been dealing with these kids for twenty years. I can tell like *that*—," he snapped his fingers, "by the smell and their behavior. That used to be all that was needed. But in the last few years the district has really gotten soft. They seem to want us to have some kind of proof of clear and present danger before we take any disciplinary action."

"Don't let down, Joe," said Tom. "You're doing a good job."

"Well..."

A shaft of light from the outside fixture shot into the alcove as one of the doors opened. Tom looked up and saw Bonnie Teague enter the gym. She was his English department chair, but that was certainly not the image she portrayed tonight. She wore a tight-fitting red evening gown and a large white heart dangled from a gold chain around her neck. She smiled and waved as she saw them.

"Hi, Bonnie," said Tom.

Joe glanced toward her, then snapped his head quickly in her direction. "You aren't on the list for supervision tonight."

"Oh, I know," said Bonnie. "I was out driving around and decided to stop by for a while to see if I could be of any help."

Joe smiled. "Do you always drive around in full evening dress?"

Bonnie smiled coyly and shrugged. "Whenever the mood directs me." She swayed her shoulders to the beat of the music. "Besides, a lot of my LENA students are here tonight, and I want to observe their creative flow."

Joe shook his head and chuckled. "I thought the board was considering not continuing that program next year."

Bonnie halted her rhythmic movement abruptly and scowled. "Absolutely not! They just reacted politically to that crazy religious-right bunch at the last meeting. They'll be making a decision next month to continue the pilot and expand the program to the whole school."

"They'll be making a decision next month, all right," agreed Joe. "But you don't know what it'll be."

Bonnie smiled and rubbed her finger across Joe's lapel. "Well...a little encouragement from you guys certainly wouldn't hurt!"

"I need some questions about the program answered first," said Tom. "That's why I asked you for some time on the English department meeting agenda. I looked at the state's basic skills test results for those kids. Their scores have been declining."

Bonnie tossed her hand downward in disgust. "Those little state tests! They're trying to measure an oil field with a dip stick! There are rivers of awareness underneath the surface. It just takes time to tap them."

"It doesn't have to be done at the expense of basic skills, does it?" asked Tom.

Bonnie turned from him, swaying in time to the music once again. She rhythmically walked away, along the foot of the bleachers.

Joe shook his head. "Rivers of awareness..."

"That's Bonnie. But at least she's interested in her kids."

"Yeah, real interested. Whenever there's a dance, the mood seems to direct her here," said Joe. "She flits up in her little red Porsche."

"Oh?"

Joe nodded. "I don't think she's missed one in three years. She saunters in, dressed to kill, gets the boys all excited, and then saunters out."

"Walt insists she doesn't mean anything by it, though," said Tom.

"Are you kidding me?"

Tom shook his head. "That's what he told me. I talked to him after I overheard some of my twelfth-grade boys making some comments. I asked him if he thought she was displaying the wrong kind of role model."

"And he probably explained it away on the basis of the program."

Tom was silent for a moment as he recalled the meeting he'd had with Walt. "You're right," he said finally. "He said he thought her actions were harmless."

"Sure. She's just reaching deep within her inner self, raising their level of consciousness!" Joe said sarcastically.

Tom laughed. "I think that's exactly what he said."

"I know." He slapped Tom on the chest with the back of his hand. "Because he told me the same thing. By the way, you'd better be on your guard. I've heard it said she'd like to raise your level of consciousness."

Tom laughed and shook his head. "Not to worry. Besides, I'm not divorced, you know. Just...just separated." The word still sounded strange coming from his lips. He had used it many times in reference to others. But he never thought it would happen to Clair and him.

The smile left Joe's face and he moved his hand from Tom's chest and squeezed his arm. "Yeah, I know. How's that going, by the way?"

"No change yet," Tom mumbled.

"I can't understand what got into Clair," Joe said. "What's it been, now? Two...three..."

"Four months."

"She knows the door's open, doesn't she?" Joe asked.

"Sure. She says she isn't ready even to think about it."

Joe shook his head in disgust. "That's absurd!" He squeezed Tom's arm again and jerked his head to the right. "C'mon. I'll buy you a glass of punch."

"Sounds good."

They stepped out of the alcove and walked along the end wall of the gymnasium toward a temporary refreshment stand. The line closest to the wall opened up, and a bright smile greeted them.

"May I help you, Mr. Carter?" the server asked.

"You sure may, Joni," said Joe. "We'd like two glasses of punch."

"All right." She picked up two glasses from a table in the center of the stand and placed them on the counter before the two men. "That'll be a dollar."

Joe pulled a dollar from his wallet and handed it to her. "Joni, do you have Mr. Kerzig for any of your classes? Do you know each other?"

Joni reached out her hand and shook Tom's firmly. "We go to the same church."

Tom squinted and placed his finger on the bridge of his nose. Then he remembered. "Of course, you're Lloyd and Sally's daughter. Good to see you again."

"I haven't seen you around church lately," Joni said.

"No," Tom admitted. "I'm afraid I haven't been very regular."

Joni put on a feigned scowl and shook her finger at him. "Well, you'd better start coming again, before staying away gets to be a habit." Joni smiled, then looked over their shoulders. "May I help you?"

Tom and Joe moved away to allow room for those behind them and walked slowly back toward the alcove.

"Now there's a girl who'll keep you in line," Joe said.

"Yeah, she's always been a good kid."

"She's in the program, you know?"

"She is?"

Yeah, but she's different from the other kids," Joe went on. "She's bright and confident. But the others are more...I don't know...self-centered."

The music suddenly stopped and a bright spotlight illuminated the center of the amplifier platform where a microphone stood. A student climbed up the stairs to the platform and spoke to the technician, who lifted one side of his sound retarders to hear what he was saying. The technician nodded and the student walked up to the microphone.

"Good evening, all!" the student greeted the crowd.

"Good evening!" the students chanted.

The student, Charlie Shaeffer, was in Tom's fourth-period English class. He wasn't one of Tom's top students, but he was popular and always in the middle of things. Tom expected him to succeed in life.

Charlie raised his finger and spoke in forced tones. "It's

riddle time! How are valentines and vice principals alike?" A broad smile crossed his face.

The crowd snickered and Charlie waited.

"They both display big hearts." Charlie raised his finger again. "Once a year!"

The students broke out in raucous laughter and looked toward Joe. He smiled and waved in response.

Charlie silenced them and continued. "You should all be very proud of yourselves. This is the most successful Valentine's Day dance ever." He pulled a piece of paper out of his pocket. "The net proceeds are..." He looked at the paper and smiled sheepishly. "On another piece of paper."

A loud booing rose from the crowd. Charlie quickly took another piece of paper from another pocket and motioned for them to be silent.

"The net proceeds are...$2,312!"

The students cheered wildly.

"And now—the person who will help us decide how to spend all this money—your student-body president...Mark Banazech!"

Charlie motioned toward the end of the platform where another student was mounting the steps. The crowd cheered and applauded in a slow, rhythmic cadence. Mark's tall, muscular frame towered over Charlie, and he rested his arm on the smaller boy's shoulder.

"Thanks, Charlie. I knew we could count on you for a big profit!" He patted Charlie on the shoulder. "Now go and put it in the bank."

"Ah, yes...interest!" Charlie turned and walked quickly off the stage.

"Well, are you all having a good time?" Mark extended his arms to the crowd.

The students cheered in response. Tom had never had

Mark in any of his classes but knew quite a bit about him. Mark seemed to have it all—he was good looking, popular, a football star, A.S.B. president, and, of course, in the program. And if that wasn't enough, his father was a successful psychiatrist and able to supplement his son's athletic scholarship with sufficient funds to send him to the most prestigious university in the state next year.

"Well, as you all know," Mark began, "the time has come for my favorite part of the evening—the president's choice dance!"

Squeals and cheers erupted from the crowd.

"Now which one of you beautiful ladies will I have the privilege of dancing with tonight?"

All of the girls screamed and shouted for him to choose them. Mark smiled as he listened to the clamoring cries. Then he motioned for silence, extended his finger, and moved it silently above their heads.

"I choose..." A hush fell over the students as Mark's finger stretched directly toward the concession stand. "Joni Irving!"

The cheer of the crowd overwhelmed the disappointed moans of the wishful girls. Tom looked toward the concession stand. Joni stood there, frowning and shaking her head.

"You can't refuse me, Joni," Mark commanded. "Those are the rules!"

"What's he trying to pull?" Joe mumbled. "He knows she doesn't go for all of this."

"Come on, Joni," Mark persisted.

Joni's arms were crossed now, and she was still shaking her head.

"Does somebody want to help her?" asked Mark.

Suddenly, six squealing girls emerged from the back of the crowd and ran toward the concession stand. They yanked open the gate, grabbed Joni, and pulled her out.

"I wonder if I should stop this," Joe mumbled. Then he shook his head. "No...she can handle it."

As the girls brought Joni to the center of the gymnasium floor, the other students formed a large circle around her. The girls patted her gently, and rejoined the crowd. Joni was still frowning as Mark jumped down from the platform and walked slowly toward her. The spotlight followed him and the other lights were extinguished, leaving the two alone in the soft circle of light.

Mark looked back toward the platform and nodded. A slow, quiet sound emerged from the speakers and then the notes of a plaintive waltz filled the room. Joni shrugged and Mark took her right hand, placing his own hand carefully behind her back. They began to dance.

"You were right," Tom said. "She's handling it."

"Well...as long as he doesn't pull something dumb."

The crowd of students were quiet as Mark and Joni danced gracefully about the spacious area. Tom sighed in relief as he listened to the pleasant music. He was glad to see that at least two young people could still do a real dance. Then, as the final chords of the slow waltz began to fade, Mark pushed Joni gently away, but held tightly to her right hand. He looked toward the platform and nodded. Suddenly the speakers exploded with a percussive sound and a deafening synthesized thump. Joni shook her head and tried to pull away, but Mark held her hand tight. The students cheered in anticipation as another explosive percussion sounded. Mark spun Joni about and then pulled her close to his body, now bobbing sensuously with the rhythm.

"I was afraid of this." Joe began to push his way through the crowd, but then Joni freed her hand from Mark's grasp. She walked quickly to the ring of students and forced her way back toward the concession stand. A moment later Joe returned to his place beside Tom.

Mark was still moving slowly in the center of the lighted area and looking around him. "Well then...someone else?" Screams gushed forth and at least fifty girls raised their hands. "All right. How about you?" Mark pointed to one girl, who screamed and entered the circle of light. "And you..." Mark continued to turn. "And you..."

Mark raised his hands above his head as the three girls approached him. He moved and spun, first with one girl, and then with another while the synthesized sounds echoed loudly through the gymnasium. The students clapped and cheered in rhythm with the beat. Joe shook his head in disgust and walked back toward the alcove.

Tom glanced toward an open spot in front of the bleachers where a white heart bobbed wildly above a red dress. The slowly circling spots of white light fell upon her face and body and cast her sensuous movements into a false appearance of slow motion. Her eyes were closed and her body swayed back and forth in the semi-darkness, while her short dark hair followed the gliding motion of her head. Most of the students were watching Mark and the three girls, but a few boys now gathered about Bonnie, clapping and chanting as they watched her dance. The music rose to a frenzied pitch and Mark's movements in the center of the circle seemed mirrored by Bonnie's on the outside. And then, after a few diminishing percussive sounds, the music stopped.

Mark and the three girls bowed to the cheers of the hundreds of students watching them while on the outside, Bonnie straightened her dress, looked around, and waved her fingers at the boys. She began walking back in front of the bleachers, followed by the small group of cheering boys. She smiled and waved to Tom and Joe as she approached the alcove. Joe, his arms folded, scowled at the boys. They stopped and sheepishly returned to the bleachers.

The lights in the gymnasium abruptly came on and the technician announced a brief intermission during which he would set up the next series of tapes.

Bonnie, fanning her face with her hand, smiled at Tom and Joe. "My, it's warm, isn't it?" She was close enough now that Tom could see the perspiration trickling from her face and down the open neck of her dress. Her heavy mascara was streaked. "These lights are too bright."

"You're getting too old for this, Bonnie," Joe said.

"Never, Joe. Someday you'll understand." She gestured aimlessly toward the platform. "The sound...the movement...," she looked at the men and cocked her head, "they hold the meaning of life!" She fanned her face again and walked out the door into the night.

"Well..." Joe looked at Tom and raised his eyebrows. "Harmless?"

"I don't know, Joe. I'm probably not the best judge. I've been accused of being out of touch with modern times."

"Goodnight, Mr. Carter. Goodnight, Mr. Kerzig." Joni was walking past them, her coat draped across her arm.

"Oh, Joni." Joe beckoned to her. "Listen...are you all right?"

"What? Oh..." She looked toward the center of the gymnasium. "Oh, that. Sure, Mr. Carter. Sometimes you just have to go along with people's games...to a point."

"Well, I'm glad you know where that point is," Joe said.

"You're not staying for the rest of the dance?" Tom asked.

"No. I was only on concession duty for the first two hours. I don't even like dances. And it's just going to get worse, because the music will get louder—and weirder!" She crinkled her nose.

The lights in the gymnasium were extinguished then, and a rapid sequence of laser beams shot through the room. A deafening beat shook the walls. Tom watched Joni move off into the partial darkness. She smiled, waved, and voiced an inaudible "goodbye."

Tom felt a hand on his arm and turned to see the school's night security guard leaning toward him. "Mr. Kerzig..."

"Oh, hi, Pete. What is it?"

"Every hour I listen to the recorded telephone messages," the guard explained. "There was one from your wife." He glanced at a scribbled note in his hand. "She sounded pretty upset. Said something about your daughter, Jennifer, being missing."

"What?"

"I don't know when the call came in," the guard continued. "Could have been an hour ago, or just..."

"You'd better go, Tom!" Joe shouted over the din of the music.. "You'd better find out what's going on!"

"Yeah, thanks," Tom mumbled.

Tom moved toward the exit, but hundreds of bodies had converged on the dance floor and it was now a sea of bobbing students. A single laser beam shown on a slowly spinning crystal. Its rays fractured and spilled out on the dancing figures. The thump of the bass and the scream of the guitars blended into an indiscernible moan as Tom pushed his way through the undulating bodies. He was jostled to and fro and his ears rang from the piercing of the wailing instruments. He watched the spinning of the light and the simulated slow motion of the dancing bodies. He felt his feet stepping unwillingly to the beat of the music. Step...step...step, two, three, four...four...four months.... He recalled the unreality of that moment...Clair..."have to get away for a while," she'd said... "find myself." He had thought at first it was a dream—a nightmare. But it had really happened. And now Jennifer...

Tom forced his way through the last group of students and burst through the door. The cool air exploded into his face and mingled with his perspiration as he ran toward his car.

2

Tom bounded up the four steps leading to the porch and banged on the door. No lights were on in the house, but Clair's car was in the driveway, so he was sure she was home. He banged again, more loudly.

The porch light suddenly glared and Tom squinted. The front door opened slowly. Through the screen Tom could see Clair. She was wearing her robe and looked as though she had just gotten up. He stared at her slim figure and momentarily forgot about Jennifer. Clair's short blond hair touched her shoulders and fell casually about the soft features of her face. She wasn't wearing any makeup. How often had he told her she didn't need it? He reached out, but the tips of his fingers only touched the rough texture of the screen wire.

"Tom?..." Clair looked at him, a question in her eyes.

"What's going on?" he asked. "What about Jennifer?"

"Jennifer? Oh!" She slapped the palm of her hand against her forehead. "I'm sorry. I guess you didn't get the second message. I called again about forty-five minutes ago."

"Is she all right?"

"Yes. I just..." Clair grinned sheepishly and shrugged, "I just forgot she was going on a field trip with her class. They went to dinner and to an astrological program. She just got home at 10:00."

A sudden wave of relief swept over Tom. But then it was quickly replaced with anger. "Astrological program? Home at ten o'clock? That still doesn't sound right."

"Oh. Well, that's because," Clair raised her fist to her mouth and yawned, "Jennifer's in a different class this semester. She's done well in her studies, you know, and her teacher recommended her for that special program."

"You mean the *LENA* program?"

"I think that's what they call it. She's been in it for two weeks now, and..."

"Why didn't you tell me about it?" Tom interrupted.

Clair gave him an exasperated look. "I didn't think you'd mind. Is there a problem? I mean, it's your school system, after all."

"I know, but I should have been told," Tom said heatedly.

"It's just another class!"

Clair obviously didn't see anything wrong with what she had done, but Tom resented being left out of decisions that affected his daughter.

"Look, maybe I should just speak with her." Tom pulled at the screen door handle, but the door didn't move. It was locked.

"Not tonight, Tom. She's asleep."

"Tomorrow's Saturday," he reminded her.

"She was tired. And so am I."

Tom hated this. Being locked out of his own house.

"I'm sorry I got you all upset over nothing," Clair continued.

Tom sighed heavily. Then he stepped closer to the screen door and placed the palms of his hands against it. "Clair, why can't we..."

Clair stepped back and shook her head slowly. "Don't start anything. Just...I'll see you next weekend when you come to pick up Jennifer."

Clair tossed Tom a vague wave and slowly closed the door. The porch light was extinguished and Tom was left standing in the darkness.

Tom had no reason to return to the dance. By the time he got there it would be wrapping up. He called Joe's home and left word with his wife about the mix-up over Jennifer and then decided to drive up the local scenic mountain road just to distance himself from everything. From the lookout point halfway up the mountain he studied the flickering lights below. Here he could put things in better perspective. Everything was smaller from here, even the problems. He was never able to stay mad at Clair, even before the separation. And now even his anger over being left out of decisions concerning Jennifer's education had mellowed into a general melancholy over the loss of his wife's presence.

Tom sighed heavily, leaned against the metal railing, and gazed out at the city. He could see the school...and their home...and his apartment. They were all still there as one in the large scheme of things. If he could only understand what caused her to pull away, then perhaps he could deal with the situation. Instead he was faced with the continual frustration of not knowing what he did, didn't do, or might have done.

Tom pushed himself back slightly from the cold railing and glanced at his watch. It was after midnight. Suddenly he heard the sound of a high-pitched engine in the distance. Headlights shone momentarily from about a quarter mile up the winding road, disappeared behind the mountains, and reappeared. The sound of the engine magnified as a red Porsche raced past him down the narrow road, its tires squealing. Bonnie's car! What was she doing up here? And why was she racing down the mountain like that?

Anxiety spread over Tom as he watched the little auto careen down the mountain road. Then his stomach lurched as the long, high-pitched sound of braked tires echoed through the mountains followed by the clatter of splintered wood, a muffled impact.

Tom bolted into his car, started the engine, and spun out of the lookout point. He turned on his bright lights and studied the guard rail as he headed down the mountain road. Then, after about a half mile, he saw the broken railing, and the gaping opening. He pulled off the road behind the fractured railing, set his parking brake, and activated his hazard lights. He was climbing out of his car when he saw the figure of a man about an eighth of a mile down the road. The man appeared to be jogging away from the crash site. Surely he had heard the crash. Why didn't he offer to help?

As Tom looked down through the break in the railing he felt some relief. This section wasn't as steep as some and it was partially wooded. Bonnie's car was about two hundred feet down the slope, its hood smashed into the trunk of a large tree.

Tom quickly slid down the slope until he reached the car. The driver's door was open and a hand reached toward it from inside the car.

"Bonnie!" Tom shouted as he slid to a stop.

Bonnie's legs were spread awkwardly across the passenger's side of the car and she was struggling to pull herself from the interior.

"Wait a minute...wait!" Tom took Bonnie's arm and prevented her from moving. The overhead light shone weakly, and he could see blood running down her face from what appeared to be a large gash in her forehead.

"Out...have to get out!" Bonnie shoved her feet suddenly against the opposite door, pushing her body halfway out of the car.

"Hold on! Your back may be injured!" Tom held her carefully under her arms and let her slide gently from the car onto the ground.

"Out...out...go!" Bonnie continued screaming and flailing her arms. Her eyes were covered with blood and she apparently couldn't see.

Tom took out his handkerchief and wiped the blood from her face. "Bonnie! Bonnie, it's Tom! Tom Kerzig! Stop moving!"

Bonnie suddenly stopped thrusting her arms about and forced her eyelids open. "Tom..." She turned her head quickly from side to side. "Where...where is..." She winced and laid her fingers against her swollen lips.

"Lie still. You slid about two hundred feet off the road. Here..." Tom folded his bloody handkerchief into a small pad and placed it on her head wound, "put your hand on this." He took Bonnie's hand and placed it on the handkerchief.

He had to get help. If only that jogger had returned. He climbed a few feet up the slippery slope, and then saw a car's headlights stop before the opening in the rail. The figure of a man appeared in the beam of the lights.

"Is anyone hurt down there?" the man called.

"Yes! She needs help! Call an ambulance!"

The man nodded and disappeared from the beams. The car's engine raced as the car sped down the road.

Tom ran back and knelt beside Bonnie. She was tossing her head from side to side moaning. Her hand fell to her chest and she pulled at the gold chain hanging around her neck. The large white heart at the end of it was crushed. She giggled. "Broken heart!"

"Try to lie still, Bonnie."

"The music, Tom. You can dance with me now."

Tom glanced into the interior of the wrecked car. The cassette was still playing and the steady thump of rock music issued from the speakers. He reached into the car and turned off the cassette.

"No!" Bonnie cried. "Turn it on. Turn it up!"

Tom shook his head, sighed, and turned the unit back on. The rock music blared again and he felt Bonnie's foot tapping against his leg in rhythm. He started to push himself back out of the car, when an object, glistening in the reflection of the dim interior light, caught his eye. It was a large crystal, hanging from the rearview mirror by a gold chain similar to the one that held Bonnie's heart. It moved back and forth slowly. The slivers of light it had captured were magnified and projected outward in a kaleidoscopic pattern. He reached out and stilled the motion.

"Yes, the crystal," Bonnie mumbled. "Let me have the crystal."

Tom gave Bonnie a disapproving look. But he removed the crystal from the mirror, pushed himself out of the car, and handed it to her. Trembling, she reached forward eagerly and took it.

"Yes, thank you." Bonnie placed her elbow against her ribs, lifted her thumb against the crystal, and dangled it in front of her eyes. The moonlight seemed to focus its soft light on the tiny pendant and be held periodically captive by the moving stone.

"Need to concentrate...meditate..." Bonnie sighed heavily as she gazed at the crystal. Her body gradually ceased its trembling and her breathing became more relaxed and regular. A moaning appeared to issue from her lips. But it wasn't a painful groan. It was a kind of chant that fell from her mouth as she exhaled. "Omm...omm...omm..."

Tom stood up, leaned back against the fender of the car, and tried to reconstruct the events of the evening. Bonnie left the dance just before he did. Why had she driven up here? He could smell no alcohol on her, or in the car. Just the speed, the recklessness. But, then, that was Bonnie.

Tom heard the sound of sirens in the distance and

looked up toward the road. He couldn't believe the motorist could have contacted them so quickly.

Tom let his arms fall against the car and breathed more easily. The cool metal reverberated with the beat of the music. The pulsating chords blended dissonantly with the approaching siren. But Bonnie's voice rose above the eerie accompaniment. Tom glanced down at her prone figure and listened to the monotonous syllable resound rhythmically from her swollen lips. "Omm...omm...omm..."

3

Tom sipped his coffee, set the cup down on his desk, and looked out the classroom windows. The early morning fog had not yet dissipated, and he could barely discern the flag-pole which stood a hundred feet from the building. He set the stack of Friday's papers aside and studied his lesson plans for the week. He appreciated having the first class period free, because it gave him the opportunity to review his students' work from the previous day and plan any needed modifica-tions to his plans. Mondays were usually good days for him, but this morning a slight headache nagged him. He attrib-uted it to a residual from Friday night's loud musical intru-sion, the concern over Jennifer, and of course, the experience with Bonnie.

Tom looked up as the door to his classroom swung open and the principal, Walt Josephson, stuck his head inside.

"Good morning, Tom. Are you free?"

"Morning, Walt. Sure. Come on in."

Walt entered the room and shut the door behind him. He was a short, slightly built man, with thin, curly hair and half-glasses which perched low on his nose. He picked up a straight-backed chair from the corner, placed it facing Tom at the side of the desk, and sat down.

"Any word on Bonnie's condition?" Tom asked.

"Well, she's banged up pretty badly. She has a concussion and some internal injuries."

"Is she still in the hospital?"

"Yes. I saw her last night. She was doing pretty well, but I think she'll be there for several more days."

"I'll be sure to visit her," Tom said.

"Good...good. Listen, I need to ask you a favor. I don't know how long she's going to be out, and I'm reluctant to bring in a substitute, because Bonnie has the LENA program. I really hate to break the continuity. Especially now, with the decision for its expansion coming up. She teaches only four periods, you know. And she has a different grade level each period."

"Yes."

"I'd like to distribute her load to some of the other teachers during their free periods," Walt said. "You've had an introduction to the program, and I think you could do a much better job than any substitute I could bring in."

Tom smiled. "When you say *you*, I guess that means you want me to take one of those assignments."

"Yes, that's right." Walt paused for a moment and lowered his head slightly as he looked at Tom over the top of his half-glasses. "You'd receive additional pay, of course."

Tom hesitated. "Well...*this* is my free period."

"I know and I'm really glad about that, because Bonnie has seniors this period, and there's no one I'd feel more comfortable about with those kids than you."

"Hmm..." Tom sighed and fanned his thumb aimlessly through the stack of compositions on his desk.

"I know you like this time to plan, but this is really a critical need."

"You have no idea how long she'll be out?"

"I don't. Not yet."

Tom removed his hand from the papers and shrugged. "Sure, Walt. I'll do it."

Walt smiled broadly and sat back in his chair. "I really appreciate it."

"Who's taking the class right now?"

"Oh, Joe's in there supervising until you get there," Walt said.

Tom raised his eyebrow and scowled. "You were pretty sure of yourself, weren't you?"

Walt laughed nervously. "Well, I just know what a caring, dedicated teacher you are and..."

"Sure!"

"Oh, one more thing." Walt stood up, shoved his hand into his pocket, and brought out a set of keys. "You'll be opening up each day, so I'll give these to you." He handed Tom the keys. "Thanks again. And...uh...Joe will appreciate it if you get there as soon as possible."

"I'll go right in."

"Great!" Walt turned and walked out of the room.

Tom lifted his briefcase from beside the desk, opened it, and tossed in his lesson plans and the compositions. He would have to spend more time in the evening on preparation, but that was okay. He looked forward to the challenge. The LENA program had previously been merely a source of curiosity to him. But now that Jennifer was involved in the program, it was important for him to learn more about it, and what better way than to teach it. He gulped down the rest of his coffee, picked up his briefcase and left the room.

When Tom entered Bonnie's room, Joe was pacing slowly back and forth at the front of the class, his arms folded in front of him. The students were intent on reading, although a few looked up as Tom came in. Without unfolding his arms, Joe waved a hand at Tom and walked behind Bonnie's desk. Tom placed his briefcase on the floor and joined him.

"Thanks for agreeing to take the class," Joe said.

"Sure, but it looks like you're doing a pretty good job."

"Not bad for an old P. E. teacher, I guess." Joe then raised his voice and spoke deliberately toward the students. "Although, I did ask them what they thought of my idea for a book I want to write some day: *Personal Reflections of a Black Athlete in a White Society*. They told me the idea was trite!" He turned away in mock injury. "So I just gave them a tough reading assignment."

A few students laughed quietly.

Joe pointed to a list on the desk. "Here's the class roster."

"Do you have a copy of Bonnie's lesson plans?" Tom asked.

"Lesson plans? From Bonnie?"

"Well, I'll look around. There must be something."

"Good luck!" Joe said.

Tom picked up the roster and glanced at the names. He knew only two of the students: Mark Banazech and Joni Irving. He looked out over the seated students. Mark sat in the back corner, his large frame slumped in his small desk. Joni sat in the front row. He set the roster down and looked at a calendar beside it. A small notation on today's date caught his eye: *Compositions Due Today*. "Well, that's something, at least," he muttered.

"Do you need anything else?" Joe asked.

"Do they all know what happened to Bonnie?"

"As much as I could tell them."

"I guess that's all, then," Tom said.

"Okay." Joe waved and left the room.

Tom looked at his watch, and saw that only about twenty minutes remained in the class period. He picked up a piece of chalk and printed *Mr. Kerzig* in large letters in the upper left-hand corner of the chalkboard. Then he stepped in front of the desk and addressed the class. "Good morning. Some of you know me, I believe. I'm Mr. Kerzig and I'll be teaching this class for a while. I'll learn your names as quickly as I can, but for a while, I'm afraid I'll be doing a lot of pointing."

The students laughed lightly and shifted in their desks.

"I'm not very familiar with the LENA program," Tom said. "Let's use the rest of our time today with a few of you describing some of the things you've been doing in class." Tom looked around the room. "Who'd like to start?" After a brief pause, a boy raised his hand. Tom nodded to him. "Yes...and give your name, please."

"Marshall," the boy said. "First of all, this is an English class, but we do a lot more than just study grammar and literature. Bonnie told us that..."

"Excuse me," Tom interrupted. "You mean *Miss Teague?*" He emphasized her last name.

Some of the students snickered.

"Well, yeah. But she wants us to call her Bonnie," Marshall said. "She says it helps break down the denial of self that we all experience."

"I see. All right. Go on."

"Anyway, Bonnie says that language is nothing more than an expression of man's inner needs and desires, and the better understanding we have of our inner being, the farther we can progress with our language."

"Okay, that's a good start," Tom said. "Let's see... Why don't we talk about something you did recently? I noticed Friday afternoon that some students were taking down a display in the back of the room. Was that for one of your activities?"

Several hands went up and Tom nodded to a girl in the back of the room.

"I'm Mary Ann," the girl said. "Bonnie says she does that every Valentine's Day It's called a love relationship simulation."

"You'll have to explain that," Tom said.

"Well, there are many kinds of love," Mary Ann began. "And many different kinds of relationships are entered into for the expression of love. The way each of us looks at love and relationships is different from others in the class, and usually different from what our parents think. Bonnie says it's really important that we analyze this in terms of our own value system."

"I see." *Of course,* Tom thought. *Values clarification. Bonnie was really big on that.* He remembered arguing with her once that he felt way too much school time was spent on it. He didn't really want to pursue this, but he would have to let the girl finish. "So describe the purpose of the simulation," he said.

"Well, two people stand up in front of the class, and pretend to be...relating." She blushed slightly and several girls giggled. "On Friday, I did one with Jim. Ah...Beth and Frank did one. And...oh, yeah...Jason and Mike."

Jason and Mike? Tom wondered what he was in for. *Don't react...not yet. Just bring it to a conclusion.* "So, explain the simulation."

"Well, the two people describe their feelings for one another and some of the things they do together," Mary Ann continued. "Then the class discusses how their feelings and actions enhance or interfere with the development of each of their personal value systems."

"Okay. Let's talk about another activity." Tom wanted to leave this subject without expressing too much discomfort. "What did you do earlier in the week?" He called on a boy near the front.

"My name's Andrew. On Monday we did creative visualization. It was great."

"Explain, please."

"Bonnie told us that the regular school program inhibits our imaginations by restricting us to the narrow field of familiar things," Andrew explained. "You know, like the classroom, the desks, the books...even the people we know. So she had us meditate for a few minutes and try to imagine ourselves...outside of ourselves. Do you know what I mean?"

"I'm not sure," Tom admitted.

"Well, if we're up here..." Andrew held his hand high above his head to illustrate. "We can still see all those real things, but we can also see ourselves. We're not limited by time and space—we can see beyond reality. And the images just whiz by!"

"What did you do then?"

"We spent the rest of the class period talking about some of the things we visualized. Then Bonnie told us to go home and practice for a few days and write a composition about our external experiences."

"That must be the composition that's due today," Tom said.

A few students gently chided the boy for telling Tom about the assignment.

"We just have a few minutes left," Tom said, "so let's talk about that assignment. I know you invest a lot of effort in your compositions and you deserve a quick response from me. So, I'll pick them up today and try to read them and make mechanical notations by Wednesday. I'll hand them back then and you can rewrite them, making the needed corrections, then turn them back in to me on Friday for grading."

The students looked at one another and shifted nervously in their desks.

"Is there a problem with that?" Tom asked.

After a few moments, Mark raised his hand. Tom pointed to him and he said, "Bonnie never has us make mechanical corrections on our compositions. She says it stifles our creativity."

A number of the students nodded.

"Hmm..." Tom scratched the back of his head. "Well...I'll tell you what. I'm teaching the class now, so we'll be doing a few things differently. I'm afraid this is one of them."

The students groaned. Their moaning soon was interrupted by the sound of the bell.

"You're dismissed," Tom said. "Just give me your compositions on the way out."

The students filed silently out of the class, tossing their compositions on Bonnie's desk as they went. Mark was the only one who did not come forward. Instead, he left through the back door. Tom picked up the stack of papers, straightened them, then looked up to see Joni approaching the desk.

She placed her composition on the top of the stack and looked up at him. "Mr. Kerzig, I just want you to know that I appreciate what you're doing."

"What do you mean?"

"The mechanical corrections," she said. "Since I've been in the program, I've had to pick up a lot of the basic skills myself. It'll be good to have some help."

"I'm glad you feel that way," Tom said. "How long have you been in the program?"

"Since the seventh grade."

"From the beginning, then. You're a veteran."

"Yeah, I guess."

"Well, I'm not sure yet what I think about the focus of the program," Tom said, "but I'll do the best I can."

"There are a lot of things I don't like about the program,"

Joni said. "Especially in English. Miss Teague spends so much time on values and visualization and inner exploration, that nothing concrete ever seems to come out."

"Well, I think her plan is to start with the inner discovery and then work toward the more concrete things."

"Maybe..." Joni hesitated, then, "It's too bad about her accident."

"It sure is."

Joni walked slowly to the door, then turned back again. "Mr. Kerzig..."

"Yes?"

"You probably don't know much about how it happened, do you?"

"No, not much."

She stood in the doorway for a moment. Then she spoke haltingly, "Maybe somebody should know. Friday night, when she left the dance..."

"Yes?"

Joni's head dropped. Then she looked up again and spoke quickly, "She wasn't alone." She turned around and left abruptly.

Tom stared at the empty door frame. It took a moment for Joni's words to register. "Wait a minute, Joni!"

Tom stepped quickly to the doorway, but he ran into Marla Vedder, who had just stepped inside.

"Excuse me, Marla! I wasn't watching where I was going."

"Oh, that's all right, Mr. Kerzig," Marla said.

Tom tilted his head and squinted. "Mr. Kerzig?"

Marla lowered her head and placed her hand to her face. "Sorry. I haven't made the transition yet." She looked up again and smiled. "Tom," she said deliberately. "It's not easy."

Marla was a new teacher this semester. She had graduated from the school just five years ago. Tom remembered her because she was one of the brightest students in his eleventh-grade English class. He had recommended her for participation in the LENA program the following year—the first year of the project's inception.

"Come in." Tom gestured broadly.

Marla shrugged and entered the room. "It's too bad about Bonnie, isn't it?

"Yeah, it really is," Tom said.

"I heard you were taking her senior class. I just thought I'd stop by and see how the first day turned out."

"Well, I guess things went well. I must admit some of the activities seem strange to me."

"Yes, the LENA program is different from the standard curriculum," Marla said. "I'm sure it will take some getting used to."

Tom nodded. "So, how were your first two weeks of teaching?"

"All right, I think. It sure is different from what I learned in college, though."

"Yeah."

"Even with the practice teaching I did, there's so much *responsibility*."

"You're in charge," Tom agreed.

Marla nodded. "It's awesome!"

Tom laughed. "You'll do fine, Marla."

"I was talking to Mr. Carter today, and..."

"You mean Joe?"

Marla smiled. "Don't push too fast. He's the vice principal, after all. Anyway, I was talking to Mr. Carter...Joe...today. He thought it would be a good idea if I had a helping teacher...one I could go to with questions."

"That's a good idea."

"So he said you were the best English teacher in the school, and I told him he was right, from what I remembered. He suggested I ask you to be my helping teacher. That is...if you wouldn't mind."

"No, I wouldn't mind at all," Tom said quickly. "In fact, you could help me, too."

"With what?"

"To learn more about LENA."

"Sure. Whatever I can tell you. Of course, it was only in its first year when I was in it, so I'm sure there have been some changes."

"You really seemed to enjoy it, though," Tom said.

"Well, yeah. They really made us feel important. Leaders of the New Age!" She moved her hand across an imaginary banner.

"Yeah, that's one of the major goals of the program. To make the kids feel good about themselves."

"I wondered about that, though, when Bonnie was talking about the expansion of the program," Marla said.

"What do you mean?"

"Well, if they offer the program to all of the students..." She paused and frowned slightly.

"What?"

"What I mean is...how can everyone be a leader?"

"Good question. But you must have learned things other than how to be a leader."

"Oh, yes," Marla said quickly. "And that's where Bonnie really helped me. You probably remember that in the eleventh grade I was very shy."

"No, I didn't notice that."

"Anyway, Bonnie helped me find my inner self and see how important I really am."

"Oh?"

"Once we realize that...really acknowledge it...there's nothing we can't accomplish."

"Maybe so," Tom said.

Marla glanced at her watch. "Oh, I have to run. Have a nice day, Tom."

"You too, Marla." Tom watched the young woman hurry down the hallway and out the double doors. He tried to determine how she was different now from when she was his eleventh-grade English student. She said she was shy. He didn't remember that at all. She was always quiet, but confident of her abilities. What was different? What was the inner self Bonnie helped her to discover?

Tom walked back to Bonnie's desk. He had just five minutes to get back to his own room, but he was determined to find something that would help him prepare for this class. He looked through all the desk drawers, but they contained no plans or even notes that related to the program. Then he remembered the adjacent office. Through the window in the door leading to that small room, he saw another desk and a number of shelves. He tried to open the door, but it was locked. He pulled from his pocket the keys Walt had given him and tried several until he found the one that opened the door.

He entered the small office, glanced quickly across the shelves. On one shelf he saw what looked like the textbooks that were used in the standard English curriculum. He went to the desk, sat down, and began a rapid search. The top drawer contained pencils, pens, and paper clips. He opened the middle drawer and saw a number of small, soft-bound books and pamphlets. One by one, he brought them out quickly, read the titles, and tossed them on the desk top.

Reading them was like listening to Bonnie talk: *Meditation for Beginners, Out-of-Body Experiences, Cosmic Humanism, Mysticism and the Global Village, The Inner Road to Enlightenment.* He pulled the drawer open further and saw a number of small items scattered about; three metal pin-on badges with pyramids on them, a stack of paste-on stickers displaying bright rainbows, and several brightly colored crystal stones similar to the one Bonnie used for her meditation chant Friday night.

At the back of the drawer was a small brown envelope. He opened it and five capsules tumbled out into the palm of his hand. They were two-toned; one end was white and the other was gray with a sprinkling of red spots. He assumed they were some kind of cold remedy. He cupped his palm and poured the capsules back into the envelope. He was about to replace it, but remembered Joe's repeated warnings about keeping substances around where students might get to them. He slipped the envelope into his shirt pocket, tossed the booklets back into the drawer, and shoved it closed.

He yanked on the large bottom drawer, but it was locked. He tried to fit several of the keys into the lock, but none of them worked.

The bell rang then, announcing the beginning of the next period. He had to get to class. He would meet with Walt this afternoon and see if Bonnie had left any lesson plans with him. He left the office and locked the door. Then he quickly placed the stack of compositions in his briefcase and rushed off to his second-period class.

4

Tom stopped by the principal's office after school, but Walt had not yet returned from a meeting at the district. Tom went into the faculty lounge to wait. A small room, it appeared crowded with the eight or ten teachers who sat around talking, drinking coffee, or reading. Tom saw Stu Welbourne sitting in a corner of the room. Stu was a tall man with stark features and a heavy mustache. He was looking through a stack of papers, an unlit pipe held casually in his left hand. Stu was the high school's LENA project chairman, and Tom saw this as an opportunity to get some background on the program. He walked over and sat in a chair next to Stu.

Stu looked up. "Hi, Tom."

"Hi. Is this the smoking section?"

"Hmm?" Stu looked at the pipe in his hand and pressed his finger down on the bowl full of tobacco. "No, I'm afraid I'd be very unpopular if I stoked this thing up in here. I'll wait until I leave." He put the papers in his lap and shifted in his chair to face Tom. "I understand you're taking Bonnie's senior class while she's out."

"That's right. If you have a few minutes this afternoon, I'd like you to go over some of the aspects of the program with me."

"Sure, I'd be glad to. What do you need to know?"

Tom laughed. "Everything!"

"Well, that narrows it down. Okay, let's see... Do you know how many project participants there are?"

"Just one target group at each grade level, I think," Tom said.

"Right," Stu said. "There are about a 120 kids at the high school. Their course of study is very structured, and they're carried through by the same teacher in multi-year subjects."

"Yeah, and I know for some of you that means a lot of preps."

"That's true," Stu agreed. "In my case, I teach the social sciences to grades nine, ten, eleven, and twelve. That means I have to prepare in geography, world cultures, American history, political science, sociology, and psychology."

"You're well rounded."

"Really! The advantage is, of course, that we have only four period assignments."

"That's true. Who are the other team members?"

"Well, there's Bonnie, of course," Stu said. "She has four grade levels of English. Lee Wong teaches four levels of physical education. Chris Donnelly has three levels of science—grades nine, eleven, and twelve. In the tenth grade, the students take the personal health and values course with Marilyn Peters, who is also a team member. And they have a year of art with Susan Reed and a year of music with Ed Staley."

"What about mathematics?"

"Oh, yes, these kids all take three or four years of math," Stu said. "But that course doesn't fit in well with the design of the program, so there's no math teacher on the team."

"Oh."

"And then, of course, the program has its own assigned counselor, Nita Masters."

"Yeah, I've heard some of the other counselors are a little

resentful about her light load," Tom said.

"Well, that position is a requirement of the program. Nita takes an active part in curriculum design and helps as needed in the classroom, so the others can't really make comparisons."

"You seem very positive about the program."

"Oh, yes," Stu responded enthusiastically. "The program has been running in this school for six years. I've had the students in my senior class for four years now and I've seen tremendous growth. The way the program is presented, it really brings out their inner potential."

"But does any of it relate to the social sciences?" Tom asked.

"Absolutely, better than anywhere else, I believe. We help them develop an awareness of their place in the world—physical, historical, social, psychological—and show them how to tap their own resources to help plan for and take part in a greater global society."

"That's great," Tom said. "I'm just having a little trouble relating those goals to the English program."

"English is language," Stu said. "And language is..."

"I know. Language is nothing more than an expression of man's inner needs and desires, and the better understanding we have of our inner being, the farther we can progress with our language."

Stu smiled and nodded slowly. "You've read the manual!"

"No. One of the students told me that this morning."

"Oh. That's a pretty good summation. Of course, it has to be worked out over the broad spectrum of oral and written expression and the study of literature."

"Yes, that's true," Tom said. "It's just that some of the activities the students described seem pretty far out."

"Well..." Stu glanced at the other teachers in the room,

leaned toward Tom, and spoke softly. "You have to understand that Bonnie is...well...on the edge of curriculum experimentation. I agree that sometimes she goes a little too far."

"You can say that again! I mean, a Valentine's Day love relationship simulation?"

Stu laughed. "Yes, the kids were still talking about that one when they got to my class. I just used it as an example of how our values are continually being bombarded, even by things that go on in the classroom."

"I don't know, Stu. Teachers are powerful models for kids. We have to be careful of what we say, how we act, and what we involve them in."

"Well, you'll undoubtedly handle the class differently," Stu said. "And that's all right. The students will adjust."

"You mentioned reading the manual," said Tom. "I don't even know what textbooks Bonnie was using, if any."

"Well, she skips around a lot, depending on the flow. Why don't you just have them work with the state literature anthology for a while? That'll give you a framework and I'm sure they can bring their past experiences to bear on their study."

"That sounds like a good idea. I think I'll do that."

"Mr. Kerzig..."

Tom looked toward the door and saw Sylvia, Walt's secretary, leaning inside. "Mr. Kerzig," she repeated, "Mr. Josephson is back now, so he should be able to see you."

"Thanks, Sylvia." Tom stood up and addressed Stu. "I'm sure I'll be talking to you again."

"Any time."

Tom left the lounge and crossed the hallway to Walt's office. When he arrived at Sylvia's desk, she was frowning.

"I'm sorry," she said. "He stopped in to see Mr. Carter for a minute. Why don't you just wait in his office? He won't be long."

Tom walked through the open door into Walt's office which was about twice the size of the faculty lounge. In fact, this room had originally been the lounge. Six years ago, when the teachers returned in the fall, they discovered Walt had switched the rooms and redecorated this one as his new office. He told them it was necessary because of the additional meetings he would be hosting as a result of their participation in the program.

The end of the room directly inside the doorway was occupied by a large round conference table which would seat a dozen people. At the other end, Walt's massive, dark-wood desk sat facing the table. On the wall behind the desk was a four-by-eight-foot display. Across the top, in large gold block letters, were printed the words: LEADERS OF THE NEW AGE. Just below that, in smaller letters: EXEMPLARY PROGRAM AWARDS. Five framed pictures hung in a horizontal row—a large one in the center and two smaller ones on each side. The picture on the left end showed Walt shaking hands with Superintendent McCray, and the one on the right end showed Walt receiving an award from the state director of curriculum. One of the other small pictures displayed Walt presenting a speech before a meeting of the local Chamber of Commerce, and the other showed him surrounded by P.T.A. leaders. The large picture in the center was taken at the conclusion of last year's program. It showed Walt shaking hands with the governor.

Tom heard the door close and turned to see Walt entering the room. Walt peered over the top of his half-glasses. "Oh, hi, Tom. Sorry to keep you waiting." He walked quickly behind his desk, opened the center drawer, tossed some papers inside, and pushed the drawer closed. He then pointed to a chair in front of the desk. "Please, sit down."

Tom sat in the thickly upholstered armchair and watched as Walt sunk into his plush, high-backed desk chair.

"Sylvia told you I was with the superintendent, didn't she?" Walt asked.

"Yes."

"And then I stopped by to see Bonnie," he added. "It took longer than I thought it would."

"How is she doing today?" Tom asked.

"Oh, better...better." Walt opened his center drawer again, fumbled through some papers, and brought out a small writing pad. He placed it on the desk before him, closed the drawer, and laughed nervously. "She said it'll just take time."

"I thought I'd visit her this evening."

"Good. She'll appreciate that."

Talking about Bonnie's accident again reminded Tom of what Joni had told him. Perhaps Walt knew something. "Uh...was she alone in the accident?" he asked.

"You mean, was there another car involved?"

"No. Was anyone with her in her car?"

"Oh...no." Walt shook his head. "She said she was just out driving around by herself. So..." Walt leaned against his desk, folded his hands, and wrinkled his forehead. "How did things go with the class this morning?"

"I wanted to talk to you about that this afternoon. But while I was waiting, I talked with Stu for a few minutes."

"Stu Welbourne? Good, good!" Walt sat back and nodded several times. "He's definitely the one you should go to with questions about the program."

"What I really need is a copy of Bonnie's lesson plans. I couldn't find anything in her classroom."

"Oh? Well, let's see..." Walt drummed his fingers on the desk, then turned quickly and pulled open the bottom drawer. He withdrew a fist full of papers, set them on his lap, and began flipping through them rapidly, mumbling the names of teachers as he passed them. "You see...ah...I'm not quite as rigid with the program teachers. Sometimes they turn plans in, sometimes they..." He came to the bottom of the stack, shook his head, and placed the papers back in the drawer. "No..." He closed the drawer and turned toward Tom. "I guess she didn't give me any for this week."

"Well, Stu suggested that I let them work in the state literature anthology for a while."

"That's a good idea."

"Any particular aspect of the program you want me to be sure to emphasize?"

"Oh, anything that helps to bring out their inner awareness and motivates them to think about global unity."

"Yes, those are the general buzz words I've been hearing," Tom said. "But you must have some specific curriculum objectives in mind for the English program."

"Well...ah..." Walt shifted in his chair. "I think they were doing something with values. Stu could probably give you a better *down-home* description." He laughed. "I spend more time with the broad administrative goals of the program."

"Okay, sure." Tom decided not to pursue this issue any further. It was clear Walt knew very little about the specifics of the program for which he was receiving all the praise.

A knock came at the door, and Tom turned to see Joe poke his head inside the room.

"Sorry to bother you," Joe said, "but I need to see you before you leave tonight, Walt."

"Yes, we'll be through in a few minutes," Walt said.

Tom suddenly remembered the capsules. He placed his hand against his chest and felt the outline of the small envelope in his shirt pocket. "Oh, Joe, just a minute. I want to give you something."

Walt raised his eyebrows and motioned for Joe to come in.

"What is it?" Joe asked.

Tom pulled the envelope from his pocket. "I found these in Bonnie's department office desk this morning." He handed Joe the envelope. "I knew you didn't want any kind of medicine lying around where it could get into the wrong hands, so I thought I'd better give it to you."

Joe pressed the sides of the envelope, looked inside, and frowned. Then he glanced at Walt and spoke slowly. "Have you told Tom everything about Bonnie, Walt?"

"Well...not everything."

Joe shook the contents of the envelope and the five two-toned capsules fell out onto the desk. Walt sat back into his chair and pulled his cheeks into a frown. "Of course, it could be nothing," he mumbled.

Joe picked up one of the capsules, placed the ends between the thumb and index finger of each hand, and twisted. "It's loose. I think it's one of them."

"Excuse me..." Tom said. "One of *what?*"

"Two weeks ago, one of the kids in the program was arrested for erratic behavior in a shopping mall," Joe said. "They found two of these capsules on him. They tested them and found they contained LSD."

"That whole capsule?" Tom exclaimed.

"Oh, no!" Joe said. "It only takes a tenth of a milligram to send you to the moon. No, it's mixed with sugar, or, worse, with the antihistamine itself."

"Was the desk locked?" Walt asked.

"Um..." Tom forced his mind back to that hurried few minutes. "No. Not the drawer these were in. The office was locked, though."

"Well, now," Walt raised his hands toward Joe, "it could have been anyone. A student...custodian...even another teacher, I suppose."

Joe frowned again. He picked up the capsules, placed them back in the envelope, and slipped the envelope into his shirt pocket. "Tom needs to know what's going on with Bonnie, Walt."

Walt sighed. "Yes, I suppose." He turned to Tom. "After the accident, when they took Bonnie to the hospital and tested her, they found out she was high."

"On LSD?" Tom asked.

"I guess. Well, I mean, we don't know," Walt mumbled. "It was something. I'm just going by what Bonnie herself admitted. She didn't say what it was."

"Do you remember that kooky seminar she went to five years ago?" Joe asked.

"Well, yes," Walt said. "But that was during the summer and it was just a part of some mind-expansion thing." He shook his head. "I doubt there's a connection."

"But what about Bonnie now, and the tests?" Tom asked.

"Well, the police got the results, of course," Walt said. "So she's charged with driving under the influence of a controlled substance."

"Oh, boy!" Tom gasped. "What's going to happen?"

"She doesn't know yet...concerning the legal action, that is," Walt answered. "But with the district, there wasn't any choice. That's what I was meeting with the superintendent about earlier today. We've placed her on administrative suspension with pay, pending the outcome of her case."

Joe tapped his shirt pocket. "We'll have to turn these over to the police, Walt."

"Wait a minute, now!" Walt shook his finger and spoke haltingly. "We don't even know what those are yet. You're always so bent on doing her in, it seems. Of course, if they *are* LSD, then it's a different story."

"The police allowed you to squelch the other incident,

Walt, because it was a student," Joe said. "And I agree that was in the best interest of everyone. But this may involve a teacher, and it..."

"*May!*" Walt said loudly. "You said the magic word—*may!* Let's not jump into the river unless we have a boat!" He spun around in his chair and pointed toward the pictures on the wall. "You talk about best interest, Joe. There's six years of best interest." He spun back toward them. "I don't want these pills mentioned to anybody until we find out what we're talking about! Is that clear?"

"You know I wouldn't say anything without finding out what they contain first," Joe said. "But I'm going to take them in right away. I should have the results in a few days."

"Come back then and we'll talk." Walt spun around again and faced the display. His head disappeared behind the high back as he slid down in his chair.

Joe motioned with his head, and Tom got up and followed him to the door.

"Thanks for letting me know what's going on," Tom said.

Joe pushed the door open slightly and spoke softly. "What Walt doesn't understand is that I don't want any damaging information being spread around any more than he does—if it isn't true." He glanced toward Walt and sighed heavily. "But I may be a little more anxious than he is to find the truth!" Joe pushed the door all the way open and stalked out.

Tom stood in the open doorway for a moment and looked back toward Walt's desk. The chair swung almost imperceptibly back and forth, a hand projected from each side, bobbing in rhythm with the motion.

5

Tom needed to stop by his classroom before leaving school, so he entered the building and walked down the now vacant corridor. It was unlit and the detail of the lockers was barely visible in the darkening of the late afternoon. As he passed Bonnie's classroom, he noticed the door was open and the lights were on. He poked his head inside and saw the custodian, Larry, pushing a large dust mop between the aisles of desks.

"Hello, Larry." Tom stepped inside the room.

"Hmm?" Larry looked up and smiled. "Oh, hi, Mr. Kerzig! I thought you'd left for the day."

"Just about to."

"You don't need to work in this room right now, do you?"

"No. Don't let me stop you." Tom started to leave, and then his glance fell on the door to the adjacent office. "Larry, do you know who has access to the department office?"

Larry stopped mopping, clasped his hands on the tip of the handle, and pointed. "You mean that room there?"

"Yes."

"Just Miss Teague," Larry said. "She uses it for all the English department books and materials. She also stores stuff in there for that club she sponsors."

"So no one else goes in there?"

"No. Nobody else."

"Hmm..." Tom turned and began to walk out the door.

"Oh...except that new teacher. I forget her name."

Tom turned back. "Marla Vedder."

Larry nodded. "Yeah, that's right. Miss Vedder. I've let her in a few times since she came. She needs to get some things now and then...since she just started, you know. Miss Teague said it was all right."

"Sure."

"In fact, I just let her in about a half hour ago."

"Okay. Thanks, Larry." Tom waved and left the classroom. Marla's room was directly across from his and as he continued down the corridor, he saw light spilling out from her open door. She was intently reading at her desk, a stack of papers before her.

Tom knocked on the open door. "Hello!"

Marla sat up abruptly, her eyes wide. "You startled me! I didn't know anyone was here." She sighed and fanned her face with her hand.

Tom smiled and walked over to where she sat. "Grading papers?"

"Yes. I keep overlooking the fact that when I give a writing assignment to all my classes I have a 150 papers to read."

Tom laughed. "Yeah, I know what you mean. But don't worry. After a while you'll become a real speed reader."

"I certainly hope so." She pointed to a chair near her. "Have a seat."

"That's okay. I can't stay long." He leaned on the corner of her desk. "I understand Larry's been letting you into the English department office."

"Yes, I need to get some books and things for my classes. Bonnie said to get anything I needed." She paused for a moment and continued haltingly, "But if you don't think I should go in there..."

"No, that's fine," Tom reassured her. "Have you found everything you needed?"

"I think so." Marla pointed to a stack of books on the corner of her desk. "I got these tonight to help me teach sentence structure."

Tom glanced at the titles on the books. "You teach ninth graders, don't you?"

"Yes."

"Sure, those should be fine. That one by Williams may be a little tough." He pointed to the one on the top.

"Yes, that's what I thought when I thumbed through it." Marla took the book from the stack and placed it purposefully to the side. This revealed a small booklet now on top of the stack: *The Inner Road to Enlightenment.* Tom sat up rigidly. That was one of the books he had seen inside the department office desk drawer this morning. "That one won't give you much information on sentence structure." He pointed to the booklet.

"What?" Marla looked at the booklet and laughed. "Oh, no. That's for some of the other activities I'm having the class do. Bonnie said it would be a good idea for me to start incorporating some of that since the program will probably be expanded next year."

"Yeah. That's what Walt's planning."

"Well, I just hope things get easier." Marla leaned forward on her desk. "When I had you for a teacher, you were just starting, weren't you?"

"That was my second year."

"Everyone in class thought you were really young." Marla placed her finger on her lips and narrowed her eyes. "Let's see...if I remember right, you have a little girl, don't you?"

"Yes..." Tom felt a hot tingling at the base of his neck. "Jennifer. She's in the third grade now."

"Not so little anymore." Marla smiled.

"No."

Marla frowned slightly. "I don't remember seeing your wife at the faculty party two weeks ago. Was she there?"

"No, we're...we're separated." Tom recoiled slightly at the sound of that word.

"Oh, no! I'm so sorry."

"Yeah, me too." Tom stood up abruptly. "Well, listen. I'd better let you get back to your grading."

"Stop in any time," Marla said, her pleasant smile now beaming again. "Don't forget. You're my helping teacher."

"Right. I'll see you tomorrow."

Marla raised her hand and waved it slowly. Tom looked at her and recalled the bright girl in his eleventh-grade English class six years ago. Her smile was the same, and her long black hair, hanging in thick curls. Nothing really seemed changed about her, except she seemed, perhaps, more determined. He smiled and left the room.

He walked across the corridor to his room and inserted the key in his door. For a moment, he recalled the booklets in Bonnie's desk. Why did Marla take one? That was the same drawer that held the capsules. He remembered Joe's words: "*Two weeks ago...one of the kids in the program... arrested... found two of these capsules on him...they contained LSD.*" Two weeks ago. Marla had started teaching at the school two weeks ago. Could there be any connection? The key suddenly felt hot between his fingertips and he dropped his hand from the door. He shook his head. Why would he even think such a thing? Of course there was no connection.

"Having trouble with your lock, Mr. Kerzig?"

Tom looked up to see Larry wheeling his cart toward him. "No, Larry. Everything's fine...just fine."

The door to Bonnie's hospital room was open, so Tom walked right in. Her's was the only bed in the room and it was adjusted to raise her head and knees. As Tom approached, he saw that a large bandage covered her nose, upper cheeks, and upper forehead. The top of her head was shaved, and the uncut hair jutted back from the shaved section in untidy clumps. Bonnie's eyes were closed, but when Tom reached the bed, they popped open.

"Pretty rough way to get some time off," Tom joked.

"Oh, hi, Tom." She raised her hand to greet him.

Tom held her hand and squeezed it. "How are you doing?"

"Better." She pressed her thumb against Tom's hand and dropped her arm to the bed. "Physically better."

"Did your head hit the windshield?"

"Yeah."

"Why weren't you wearing your seat belt?"

Bonnie shrugged. "My reading didn't indicate an accident that day."

"You're kidding, I hope."

Bonnie shrugged again and turned her head away. She then turned back and shifted her body on the bed. "Walt tells me you're taking my seniors."

"Yeah."

"I'm glad. I know you'll do a good job."

"How long will you be in the hospital?"

"They want to monitor my head for a while," she said. "The doctor said I should be released Wednesday or Thursday. But I won't be coming back to school for a while."

"Yeah, I know."

Bonnie's head snapped toward him, her eyes slits beneath the bandages. "Did Walt tell you about the charges?"

"Yes."

"He had no need to do that!"

Tom put his hand on her arm. "He and Joe thought I should know. I'm sure you wouldn't want me to hear about it indirectly."

"There shouldn't be any way for it to come out...*indirectly*."

"Well, you know, these things have a way of getting out," he said.

"Great!" She clenched her fist and pounded it on the bed. "Did Walt tell anyone else."

"I don't know."

"It's all a big mistake, you know."

"What?" he asked. "The positive drug test?"

"Test...test...test! I knew you'd react to that. You just love test results!"

"This is a little different, Bonnie, don't you think?"

"The police aren't infallible, you know," she said.

"But what else could have caused the positive test?"

"Who knows! I'd been taking aspirin for a headache and a prescription drug for PMS. You'd think they'd do some more checking before they bring me up on a D.U.I. charge." She turned her head toward him again, her eyes filled with tears. "And you'd think Walt and the superintendent wouldn't decide right away to put me on suspension."

"They didn't have any choice," Tom said. "It's a board policy."

"Well, it's a stupid policy!" she muttered. "Stupid test...stupid situation."

Tom took her hand and spoke lightly. "You're being redundant."

A faint smile crossed her lips. "Absurd, asinine, half-witted, irrational, ridiculous, senseless, witless. Is that better?"

"Much better for an English teacher!" Tom squeezed her hand.

Tom decided not to tell her about finding the capsules...not now. Walt could be right. They might not be related. But then he remembered what Joni had told him. That might be related. "Bonnie," he said cautiously. "Were you alone at the time of the accident?"

Bonnie jerked her hand away from him and frowned. "Why do you ask that?"

"Well, it could make a difference. I mean, especially if someone else was driving."

"Do you think I'd be sitting here with a D.U.I. charge if someone else was driving?" Bonnie shifted in her bed so that her body was partially contorted on the angular mattress. "What made you ask if I was alone?"

"Well..." He was reluctant to answer. "It was just something Joni said."

"Joni? You mean Joni Irving?"

"Yes. She mentioned to me that after the dance you might not have been alone."

"Why would she have said that?"

"I don't know," he said. "I thought you might be able to tell me."

Bonnie sighed and let her body fall back into the contour of the bed. "I have no idea. I mean, I left at the break."

"So did Joni," Tom said.

"Where did she see me? In the parking lot? It was very dark, you know. She might have thought she saw someone." Bonnie shook her head slowly. "You know, Tom, you'll probably notice this in class, but Joni isn't really...well, she isn't really with the program. She always tends to see things as black and white, when explanations for phenomena are really much more complex. I don't know... Maybe that same problem slips across into her physical perception of things."

"So there was no one with you?" Tom pushed.

"How many times do I have to tell you?" Bonnie's voice crackled with irritation.

"Hey, c'mon, Bonnie. I'm just trying to find anything that might help you."

"I'm fine." Bonnie closed her eyes. Then she opened them, smiled faintly, and patted Tom on the hand. "I'm fine!" She sighed and forced her body toward him again. "So, how did things go in class today?"

"Pretty well." Tom smiled. "It would have been easier if you'd left a lesson plan."

"Walt stopped asking me for lesson plans. I think he finally agreed with me that they are just too limiting. That's something you'll learn from the program, Tom. When you get in that class with those bright kids, things just open up!"

"Couldn't you at least jot down some general notes on where you're headed?

Bonnie closed her eyes, raised her chin, and spoke dramatically. "I, too, am untranslatable. I sound my barbaric yawp over the roofs of the world!"

"You're supposed to *teach* Whitman, not *be* him."

"That's where you're wrong," Bonnie said. "You have to become the essence of life before you can teach it. You have to become one with all who have experienced that unity! You'll understand." She nodded slowly. "One week with my kids and you'll understand."

"Well, I did get a glimpse of that today."

"Good," Bonnie said. "Just open up and let them fill your vessel."

"Well, you did, at least leave one translatable yawp." Tom smiled. "The compositions due today."

"Oh, yes! Did you pick them up?"

"Yes."

"I'd love to see them!"

"Well, maybe later," he said. "I'm going to make mechanical marks and return them Wednesday for the kids to rewrite."

"Mechanical marks?" Bonnie cried loudly. "That wasn't a grammar exercise! It was a creative composition!"

"Creativity and accuracy can go hand in hand," Tom said. "They have to get the mechanics somehow. What better way than through their own work?"

"Mechanics are secondary to inspiration."

"In the real world, people want their inspiration presented correctly."

"In these kids' real world, they'll decide how important mechanics are to their goals," Bonnie said. "If they decide they're important, they'll pick them up in an instant. If they decide otherwise, they'll have secretaries to worry about the mundane things."

"They won't even know how to decide unless they've had the experience."

"You're going to stifle their creativity!"

"So your kids told me," Tom said.

"So you're going ahead with it?"

"I told them there were some things I would be doing differently. And this is one of them."

"Oh!" Bonnie let out an exasperated sigh and pounded her hands on the bed beside her body. "What are you going to do for the rest of the week?"

"We're going to study the state literature anthology for a while."

Bonnie closed her eyes tightly and pressed the fingers of one hand against her lips. "All right, all right. Have them relate

Whitman to the twentieth-century American realists. Have them show how his sense of oneness with the universe would have helped their characters come to a full realization of their potential, despite the chaos of the world about them."

"Bonnie, they had twentieth-century American literature last year," Tom reminded her.

"It's just a vehicle. It's not what they study. It's what they bring of themselves."

Tom shook his head and spoke resolutely. "Twelfth grade is European lit, Bonnie. Do you have a preference in that area?"

Bonnie looked at him with pursed lips for a moment. Then she turned her head and spoke without feeling. "Very well. Do the same exercise with the French realists." She turned toward him and spoke almost threateningly. "They can still use Whitman as the comparator, can't they?"

"Sure. That's a reasonable use of previous knowledge to lead to an understanding of new content."

"All right. Get them started on...oh...Proust, Gide, Camus, and Sartre, of course." She leaned up on her elbow. "But, whatever you do, weave in humanistic positivism wherever possible. They mustn't be left with a feeling of despair."

"I'm not a nihilist, Bonnie," Tom said.

Bonnie laid back again, and spoke through her teeth. "I want to be out of here! I want to be out of...this! I want to be with my kids. I want to feel..." Bonnie's eyes suddenly opened wide, and with her body rigid, they darted about the room.

"Bonnie, are you all right?"

"The ceiling...it's beautiful...so many colors."

"What?" Tom looked at the ceiling. It was the same drab color as the rest of the room.

"The lights..." Bonnie continued. "Spinning... It's all right. They won't hurt me... Just spinning." She closed her eyes and sighed deeply.

"What is it, Bonnie? What's the matter?"

She opened her eyes and smiled at him. "It's all right, Tom. It's just my head injury. They told me some weird things might happen from time to time. I'll be okay by Wednesday."

"Well, I'd better be going. You need to rest."

"Come over after I get home. I want you to keep me posted on how my kids are doing."

"All right. And don't worry. If it is just aspirin and a prescription drug, they'll get it straightened out. Everything will be all right. You'll see."

"I'm just gliding with the flow, Tom." Bonnie made a broad, undulating gesture with her arm.

He waved at her and walked to the door where he was met by a huge bouquet of flowers coming in. The flowers shifted to the side then, and Mark Banazech's head became visible.

"Oh, hello, Mr. Kerzig."

"Hi, Mark."

"Mark, is that you?" Bonnie struggled to raise herself.

"Yeah. A few of us decided some flowers might cheer you up and I was elected to deliver them." He walked over to the bed and placed the bouquet on the side stand.

"Oh, they're beautiful!" Bonnie gushed. "Aren't they beautiful, Tom?"

"Absolutely. And you keep that smile going!"

"Here, Mark." Bonnie gestured to a chair near the side stand. "Sit down. You can stay for a while and talk, can't you?"

"Sure."

"Goodbye, Tom," Bonnie said. "Thank you for coming."

"Sure, I'll see you later. See you tomorrow, Mark."

Tom left the room and walked quickly through the wide

hospital corridor toward the elevator. He wanted to believe Bonnie, but he'd never heard of charges like this being brought unless the police were sure of their facts. And what about Joni's statement? Why would she have said anything if she hadn't seen...what? Too many inconsistencies—everywhere. But he had to give Bonnie the benefit of the doubt for now.

He stopped before the elevator door and pushed the button. He closed his eyes and pressed his thumb and forefinger against the bridge of his nose as he tried to mentally construct some literature study activities that would suit his style and yet meet Bonnie's program needs. If she had her way, she'd use Whitman's "Song of Myself" as a springboard to every literary study. How often had he seen her before school in the morning, sitting cross-legged on top of her desk, looking through the window with unopened eyes toward the warmth of the rising sun, muttering lines from this author's celebration of his oneness with the world. Suddenly, Tom found himself caught up in the excitement of the coming study. The pantheism of Whitman and the atheism of the French realists... Yes, he could spend the rest of the semester on that, if he had to.

A bell rang and Tom opened his eyes to see the doors to the elevator sliding open. Two nurses, dressed in sparkling white stepped out, laughing. He glanced at the indicator above the door and saw a red arrow, pointing down. The open elevator stood expectantly—a vessel, waiting to be filled. Tom entered and the doors slid closed behind him, leaving him captive for a moment in this tool of reality. The elevator lurched into movement and he was filled suddenly with a weird mixture of fear, doubt, and excitement. Did elevators ever fail? Were tests ever wrong? Did Whitman ever cry?

6

Tom's apartment was only a few miles south of the hospital, but somehow his car headed west, toward their house—the one he'd had shared with Clair and Jennifer until four months ago. At first, he casually blamed the misdirection on habitual response. That had been his destination for ten years, after all. But he'd driven by the house a lot lately. He knew the real reason was because he didn't want to lose the image; their home, the three of them, together. It could be again—*would* be again. *How long, Clair?* he thought. *When will your freedom become a bondage to you?*

He turned at the familiar street light, half hidden behind the thick branches of the huge oak. He directed the car slowly down the narrow street and pulled to the curb across from their house. He turned off the lights but left the engine running. The study was in the front of the house and the window to that room glowed brightly. Clair must be in there working on a case. She had finished her education last June and had gotten the job as a social worker for the welfare department in August. That was when their relationship began to slip. No, it was before that. She had become distant during her last year at the university—almost unapproachable. He had attributed this to the stress involved in completing her degree. But the stress seemed to continue after she began her job. "Need time to learn the ropes," she had told him as she spent hours in the study at night, mulling over her cases. He tried at first to do his work there, too, alongside her. But she became irritated by his presence. Then, in October...

The engine rumbled quietly and Tom reached forward and switched off the heater, whose warmth was now becoming oppressive. He turned on the lights, glanced in his side mirror, and pulled away from the curb.

Tom's apartment was small, but adequate. He adjusted the lamp beside the couch, leaned forward over the low table in front of it, and picked up the cup of hot coffee with both hands. He sipped it cautiously as he glanced at the stack of compositions from Bonnie's seniors. He chuckled as he recalled her anger when he told her he planned to mark them for mechanical errors. He wondered for a moment if he was being too inflexible. It was her class, after all. Perhaps he shouldn't make such a big deal out of it.

He set his coffee down and picked up the top paper. He sat back and began to read the messily handwritten page:

Out-of-Body Experience
by Kyle Phillips

Monday we did a classroom meditashun and many strange things happend so Bonnie told us to write about one that we did. I went home and tried it was hard at first because my mother wanted me and my brother to help her. I told her I had to do some homework and she said I didn't look like I was working. But I finely convinced her it was important.

Tom tossed the paper back on the stack in disgust. No, he wasn't being too inflexible! He couldn't believe Bonnie would want work like that to go uncorrected. Marking their papers and having them rewrite wouldn't stifle their creativity. It would heighten it by giving them a greater sense of accomplishment. Bonnie wasn't there to contest it, anyway. He would just do what was right.

He leaned over the table and browsed slowly through the first few papers on the stack. The first one wasn't a fluke; all of them had problems. Tom wondered, *What about Joni's paper?* He leafed through the compositions and finally pulled out Joni's paper. To begin with, it was typed. That certainly helped. And the separate title page was neatly centered:

An Out-of-Body Experience
A Composition for English IV
by Joni Irving

The composition was several pages long and as he fanned through the pages, he couldn't spot any errors. He took another sip of coffee, sat back against the lumpy cushion at the corner of the couch, and began reading.

Getting out of the body isn't difficult. No, it's easy, deceptively easy. There are anxious thoughts inside, stirring up turmoil. I can feel them, battling against the law of my mind. Their hidden counterparts are already there, on the outside. I can hear their great swelling words, and my thoughts are flattered away from my mind.

"I will fly away in a dream," I muse. Yes. I will chase myself away from the presence of the light, like a vision, searching for the night. But first, there's a small window, bumping against my wish, but showing a glimpse—a glimpse of what's outside.

Others are there, in the shadows. No, they are the

shadows. And glowing from their centers is a mark, placed there in ages past, for the garden once green has perished. The light from my window cuts through the darkness and I push my wish aside so that I see. The shadows fly about, casting their glow before them, and huddle in the warmth of themselves.

A greater shadow is there, a silhouette vaguely painted in a pastel of gray against the gray of the night. It whisks by quickly, places a veil over my window, and then hovers lightly above the huddled group.

"Watch," it says, "for those once alienated will see. The darkness is not dark. The secret lies within— beneath reality." The greater shadow extends a nebulous appendage and thrusts it deep into its center. "Watch the aura!" The appendage discharges itself and a roughly cut crystal radiates with subtle hues of light. "Watch!" the shadow repeats, and the appendage circles above its head, a dull rainbow shimmering above the hint of a deep face.

"Now you do it," it coaxes. "Find yourselves!"

One by one, the members of the huddled group reach within their glows and pull forth dimly effulgent semicircles. They sway from side to side, admiring themselves in the mirror of the greater shadow.

The greater one then stands upright and becomes as a person. "I am the master. Follow me." He reaches up to the seven colors about his head and spins them. They whirl crazily as he speaks. "Our deity is unleashed!" he shouts. "We will build a city. Follow me. We will have a feast! There is nothing to fear."

The masses flutter after him. Above them, in the darkness, darker clouds cast waterless raindrops, and the late autumn trees thrust their barren branches upward, their roots yanked mercilessly from the rocky soil. The dark master shoves them aside as he passes.

"Here," he says. "This is the place." He wipes the scum from the trees, throws it before him, and it becomes a carpet of scum upon the ground. "The thief awaits in the night," he says. "But I will protect you."

The dark master wrenches one of the barren trees from the surface and scratches the outline of two roads on the ground. The fork of the roads rises up suddenly and bumps against my small window, hiding its light. But the dark master is there, standing glowing at the fork. He gazes into his crystal as he points a golden arrow to the left.

"Let the children come," says the dark master. "The way is clear. The road is good. Let the children come!"

My thoughts want to follow, but my mind asks, "Why, dark master? Why do you call?"

He points a black shimmering finger toward the nonexistent sky and a white dove floats silently by, a brilliant lotus flower hanging gently from its beak.

"Freedom!" he says in empty, swelling words. "See how she flies! You can fly, too."

My warring thoughts are struggling to be free, but my mind envelopes them with a gentle embrace and calls out, "But there is a greater light!" And even there, above the folds of overpowering darkness, its brilliance gleams, undiminished.

"That is but a fleeting star," says the dark master. "Yours is greater! Follow me and you will be exalted above the throne!"

He turns and begins walking down the dark road and my thoughts reach out to follow.

"Let the children come!" he shouts. "I am excited by your presence." He waves his arm from side to side as he walks, and forms of death rise from the ground before him. The dust from their graves hovers noiselessly about his feet.

"But what of life?" wonders my mind, softer now in the depths of periodic doubt.

The dark master stops and plucks a handful of shriveled fruit from the gnarled trees beside the road, smiles at me, and plunges the fruit into the shadow of his mouth. "What of life?" he mocks kindly.

"But when the fruit is gone..." wonders my mind.

The dark master lays his head back in thundering laughter. His head lurches forward toward the trees, and he vomits. The discharge casts itself upon the dry branches and hangs there in the likeness of a fruit. He reaches out and picks it and eats again. "Sustenance is ours!" he shouts amidst his laughter.

The other shadows now join his feast. They eat the sparse fruit from the gnarls until it is gone. And then they, too, fall back in laughter and imbue the branches with their vomit. And then they clamor about the trees and replenish themselves with the filth of themselves.

"Let the children come," shouts the dark master through his laughter. "For here is where we will build their tower."

The huddled shadows continue their eating and retching. But when the refuse rises about their feet, they cry out, "What now, dark master?"

"We build," he says gently. "We build to your glory!" He begins gathering the refuse and placing it in a neat pile. The others follow his lead, and soon the pile reaches to the darkness above.

The dark master watches them and nods in approval. "This is for your glory. In the name of Ashtoreth, Chemosh, and Milcom."

The pile now forms a gigantic pyramid and the shadows begin circling it, chanting the names that the dark master has given them. And then, from the top of the pyramid, a faint form descends.

"See—she comes again," says the dark master. "The dove, with the flower of peace!"

And now the descending form becomes many, and their size increases. They are not doves, but vultures, and from their beaks hang sharp thistles, which tear at the faces of the huddled masses as they pass. But the shadows throw their heads back in laughter as the blood streams from their wounds, and they continue their marching and chanting.

My window suddenly glows with the close form of the dark master. His red teeth glisten as he speaks softly to my warring thoughts.

"Leave the body," he urges. "It's so easy. You will be glorified like the others! There will be pleasure and wonder and power!" He backs away now, but his teeth still glisten as he beckons with a dark appendage. "Let the children come!"

But the rays from the distant star pierce the smallness of my window, and my warring thoughts fall back and nestle quietly within the comforting of my mind. "It's easy to have an out-of-body experience," I muse. "Deceptively easy."

And even now, with my window open to the blinding light which covers the night, the words of the dark master beckon—and will continue to beckon, "Let the children come...let the children come...let the children come..."

With a trembling hand, Tom wiped a stream of perspiration from his forehead. The images were so powerful, so unlike anything he would expect from Joni. Were these just words? Or were they disturbed imaginings, dredged up by Bonnie's bizarre assignment? Joni had told him she didn't even like the program, and yet this composition seemed to suggest that she was participating wholeheartedly in the pronouncements of mystical experiences. She seemed to have things so together, much more so than the other students.

Tom's imagination suddenly departed from Joni, and enveloped the image of Jennifer. He cast her forward in time and she became a replica of Joni. Yes. They would be alike. Jennifer, too, was bright, discerning. Would she also be driven toward such bizarre conceptions?

Tom stood up and began to pace nervously. He was suddenly filled with an overpowering desire to learn more about Joni. Maybe he should talk to her parents. He stopped in front of a small telephone table, opened the drawer, and pulled out the phone book. He flipped through the pages until he found the number for the Irvings. He removed the receiver from its cradle, a low buzz issuing from its ear piece. He stood there motionless for a moment, then replaced the receiver and shook his head. What would he say? "Hello...your daughter wrote a strange paper"? No. He'd better think about it for a while. Besides, Walt had told him that if he had any questions about the mental or emotional states of students in the program, he should first talk to Nita Masters. Yes, he would do that...tomorrow, during lunch. Maybe Nita would have some answers.

Tom started to walk away from the telephone table, but then he stopped, sighed, and picked up the receiver again. His finger fell on a number code button and the sound of seven rapid beeps filled his ear. There was a moment of silence and then the sound of ringing. Once. Twice. Three times.

"Hello?"

Tom bent forward slightly and raised the mouthpiece. "Clair..." There was silence on the other end, so he spoke again. "Clair...it's...it's Tom."

Silence...and then, "Tom, it's awfully late."

Tom glanced at his watch. It was only 9:30. "I didn't think you'd be in bed already."

"I wasn't. It's just... What do you want?"

"I was just grading some compositions," he said, "and I got this really strong feeling, like...I just wanted to talk to you."

Clair's heavy breathing was clearly audible as he waited. "Tom, this isn't helping anything, you know," she said finally. "If there's something you need to say, then, okay. But calling me just because you want to talk makes me uncomfortable."

"Yeah, I know. Remember Joni Irving, from church?"

"Lloyd and Sally's daughter? A little. Why?"

"Do you remember her being...pretty stable?" he asked.

"Well, I think so. I didn't know her that well. Lloyd and Sally kept a pretty close rein, as I recall. Why? Is anything wrong?"

"No. I just wondered if you remembered her. Bonnie Teague was in an accident Friday, and..."

"Oh, really? Is she all right?"

"Yes, she'll be fine," Tom said. "I'm taking her senior class for a while and Joni is one of the students."

"Oh." Another long pause. Clair spoke again with a slight irritation in her voice. "Is there anything else?"

"No. Oh,...how's Jennifer?"

"She's asleep."

"I mean..."

"She's fine, Tom. You'll see her this weekend."

"Yeah." He sighed deeply and ran his finger along a wrinkle in his forehead.

"So...I'll see you this weekend, then."

"Okay, Clair," he said. "Thanks for talking. Bye."

Tom slowly replaced the receiver. He walked to the couch and lay down. He was irritated with himself for calling her. He didn't want to do anything to jeopardize what little relationship they had left. "What a day!" he mumbled. He couldn't believe that just that morning he had walked into Bonnie's class for the first time. Visions of the day's activities whirled through his mind—the students' strange descriptions...Marla...the capsules...Walt's frightened response...the visit with Bonnie...and Joni's paper. What a conclusion! The dark master...beckoning... *What are you trying to say, Joni?*

Tom rose from the couch and walked to the window. The quarter moon was out, its light spilling subtly on the landscape. A slight breeze moved the branches of the trees as their leaves caught its power. And below, the shadows danced about in vague response.

7

Tom arrived at school early the next morning so he could gather his thoughts for the coming literature study with Bonnie's class. He still had positive feelings about the general area of study they had agreed upon, but on reconsideration, he found he did not completely concur with Bonnie's selection of authors. Sartre was a bit heavy, even for these students, although Tom decided he could extract enough from his work to provide a philosophical viewpoint for comparison. He was sure the students could relate to Camus and his struggle against the absurdity of life. But he decided against including Proust and Gide who were a little too perverse in their outlooks on life. While valid points about the morality of relationships could be drawn from them, the journey toward those conclusions might lead away from the major focus. He shuddered as he remembered the girl's description of Jason and Mike participating in a love relationship simulation. Yes, a study of Proust and Gide would definitely lead them astray. He decided to substitute Malreaux.

The students seemed eager to engage in discussion that morning, and Tom was pleased to discover that Bonnie apparently had given them a fairly good grounding the previous year in American Literature. They knew Whitman's work backward and forward, of course, but they also seemed to have a good grasp of the alienation motif prevalent in the twentieth-century American writers. This would be a good starting point for their study of the French authors. The class period was nearing an end, however, and he realized he would need to bring the discussion to a close and help the students focus on the coming study.

"I'm really impressed with your knowledge of Whitman and the other Americans," Tom joked, and the class responded with good-natured laughter. "Our study comparing these with the French authors should be very productive. In the few minutes we have remaining, I'd like to suggest an approach for this study." He moved to the board behind him and picked up a piece of chalk. "Several of you used this term with regard to Whitman, and I think it's one we should focus on." Tom turned and wrote the word *Pantheism.* "This is the word used for Whitman's view of the world. God is everywhere and everything is a part of the universal good." He turned back to the class. "This resulted in Whitman's apparent optimistic view of life and his place in it. By contrast, the French writers we're going to study, as well as many of the twentieth-century American writers you mentioned in our discussion, did not share this view. They began from a much more pessimistic view of life—alienation, leading to a sense of absurdity. Their outlooks could be better described by the term 'Atheism'." He turned to the board and printed the words *vs. Atheism* beside the other one.

Tom set the chalk down, stepped in front of his desk, and leaned against it. "As an initial exercise, I'd like you to think about these two terms for a moment, and then write down a one- or two-sentence reaction to this approach. I think this will help me structure the study in a way that will be best for the class."

There was a brief shuffling noise as the students removed paper for the exercise, and then they bent to the task. Tom glanced toward Joni's desk. She wrote something quickly, placed her pen down, and sat back. She seemed depressed today. She participated only briefly in the discussion, and then in a quiet, detached way. He wondered if something about the topic bothered her. But she had seemed upset from the moment class began. The images in her composition still haunted him, and as he watched her now, sitting pensively, he tried vainly to relate the person to her work. Perhaps he should talk to her after class. She might say something relevant, provide some clue.

His thoughts were interrupted by the ringing of the bell. The few students who had not yet finished the exercise scribbled a final word or two and prepared to leave.

"Just leave your sentences on my desk as you go," Tom said. "Oh, I began the process of marking your compositions last night, and believe me, they *needed* marking! I'll try to finish them tonight and return them to you tomorrow for you to correct and rewrite."

The students began filing out of the room, dropping their papers on his desk as they went. Mark Banazech came forward, placed a sheet on the desk, and then held out another paper.

"I didn't hand this in yesterday," he said.

"I know. I wondered what happened."

"Well, I usually do these creative visualization assignments in pretty rough form," Mark explained. "That's what Bonnie seemed to want. But I really can do a better job with mechanics if I try. So I rewrote it, and I'd like to turn it in now, if that's okay."

Tom smiled. Maybe his message got across more quickly than he'd hoped. "Sure, that's all right this time. If you're going to turn something in late again, though, let me know ahead of time."

"That's fair. Thanks." He handed Tom his composition, turned, and moved his large frame slowly out the door.

Tom turned back in hopes of catching Joni, but she had already left. He placed Mark's composition on the desk, then picked up and straightened the rest of the papers the students had left. He leafed through the pages and chuckled as he read some of the remarks: "Sounds cool"..."Whitman again!"..."I think a study of the French writers will be neat." But he was curious... He flipped quickly through the papers until he came to Joni's. Her reaction was brief, and was stated in an unusual combination of cursive and manuscript: "*Pantheism* IS *Atheism.*"

"Good morning, Tom!"

"Hmm?" He looked up to see Marla standing in the doorway. "Good morning, Marla." He set the papers on his desk and walked over to greet her. "How did the exercise on sentence structure go today?"

Marla made a face. "Not too well, I'm afraid. I thought the students would do a lot better than they did."

"One thing you have to learn as a teacher is not to get frustrated when your expectations aren't realized."

"That's hard to do. Listen, do you suppose you could meet me in the cafeteria for lunch and take a look at what I'm trying to accomplish?" She put on a wide smile and raised her hands. "Help!"

"Sure, I'd be glad to..." Then he snapped his fingers as he remembered. "Oh, no, I can't. I'm meeting with Nita Masters during the lunch period."

"Oh..." The smile left her face and her shoulders dropped.

"Another day I'd be happy to."

"Sure. That'll be fine. Well, see you later." She waved and walked away.

Tom erased his notations from the board, gathered the papers, and headed back to his own classroom.

Nita had worked as a counselor at the school since Tom started teaching, but he had rarely spoken with her, since she was assigned specifically to the students in the program. As he entered her office, she looked up, smiled broadly, and rose from her desk. She was a tall, attractive woman, and her brown hair was gathered neatly behind her head.

"Hello, Tom!" She walked over briskly and shook his hand. "I'm glad to have a chance to talk with you."

"I appreciate your taking the time."

She placed her hand behind his elbow and pointed toward two upholstered chairs in the corner of the room. "Let's sit there where we can be comfortable."

A bright serape hung on the corner wall behind the chairs, and a low glass table, bearing a small vase of flowers, sat in front of them. This area stood in stark contrast to the rest of her office, which was filled with book shelves and filing cabinets. A small section of wall behind her desk was reserved for a cluster of framed degrees and a picture of Sigmund Freud. Nita curled back in one of the chairs, her hands folded in her lap.

"This is great!" Nita laughed. "You've been in the program for only one day and already you're making use of my services!"

"Well, it's probably *because* I've been in the program for only one day. Maybe there's no reason for me to be concerned."

"Well..." Nita smiled and raised her palms. "Try me out!"

"I've been teaching for seven years and I've never seen anything like..." Tom shifted nervously in his chair. "Are these kids ever...ah...bothered about things...things in the program, I mean?"

"Sure," Nita said. "They're normal, flesh-and-blood members of the student body. Concerns are going to get to them from time to time."

"I guess it's just that they seem...different in some way."

"Good! That means the program is having an impact."

Nita leaned forward and touched his arm. "Being thrust into it suddenly as you have, you are going to be more aware of it, of course. In a sense, it's a matter of degree. You've studied Maslow, and you're aware of his hierarchy of needs."

"Yes."

"Well, in the program, we just spend more time on the higher-level needs—self-actualization and transpersonal awareness. And that can lead occasionally to somewhat volatile situations. Usually the teachers can handle them without any trouble, but in some instances, I'm called on to help."

"Can you give me an example?" Tom asked.

"Like with Bonnie's class?"

"Yes, if you can."

"Well, let's see..." She rested her chin on her hand and squinted. "This one's pretty extreme, but it will serve to illustrate. Last year Bonnie was conducting an external awareness exercise with her seniors, and..."

"You mean *out-of-body*."

"Yes, I think that's the working terminology."

"That'll be a perfect example."

"Good. Well, anyway, during the exercise, one of her students gave a vivid description of himself in a somewhat ethereal relationship with his father and mother. At the end of the period, though, he didn't seem to snap out of it. He remained somewhat withdrawn, almost catatonic. We discovered his parents had been killed in a plane crash and he was having a hard time dealing with it."

"That sounds bad."

"Well, our teachers are supposed to be aware of any personal problems that might get in the way of the flow of consciousness," Nita said. "Bonnie usually does an excellent job of that. But this one slipped through the cracks."

"What did you do?" Tom asked.

"I brought him to my office and worked with him the rest of the day," Nita said. "I met with him daily to bring him back to reality. Within a week he was completely all right."

Tom visualized Bonnie at the front of the class, urging her students toward some strange, mystical experience, and the back of his neck bristled. "I just don't understand why we're involved in activities that can lead to this type of reaction."

"That was a very unusual case."

"But still..."

"Let's use athletic competition as an example," Nita interrupted. "Coaches push their team players to the limit of their endurance. And not infrequently kids get hurt during the competition or in practice. But they heal and go on to better and higher achievements."

"I don't see how that—"

"Excellence!" she interrupted again. "Coaches want their players to reach down to the core of their physical abilities and perform to their greatest potentials. That's a good analogy to the LENA program goals. We want our students to reach down to the core of their beings and emerge as competent, whole, excellent members of...no...*leaders* of the coming world."

"Hmm..."

Nita tilted her head and smiled questioningly at him.

"I'm having difficulty with the analogy," Tom said.

"Give it time. You'll fall into the pattern."

"I guess."

"In the meantime, let's get to the reason you came. You must have a specific student in mind."

"Yes."

"Who is it?" Nita asked.

"Joni Irving."

"Yes, I know Joni." Nita rose and walked to the filing cabinets. "And her parents, as a matter of fact." She pulled out a file drawer, flipped through a number of tabs, and removed a folder. Then she closed the drawer, returned, and sat again. "Joni's been with the program from the beginning." She opened the folder and began browsing through the records inside. "She's a bright girl, Tom."

"I know that," Tom said.

"She's done extremely well in all of her classes. There is one significant fact about her, thought

"What's that?"

"She's one of only three program participants whose parents requested the students be exempted."

"From..."

"From tenth-grade health and personal values class."

This class was required of all tenth graders, unless their parents requested an exemption. It was originally designated simply as "health," but fourteen or fifteen years ago it was redesigned to include an in-depth study of reproduction, personal sexuality, and current mores in sexual behavior. The course had engendered such a controversy that the administration and board reluctantly provided for the exemption procedure.

"But that's not unusual, is it?" Tom asked. "Many of the students are exempted from that course."

"But only three program participants. The exemption is much more significant in their cases."

"Why is that?"

"Well, the kids never exempt themselves," she explained. "It's the parents."

"Yes..."

"The LENA students are being shown the tremendous importance of developing their own values and making their own decisions," Nita went on. "This leads them to a much greater inner struggle in instances where the parents are overly restrictive."

"Do you think this is the case with Joni's parents?" Tom asked.

"Well, I know they belong to a very conservative church."

"I know. I go to the same church."

"Really?" Nita sat back with an amazed look on her face.

"Well, *went* to..." Tom shrugged. Why did he mention that? It didn't matter. It was inconsequential.

"But Joni's parents have a very fundamentalist view," Nita continued. "You're different from them, Tom. You're more...balanced."

Tom wasn't sure what she meant by that. He didn't know Lloyd and Sally well, but from what he remembered, they were as well balanced as he. Joni was their only child and they were always doing things together as a family. They seemed happy...all of them.

"There must be something specific about Joni that has you worried," Nita said.

"Yes, it has to do with those...what did you call them...*external awareness exercises.* Bonnie had the class do that last week and write a composition about it." He handed Joni's composition to Nita. "Here's Joni's. I'm concerned. It seems so completely out of character for her."

"Let's see." Nita took the composition, tossed back the title page, and read intently for a moment. Then she raised her eyebrows. "Boy! This is pretty heavy." She flipped to the next page and her eyes scanned quickly to the bottom. She repeated that several times until she reached the end of the composition. "Well, she certainly is an excellent writer, isn't she?"

"But what about all the strange images and negative portrayals? Is that normal?"

"As I said, she's struggling to release her own personality from the repression of her parents. This is her opportunity for an outlet. It's probably very healthy."

"I didn't interpret anything in the paper that would show a struggle with her parents," Tom argued.

"Well, of course I don't know the particular instructions Bonnie gave them for this exercise. That could be a factor, too."

"I suppose."

"Listen, I'm going to visit Bonnie tonight," Nita said. "Why don't I take this to her and ask her to read it? I'll see what she thinks."

"I need to hand the compositions back to the students tomorrow."

"Well, I'll take a copy to her." She leaned forward and called out the door. "Karen, will you make a copy of this for me, please?"

A young clerk walked into the room, took the composition, and left.

"I'll have Bonnie look it over," Nita said. "From what I can tell, though, it's indicative of some healthy inner struggle. It may also be a natural release of creative expression. A little dark and foreboding, but she has a marvelous way with words, doesn't she?"

"Yes."

"Bonnie certainly does a good job with those kids."

Tom nodded. He wondered whether Nita knew about the drug charge. Probably not. Walt wouldn't tell anyone who didn't absolutely have to know.

"I wouldn't worry too much about Joni," she said. "She just needs some room—needs to find herself."

Her words pierced Tom's mind like a dagger. They were Clair's words, in that moment of unreality. "I have to get away for a while," she'd said. "Find myself." *Maybe she just needs room,* he thought. *How much room? How much time?*

The clerk returned then with the original and the copy of Joni's composition. Nita kept the copy and gave the original back to Tom.

The intercom on Nita's telephone buzzed and she excused herself. She sat casually on the corner of her desk and picked up the receiver. "Yes? Hello, Walt. What can I do for you?... Who?" Nita stood, let out an exasperated sound, and shook her head. "All right. I'll be right there." She hung up the receiver and stood for moment with her back turned, drumming her fingers on the desk.

"Problem?" Tom asked.

Nita turned around and leaned back against her desk with her arms crossed in front of her. "I have to meet with Walt and some parents. It's about one of the girls in the program. I helped her through a *decision* to get an abortion, and now the parents are angry because they weren't notified."

"Why weren't they?"

"The girl didn't want them to be."

"Didn't want them...how old is she?"

"Fifteen," Nita said.

Tom couldn't believe what he was hearing. "You counseled her into getting an abortion without..."

"No! No, I said I helped her through a decision. That's what the program is all about, Tom. Responsible personal decisions." She looked toward Walt's office and shook her head again. "She made the right decision for her...and her parents are complaining. They aren't the ones who'd have to deal with the consequences of an unwanted child!" She briskly walked to the door, paused, and turned back toward Tom. "I'm sorry to have to cut our time short. I need to see if I can defuse this situation. The perils involved with creating responsible members of society!" She walked out the door.

Tom still wasn't sure he completely understood what he

had just heard. If Jennifer, when she became fifteen, got into a situation like this, and he wasn't notified, he'd... That would be only seven years from now! A chill shot up his spine as he thought about the possibility of his own daughter meeting with Nita, asking for counsel...asking that he not be told.

Tom shook his head convulsively and stood up. There must be more to it than he knew. But what of Joni? Was he just to wait now? For what? Advice from Bonnie? No. He stepped over to Nita's desk and removed a small address book from his coat pocket. He found the Irvings' telephone number, picked up the receiver, and dialed. After a few rings, Joni's mother answered.

"Sally?" Tom said.

"Yes."

"This is Tom Kerzig...from church. I don't know if you remember..."

"Oh, yes, Tom. Of course. How are you?"

"Fine, thanks."

"Joni told us you're taking Miss Teague's class for a while. She's very happy to have you as a teacher."

"That's good. I'm glad," Tom said. "Listen, that's what I'm calling about. I'd like to talk to you and Lloyd about something."

"Is there a problem?" Sally asked.

"No. I just think I need to talk with the three of you, to get some idea of how Joni views the program and the class. It would be helpful to me."

"Well, certainly."

"Are you going to be home tonight?" he asked.

"No, I'm sorry. We're going to a church program. How about tomorrow night?"

Tom thought for a moment. "No. Tomorrow and Thursday are bad for me."

"And we'll be out on Friday," Sally said. "Would next week be soon enough?"

"Well, I suppose." But it wouldn't...not really. Something was going on, some turmoil, hidden in the words of Joni's paper. Why did he feel this compulsion to hurry to resolution? Nita wasn't particularly concerned. But there was just something.

"Tom, I get the impression we shouldn't wait until next week," Sally said after a pause.

"I would feel better if we didn't."

"Listen, we'll be back from church by 9:00 tonight. Would that be too late for you to come over?"

"No. No, that would be fine!"

"Why don't we do that, then? Come about 9:30, just to make sure."

"That'll be great. Thanks, Sally. I appreciate it."

Tom replaced the receiver and a deep sigh passed over him. Yes, this was better than waiting. Tonight they'd find some answers. He visualized their meeting. They were always happy, smiling. Joni, too. They would be tonight. He was sure of that. But what of Joni's dark master, ripping barren trees from the soil, and thrusting the vomit-filled fruit into the shadow of his mouth? "She just needs some room— needs to find herself," Nita had told him. Would the dark master lead the way? Or Nita? Or Bonnie? And what of Clair? "I need to find myself," she'd said. Who was her dark master? And what of Jennifer? How would she know? Who would be the counselors in her life, helping her decide? *The way is clear, the road is good,* he said. *Let the children come...let the children come.*

Tom looked toward the doorway in time to see Joe pass by, do a quick double take, then step inside.

"Are you subbing for Nita, too?" Joe asked facetiously.

"Sure. I had another free period during my lunch hour, so why not?"

Joe laughed. "You know, I'm still waiting to challenge you to another racquetball set."

"Yeah, we need to do that sometime."

"Well, the P. E. teachers are meeting tonight to discuss plans for the school's spring Olympic festival. I have to sit in on the first part of that meeting, but I'll be out by 7:30. Why don't you meet me at the gym then?"

"Oh, I don't know if I can tonight, Joe," Tom said.

"All work and no play..." Joe chided.

"No, it's not that. I'm meeting with some parents..." But then he realized his meeting with the Irvings wasn't until 9:30. A game of racquetball would be a good release. He could finish marking the compositions while he ate supper in the classroom, meet Joe for a short game, and still have time to get to the Irvings'.

"And?" Joe coaxed.

"Sure, Joe. That sounds good."

"Great! I'll meet you at the south door." He waved and walked off.

Tom glanced at his watch. The lunch period was almost over. He walked quickly to his classroom to prepare for his fifth-period class.

8

The sound of the small hard ball smacking against the walls and ceiling of the racquetball court was punctuated by periodic grunts from Tom and Joe and the squeaking of their shoes as they raced back and forth in energetic competition. The school had six courts adjacent to the gymnasium which the faculty members were allowed to use in the evening. Tonight Tom and Joe were the only ones in the building. The noises from their game seemed magnified by the contrasting silence about them.

"Ah!" Tom reached unsuccessfully for a rebound from the corner. "Nineteen-eighteen." He retrieved the ball and tossed it back to Joe at the serving line.

Joe smiled and bounced the ball three times. "Watch out! I'm pulling ahead."

"False sense of security," Tom said.

Joe put the ball into play again. "How's it going with Bonnie's class?"

"Pretty well." Tom returned the volley. "I'm not doing everything the way she'd like, but the kids seem to be responding."

"They're getting a better deal out of this than they think. Ah! Missed it! Your serve."

Tom got the ball and stepped to the serving line. "Bonnie does a pretty good job in the classroom," he said as he served the ball.

"Ugh," Joe shouted as he ran unsuccessfully to return the serve. "You knew that would distract me, didn't you?" He picked up the ball and tossed it to Tom. "Nineteen-nineteen."

"I'll have to remember that strategy," Tom joked and served again.

"So how do you know?" Joe returned the ball more slowly this time.

"How do I know what?"

"How do you know Bonnie does a pretty good job in the classroom? Have you observed her?"

"No, not really," Tom said. "I'm just going by what she says and the way the students seem to be doing."

"Oops, you got me again," Joe said as his return struck the floor.

Tom reached out and grabbed the ball as it rebounded from the front wall. "Game point! Are you ready?"

"Yeah..."

Tom dropped the ball to the floor and struck it hard. It bounced from the front wall to the side wall and sped toward the back corner of the court. Joe raced after it, but it hit directly in the corner and dribbled away from his reach.

"Were you saving that one for now?" Joe cried.

Tom laughed. "Pretty lucky, huh?"

Joe wiped his forehead with his sleeve. "All right, that gives you two out of three. I concede!" He opened the low door, reached outside, and brought in two small bags. "Unless you want to risk three out of five."

"No way! I'll never get a shot like that again."

They placed their rackets and sweatbands in their bags, zipped them up, and stooped as they exited the court.

"Bonnie's kids don't do as well as they should on the

state tests, you know," Joe said, continuing the conversation.

"Yeah, we were talking about that the other day. But that may be a function of the LENA program emphasis."

"Oh, speaking of the LENA program. Have you seen the new combination room yet?" Joe asked.

"No. Is it finished?"

"Just about." Joe beckoned with his finger and stepped across the hall toward another small door. He took his keys from his pocket and unlocked the door. "Come on."

Joe pushed the door open and they entered the dark room. The smell of fresh paint filled Tom's nostrils. He heard a click and the room became flooded with light. They were in another racquetball court. This one, however, had a new hardwood floor and bright paint. One entire wall was glass.

"Lee got a special grant from the state to build this for his P. E. unit," Joe said. "I think it's somewhat excessive, but..." He walked to the corner of the room and placed his hand on a recessed panel. "This contains the controls to the adjacent work-out room." He pushed a switch and a flood of light suddenly shone through the glass wall. On the other side of the glass was another room, similar in size, but outfitted with several body-building and exercise devices.

"That's pretty impressive," Tom said.

"Lee sold it to the state with the idea that he needed to conduct what he called *unheeded observations*. This is one-way glass. From the other side, this is just one huge mirror."

"Boy!"

"In actuality, Lee can supervise one of his classes in there, while he plays racquetball in here," Joe said. "There's a communication device, so he can hear everything that's going on, and talk to them if he wants to. That's the only way, in fact." He tapped the glass. "This is completely sound-proof."

"This entire court could be converted into an observation

room," Tom suggested, "so larger groups of people could do the unheeded observing."

Joe smiled. "Ain't gonna happen!" He pushed the switch again and the adjacent room became completely dark.

Tom stooped through the door and waited in the corridor as Joe turned out the court lights and joined him. They walked down the corridor toward the exit.

"Well, it's another facility for the kids," Tom said. "I guess that's what counts."

Joe reached to turn off the corridor lights, paused, and turned toward Tom with a perplexed look on his face. "How do we really know if the kids are getting everything they deserve?"

"Well..."

"Let's take you, Tom. I consider you to be an excellent teacher. But I'd have a hard time verbalizing the reasons. Do you ever wonder if you're doing right by the kids?"

"Sure I do. All the time."

"Look at this new court," Joe said. "It's a closed-up, isolated box. But I'm not sure it's much different from any other teaching station."

"What do you mean?"

"Sometimes I look around the campus." Joe gestured with his arm. "I see it as seventy little boxes, each one with a teacher in it. Then we pour in the students and hope that something goes on inside those boxes that will help them grow toward responsible adulthood."

"That's not a bad analogy," Tom said. "We *are* insulated—so insulated." He recalled the varying experiences he'd had with all of the students in his six classes. He always assumed he was giving them the best possible instruction, but he often wondered how he could really measure his success. Even within the bounds of a relatively confined course of study, there were many choices. And choices elicit values. He recalled his choice of literary samples for Bonnie's class. He had deliberately excluded Proust and Gide, but Bonnie would have used them extensively. Who was right? And was there really any way to tell?

The corridor fell into pitch blackness as Joe turned off the lights and then became slightly illuminated as he opened the door to the lighted entry. They stepped outside, letting the door close behind them.

"Well, if you come up with any new ideas on how to measure successful instruction, let me know," Joe said. "I have to do several teacher evaluations every year, and, I have to admit, sometimes I feel like I'm stabbing in the dark."

"I wouldn't like that job."

Joe placed his key inside the lock to the door, but before he could turn it, a shrill whistle split the air.

Tom looked in the direction of the sound and saw Lee Wong walking toward them, waving. Lee was a short, dark-haired man with a muscular build. A taller figure walked behind him. As they neared, Tom recognized the second person as Mark Banazech.

"Hi, Lee," Joe said. "Is your meeting over?"

"Yes, we wound things up about fifteen minutes ago."

"Hi, Mark," Joe said. "What are you doing here tonight?"

"I asked Mark to come to the last part of the meeting," Lee said. "He brought some ideas for the Olympics from the student council. We thought we'd get in a couple of games before we left. Don't bother locking up."

Joe removed his key from the lock. "It's all yours. Oh, we took a peek at your new toy."

"The combination court?" Lee asked.

"Yeah."

"I'll begin using it next week," Lee said.

"Well, if ever you can't find me, I'll be in there," Joe said. "It's the best spot on campus."

"I'll remember that."

Lee and Mark waved and started inside. Then Mark turned back. "Oh, Mr. Kerzig, did you finish marking the compositions?"

"After school this afternoon," Tom answered.

"How did mine look?" Mark asked.

"Well, as I recall, you had only two or three errors. I'd say you did pretty well."

Mark smiled. "I'm glad I rewrote it before I turned it in, then." He followed Lee into the gymnasium.

"Now there's a good example," Joe said as the door closed. "He's a bright kid and seems to have everything going for him. Somehow, though, I have the strange feeling he's not quite ready to step out into the world in June."

"Well, you know, I always assumed he was a real scholar, too," Tom said. "But now I'm not so sure. That composition he was referring to... He rewrote it to make it as accurate as possible, but it still exhibits a struggle with terminology. Those are the errors I mentioned. He uses a lot of big words apparently without knowing what they mean."

"Hmm...that fits my impression. Kind of a *put-on* intellectualism."

"You might say that."

"It seems to have served him well, though," Joe said. "He's done extremely well in his classes."

"Yes."

"Maybe that's why he always seems so—this may seem a little strong—so...arrogant."

"I've sensed that with a lot of the students in Bonnie's class," Tom said. "The LENA program seems to encourage that trait."

"It doesn't have to, though. It doesn't seem to have affected Joni Irving that way."

"Yeah, that's true. Oh, that reminds me..." He glanced at his watch. It was just after 8:30. "I have to get cleaned up. I'm meeting with the Irvings tonight."

"That's a late meeting," Joe said.

"Well, we both had schedule problems." He didn't want to tell Joe about his concern. There may be no reason. "Thanks for the game, Joe. I'll see you tomorrow."

"Yeah. The next time we play I won't let you win!"

Tom laughed and walked rapidly toward the parking lot. The cool night air brushed the remaining perspiration from his forehead and face. As he passed by the school buildings, he chuckled as he recalled Joe's comparison of the classrooms with boxes. Pour them in, pour them out. Same ingredients, different cooks. What makes the difference?

By 9:25 Tom had arrived in the general neighborhood of the Irvings' house. He pulled over to the curb, turned on the dome light, and studied a map to find the exact location. Their house should be about two blocks to the right. He set the map down, turned off the light, and proceeded. Glancing at the addresses on the houses as he drove, he slowed as he saw flashing red lights in the distance. As he neared the flashing lights, he saw that they emanated from two police cars and an ambulance. A spotlight from one of the police cars shone on the porch of a house, making its address clearly visible. It was the Irvings'.

Tom pulled up behind one of the police cars and stepped out onto the street. A few people stood on the porches of the nearby houses, watching. Tom shut the door, stepped up to the sidewalk, and walked toward the Irvings' house. Two uniformed police officers stood on the porch, talking quietly. They looked up as two ambulance attendants wheeled a gurney out the front door and down the stairs to the ground level. A figure on the gurney lay hidden by a sheet which covered it completely. Tom approached them, but they motioned him back, and wheeled the gurney to the back of the ambulance.

Tom heard a deep sobbing and he looked up to see Lloyd and Sally Irving coming out the door, accompanied by a large, heavyset man. Sally's face was buried in her hands, and she was being led by Lloyd, who walked forward slowly, his eyes locked in a blank stare. Tom walked up quickly to meet them.

"Lloyd...Sally. What is it?" he asked. "What happened?"

The heavyset man stepped between them and took Tom's arm. "Please don't try to talk to them now."

Lloyd looked over and slowly blinked his eyes. "It's all right, Inspector. He's a friend. He's...he's one of Joni's teachers."

Sally looked up now. Her eyes were red, her face drenched with tears.

Tom stepped in front of them and touched their arms. "Lloyd, what..."

"It's Joni," Sally sobbed, and the tears flowed again.

"She's...she's dead, Tom," Lloyd said stiffly. "Joni's dead."

"What?" Tom looked toward the ambulance and saw the attendants push the gurney inside and shut the door.

"Please, sir." The inspector took Tom's arm again and pulled him back. He motioned toward the two uniformed officers, who then stepped up beside Lloyd and Sally.

"What...what do we..." Lloyd began mumbling incoherently.

The inspector drew his hand across his face and spoke to them softly. "They'll take you. We just have to get some information. I'm sorry."

Lloyd nodded and led Sally before the officers. They got

into the back seat of one of the police cars and the officers got in the front. The flashing light on the ambulance was extinguished and the vehicle slowly pulled away from the curb. The officer in the police car turned off the circling light also and followed the ambulance.

The inspector silently watched the vehicles for a moment. He sighed heavily and turned to Tom. "You're a friend, they said...a teacher?"

"Yes. I'm Tom...Tom Kerzig."

"I'm Inspector Gruber." He looked toward the house and shook his head. "I hate this!"

"What is it? What happened?"

"We had a tragedy here tonight," Gruber said. "A real tragedy."

"What happened?"

"I don't understand it. I can't explain it." He took Tom by the arm and spoke intensely. "Maybe you can tell *me*...tell me why a young girl with everything going for her would take her life."

"No...no!" The inspector's words fell on him like a knife. He struggled to speak. "No...she wouldn't..." And now the image of her parents' grief plunged more deeply into his consciousness. "Lloyd and Sally...didn't they tell you...she wouldn't..."

"Sure they did. But parents always say that. It's a terrible thing to deal with."

"But how do you know...I mean...how did it happen?"

"The parents came home from a church meeting and found her in her room. She was already dead." Gruber held out a plastic bag. "We found these. And she had a needle puncture in her arm."

Tom looked at the bag. Inside was a small hypodermic needle and three capsules—two-toned, white on one end and gray with a sprinkling of red spots on the other.

"We won't know for sure until we get the lab tests," Gruber said. "But it's a pretty sure thing." He folded the bag carefully and placed it in his inside coat pocket. "And there was a note."

"May I...may I see it?" Tom asked. "She wrote something in class. That's why I came tonight...to talk to them. She wrote something that concerned me."

Gruber thrust his hands in his pockets, spat on the ground, and spoke harshly. "What are you people in the schools doing with these kids?"

"What do you mean?"

"Can't you teach them to stop playing with their minds? Can't you show them what happens?"

"I know. We do...I do..."

Gruber sighed again and placed a hand on Tom's arm. "Sorry. I don't mean to take it out on you. It's just that I get so angry "

"Inspector...those capsules. Are they common?"

"We'll have to wait for the lab tests."

"I mean the appearance," Tom said.

"The shell?"

Tom nodded.

"We've seen quite a few of them in the last two weeks. I think one of your students recently got busted with some of them."

"Yes. So I hear."

Gruber walked toward his car. Then he turned back and cocked his head. "Look, Mr. Kerzig, do you have any information I should know about this girl?"

"I might."

Gruber rubbed his hand across the back of his neck.

"What time do you finish teaching?"

"Three o'clock."

"I'll meet you in your room at three o'clock tomorrow." Gruber walked quickly to the driver's side and opened the door.

"I'm in room number—"

"I'll find you." He sat heavily and closed the door.

Tom watched as Gruber leaned forward under the circling glow of the red light and started the car. The car moved ahead slowly, the crimson illumination falling vaguely on the trees as it passed. Then the flashing light went out and the vehicle sped off into the darkness.

Tom felt himself step impulsively toward the Irvings' house. His foot fell on a wide crack in the sidewalk leading to the porch and he halted. Without the glaring beam of the spotlight, the house was dark now. He glanced at windows which were visible along the front, and wondered which one, if any, led to Joni's room. The window...it bumped against her wish. Why? What was her wish? *I will fly away in a dream. I will chase myself away from the presence of the light, like a vision, searching for the night.*

Tom turned around and walked toward his car. His mind reeled from the reality of her death. He had just read her paper last night. Last night. Why didn't he call then? Talk to them, tell them...anything. Instead he had waited, talked to Nita. Why?

Tom placed his hand on the cold metal of his door handle and leaned heavily on the roof of the car. He shuddered slightly. He opened the door, got in, and closed the door behind him. The interior of the vehicle closed in about him like a box and he felt suddenly more secure...insulated. He put his hand to his face and wiped away his tears. *Whose box were you in, Joni? Who poured you out? Only two days. No excuse. I should have done...something.*

Tom started the car and turned on his headlights. The bright beams shone on the vague form of a tree beside the road. In the darkness its branches appeared gnarled and the leaves hung like shriveled fruit, swaying gently in the shadows. *"What of life?" mocks the dark master. The fruit is gone. The fruit is gone.*

9

Tom arrived at school early the next morning at Walt's request. When Tom had called him the night before to inform him of Joni's death, Walt had suggested they meet before the other students were told. Apparently no one else knew about it, because the teachers and other staff members milling around in the office were conversing in their normal jocular manner. Walt was leaning over his secretary's desk looking through some papers, and as Tom approached, he looked at him over the top of his half-glasses without moving. He stood upright and motioned for Tom to follow him. They entered Walt's office and the principal closed the door behind them.

"Good morning, Tom. Thanks for coming early."

"Sure."

Nita was seated in one of the upholstered chairs in front of Walt's desk. Another chair sat empty beside her.

"Sit down, sit down." Walt pointed to the empty chair.

"Hello, Nita." Tom sat down and looked over at Nita, who was staring at the wall behind Walt's desk.

Nita looked at him with a slight smile. "Hi, Tom." She lowered her head and picked at one of her fingernails.

"Well, now, let's see what we're about." Walt sat in the large swivel chair behind his desk. "I told Nita what happened, Tom. And I asked her to meet with us this morning."

"Sure. That's a good idea," Tom said.

"No one else knows, though," Walt said. "That's why I asked you both to come in early. We need to think about...well...what to say. I mean, how to tell everyone. The other students, of course, and...well...everyone. This is a very critical time. With the board meeting next month to approve the expansion of the program, it's important that nothing happens that might...well...hinder their decision making."

"I don't see how this could affect that decision," Tom said.

"Joni was in the program," Walt said. "Think about it. Two weeks ago a LENA student was arrested while under the influence of LSD, and now Joni's suicide from an overdose of—"

"Suicide hasn't been established yet," Tom interrupted.

"Well, after you called me last night, I contacted that police inspector," Walt said. "Ah...what's his name?"

"Gruber."

"Yes. Inspector Gruber. He told me he was quite certain it was suicide. I mean, the hypodermic was found, and she did have a puncture in her arm. I think we can safely accept his assumption."

Tom sighed and glanced over at Nita. She raised her eyes to his momentarily, then dropped them again.

"But, you see, some people will try to make something of this," Walt went on. "You know, the program is too demanding, pushed her to the brink. We know that's not the case, naturally, but I promise you, some of the crazies will make that claim."

"I don't understand, Walt," Tom said. "What are you trying to do?"

"We have to make it very clear that the LENA program is not bringing out this kind of behavior." Walt leaned out on the center of his desk and looked at Nita over the top of his glasses. "Nita, what do you think? Did you have a chance to look over Joni's file?"

"Yes, I did. Well, actually..." She glanced briefly at Tom. "Tom and I were discussing Joni just...just yesterday."

Yes, Nita, Tom thought. *Just yesterday. You remember. I came to you because I was concerned about Joni's state of mind. You told me not to worry. You told me her composition was indicative of some healthy inner struggle or just a natural release of creative expression. Not to worry...*

"We talked about her background," Nita went on, "and how she was somewhat different from the other program students."

"Yes?" Walt took a pen from his pocket and poised it over a yellow writing pad.

"The others don't come from such conservative religious families," Nita explained. "I told Tom that she was one of only three program students whose parents excluded them from the health and personal values course."

"Oh?" Walt scribbled on the pad. "She didn't take the course?"

"No. And...ah..." She glanced at Tom again. "Tom showed me one of her compositions. It showed what seemed to be a real struggle against her parents' fundamentalist beliefs."

"A healthy struggle," you said... "just a healthy struggle..."

"Yes, that sounds reasonable." Walt wrote hurriedly on the pad. "If she had taken the health and personal values course, she could have dealt with that struggle more effectively, couldn't she?"

"I believe so," Nita said.

"Walt, you're making too many assumptions too quickly," Tom said.

"Well, everyone is going to be making assumptions,"

Walt said. "We just have to make sure they make the *right* ones."

"But how do you know—"

"All right!" Walt grossly placed a period at the end of his notations, picked up the pad, and through the half-lenses, moved his eyes back and forth as he read what he had written. "This will be enough." He replaced the pad on the desk and tapped his pen on it. "Now, we need to decide how to tell the students."

"I can do that," Tom said.

"No, you haven't been with the program long enough," Walt said. "You don't understand these kids. They're very...ah...sensitive." He set his pen down, looked at Nita, and folded his hands before him. "Nita, I want you to go to Bonnie's class this morning and tell the students what happened. Counsel them. You know...the way you showed the teachers in that one in-service session we had."

Nita sat back stiffly in her chair, her hands clutching at the curved wooden arms. "I don't know, Walt. I feel a little strange about this."

"We all feel a little strange," Walt said gruffly. "One of our students has committed suicide!"

"I mean, I haven't met with these students as a group," she said haltingly. "Maybe..." Nita looked at Tom as she continued, "Maybe Tom *should* be the one to tell them."

"No. Tom hasn't had the training," Walt said. "You're clearly the right one to do it."

"It always seems simple in the workshop simulations," Nita said. "But this is real. I'm not sure I'd know how to start."

"All right. Listen..." Walt sat back and wiggled his chair slightly back and forth. "I'll go up, too. I'll make the announcement and you do the counseling. How does that sound?"

"Yes. That's better."

"I'd like to be there, too, Walt," Tom said.

"What? Oh. Oh, yes, of course. We'll all go." He slapped his hands on the desk, stood, and looked at the clock on the wall. "We have about fifteen minutes. Nita, you and Tom go on up. I'll break the news to a few people here and then I'll join you." He strode across the room, opened the door, and left.

"Well, I guess we'd better get going," Tom said.

"Tom..." Nita placed her hand on his arm. "It's so terrible about Joni." Her hand squeezed tightly into his flesh. "I'm so sorry."

"So am I, Nita. So am I."

Tom, Walt, and Nita stood at the front of the classroom as the students filed in. A few of them broke from their talking and laughter long enough to cast a puzzled glance toward the three of them, but most just marched energetically in, sat, and became intent upon finishing their conversations before they were interrupted by the tardy bell. Tom studied the students' faces as they sat down. None of them apparently knew. He felt a twinge of pain in his head as he looked at Joni's empty desk. The students' laughter merged into an indistinguishable noise and he momentarily imagined her sitting there, quietly, with her faint, confident smile.

The ringing of the bell cleared Tom's head. The students reluctantly turned from their conversations and waited expectantly for one of the adults to speak.

Walt stepped forward and smiled. "Good morning, students. I guess you're wondering why we're all here today." He fidgeted nervously. "I'm afraid we have some very sad news. It's about Joni."

The students waited quietly.

"Last night..." Walt cleared his throat and continued. "Last night, Joni committed suicide."

The classroom became a bedlam of shock and denial. A group of girls near where Joni had sat gasped loudly and reached out to touch her desk, tears streaming from their eyes. In the back of the classroom, Mark and several other students looked at one another and shook their heads in disbelief.

Walt raised his arms and quieted the students. "I know what a terrible blow this is to you. That's why I've asked Ms. Masters to be here this morning. She's going to spend a little time with you and help you through this period of shock."

Walt motioned to Nita. Then he took Tom by the arm and they moved back into the corner of the room.

Nita walked slowly forward. "I'd much rather meet with you in a happier situation. I'm sure we all would. But we know we aren't always faced with happy circumstances, are we? You've talked about that in your studies a lot, haven't you? You've learned that, sometimes, things happen that are...contrary to the feeling of universal peace and unity we're all striving for. Things happen that can damage our inner focus, detract from our knowledge that we have the power to...to overcome disappointments and unhappiness."

A girl in the front row raised her hand and spoke through sobs. "Why? Why did she do it?"

Nita glanced at Tom, sighed, and began walking back and forth across the front of the classroom, gesturing as she spoke. "We can't be sure yet. But you all know that influences outside ourselves—peers, employers, teachers, parents—certain influences try to push us into molds—certain manners of thinking, ways of acting. All of us have these influences. Joni certainly did, perhaps more than the rest of us. You all know how important it is to be able to exercise your own wills, establish your own values. This is difficult when people you

rely on, people you trust, are...restrictive of this will and negative toward these values. This can lead to a feeling of
extreme frustration and indecision. It can lead to a feeling
that existence is fruitless. Many of you have experienced this
feeling, haven't you?"

There was a moment of silence as members of the class
looked sadly toward one another.

"It's important that we get these feelings out," Nita said.
"Close your eyes...everyone."

The students sat upright, folded their arms before them,
and closed their eyes.

"Now, quietly, ever so quietly reach down and pull out
some of your hidden fears. People have influenced you, too,
haven't they? Forces have thrust themselves on you, making
you doubt your own power. Draw these feelings out. Let
them be shown."

A few students began swaying forward and backward,
and a low hum passed from their closed lips. Others followed
suit and soon two-thirds of the class was swaying and humming.

"All right," Nita said. "Now remember what you've
learned. How do we deal with this?"

"Sadness is false, because it is contrary to my inner feeling of harmony," a boy in the middle of the room spoke
without changing his position or opening his eyes. "I am still
in charge. I can cast it out...deny it."

"Good," Nita said. "Others, please. How do we deal
with this?"

"All experience is a positive aspect of my aura," a girl
offered. "Even loss is gain, because I am still here. I am
vibrant and alive."

"Yes, yes," Nita encouraged. "Let the feelings rule."

"There was something different about Joni," one boy

said. "I couldn't know her...didn't feel the unity. Was she in touch with her karma? Who knows?"

"Joni is gone now," Nita said. "Think of *our* feelings. How...how do *we* deal with this experience?"

"Death is a stopover," another boy said. "We will all experience it momentarily in our journey from one existence to another. It is nothing."

"It is nothing, but now we have the essence," a girl said. "We have the power to be anything we want in this existence and to overcome all negative influences."

"Yes. Yes, feel the power of overcoming," Nita encouraged.

"Didn't feel the unity," the other boy repeated. "Joni... where is she? What level...who knows?"

"No, our own feelings." Nita glanced quickly over to where Tom and Walt stood in the corner, her eyes were wide, fearful. "Joni is gone," she repeated intensely. "This is an exercise for *us...our* feelings...*our* resolution to maintain."

"I think I do," a girl said in the back of the room. "It's just a shadow now, but I think I see something. There's a light inside it and it's growing."

"Wait," Nita muttered. "Don't leap so far. Don't..."

But the girl didn't seem to hear her. She continued her swaying, in a greater motion now, and her voice became loud and desperate. "Yes, I think it's Joni. I can see her now, and she's smiling. And I can almost hear her voice. *All is well...all is well..*"

Nita walked quickly to the back of the room and placed her hands on the girl's shoulders. "Yes, if she could, she would tell us that." Nita was stammering, struggling with words. "And she would say...come back to now...come back to now and be the feelings of ourselves. Someone else, please...back to now... What are the feelings of ourselves?"

"All is well," another girl said.

And then, throughout the classroom, the chanting echoed, "All is well. All is well. All is well. All is well."

"Yes, all is well." Nita returned to the front of the room. "And now, let's *see* our reality. Open your eyes. Open your eyes and realize that we are here and we are in charge. The unity continues."

One by one the students stopped swaying, opened their eyes, and dropped their arms to their desks. Finally, all sat quietly looking at Nita.

Nita closed her eyes and sighed deeply. Then she opened her eyes and smiled. "All is well, people. All is well!"

Nita walked over to Tom and Walt. "Tom, is there something..." she whispered and then glanced back at the students, "is there something quiet they could do for a while?"

"Yes, we're studying out of the Anthology," Tom said.

"Page?"

"Uh..." Tom struggled to visualize the notation in his lesson plans for today. He planned to begin with an introduction to the philosophical viewpoint of Camus. "Yes, now I remember. Page 327."

"Thanks." Nita walked back to the front of the classroom. "We're going to channel our thoughts into some quiet reading for a while, class. Mr. Kerzig will be working with you in a few moments, and in preparation, will you please begin reading in the Anthology, on page 327?"

The students quietly picked up their books, placed them on their desks, opened to the assigned page, and began reading.

Nita turned and rejoined Tom and Walt. "All right. It's done."

"That's marvelous!" Walt exclaimed quietly. "I don't know what you were worried about, Nita. You did a great job!"

"I don't know for sure. They may still be repressing..."

"No, they're fine," Walt insisted. "And they'll remember what you told them. That's what comes of all the restrictions and negative influences."

"I don't remember saying exactly that," Nita said.

"You did fine, just fine." Walt patted her on the arm. "All is well. All is well." He smiled and walked out of the classroom.

Nita started to follow Walt, but Tom took her by the arm. "Wait, Nita."

"What?" Nita was not smiling, but the fear was gone from her eyes. "It's all right, Tom. They're all right now."

"No. No, I don't think so. What happened, Nita? What was that all about?"

Nita studied the students for a moment, then she motioned for Tom to step outside with her. Once there, she spoke softly, but intensely. "I'm going to have to speak with Bonnie. She's got those kids too far out on the edge. They're too ready to—"

"I know," Tom said. "One moment they were sharing their grief, and the next, they were playing some kind of extrasensory game."

"But you see..." Nita paused and slowly shook her head. "I just need to talk with Bonnie. She has to work harder on the restraining mechanisms."

"Nita..." Tom frowned and shook his head. "I haven't had any training in this kind of thing."

"I know, Tom. And that's all right. You'll be good for them while Bonnie's out. You'll provide a good, steady, non-disturbing influence. I'll work with Bonnie on her approach when she gets back."

Tom started to respond, but then he held back.

"They really are fine now, Tom."

Tom glanced quickly into the classroom. "How about next period, or tomorrow, or next week?"

"The other teachers will know what to do. Call me if you need me." She smiled and walked briskly down the corridor.

Tom returned to the classroom and surveyed the students, their eyes still intent on their reading. At least they were attentive. He had to give that to Nita. She certainly brought them around. But from what? How did they leap in and out of such a mystical experience so quickly? *Nita may think everything is all right now,* thought Tom. *But in the midst of it, she was terrified.*

Tom stepped behind the desk and picked up his copy of the Anthology. He flipped through the pages to the assigned section. They would be studying the philosophical viewpoint of Albert Camus. The Anthology contained an excerpt from his essay, "The Myth of Sisyphus." The excerpt was the segment entitled, "An Absurd Reasoning." A chill suddenly shot through him as he realized that the first subsection was entitled, "Absurdity and Suicide." He looked up impulsively and considered changing the assignment, but, of course, it was too late. He read the first four sentences of the excerpt:

> There is but one truly serious philosophical problem, and that is suicide. Judging whether life is or is not worth living amounts to answering the fundamental question of philosophy. All the rest— whether or not the world has three dimensions, whether the mind has nine or twelve categories— comes afterwards. These are games; one must first answer.

Any other time he would have viewed this as an outstandingly well-related assignment—taking a relevant current event and using it as a springboard to discovery. But this event, at this time, with these students... But it was done. He would just have to make the best of it.

By the end of the day, Tom was exhausted, and when Inspector Gruber entered his classroom, he was leaning back in his chair, with his feet on his desk. The large man smiled, pulled up another chair beside the desk, and sat down.

"You look beat," Gruber said.

"Yeah, it was a pretty rough day."

"I don't know how you do it. I couldn't work with a bunch of kids like that all day."

"No, it's not that. It's just...everything."

"Yeah, I didn't sleep much last night, myself," Gruber said. "I kept thinking about that little girl. I can work with kids that get into trouble. But this..."

"You get the worst to work with all the time," Tom said. "In that respect your job is a lot harder than mine."

Gruber slumped down in his chair. "All right. What can you tell me about Joni Irving?"

"First of all, I'm a little limited. I just took over this class on Monday, so I saw Joni in this setting for only two days."

"Yeah, that really isn't much time," Gruber said. "So, what can you..."

"I also knew her from church, though. And her parents. I knew them well enough to think that what happened just doesn't make sense." Tom paused as he caught a fleeting recollection of Joni sitting in class...and then lying on the gurney. "But then...neither did her composition."

"Composition?"

"Joni is in a special program here at school called LENA. It's a quasi-acronym for Leaders of the New Age."

"Yeah, I think I read about that in the paper," Gruber said. "It's supposed to really push their mental capacities."

"Yes, that's part of it. They get involved in some rather unusual activities. One of these is an external awareness exercise. They refer to it as an *out-of-body experience.*"

"Sounds weird."

"Well..." Tom reached inside a folder and pulled out a copy of Joni's composition he had made for Gruber. "This is a composition Joni wrote as part of that exercise. She turned it in on Monday, and then, on the very next day..." Tom paused and wiped his eyes. "I don't know if there's anything significant here, but it just didn't seem to match my perception of her."

Gruber narrowed his eyes and scratched his cheek aimlessly as he read the first page. "Well, I don't know. We might be able to find some relationship with the note she left."

"The note. Could I see it now?"

Gruber set the composition down. "I couldn't let you see it last night. I had to enter it into evidence." He pulled a folded sheet of paper from his pocket and handed it to Tom. "Here's a copy of it. We pulled it out of the typewriter in her room."

Tom opened the sheet. In the center of the page were two sentences:

Death is the penultimate cakra!
All else is illusion.

"Maybe you can help me with this. What's a *cakra?*" Gruber asked, pronouncing it with a "k" sound.

"Actually, it's pronounced *chakra.*"

"Really? What does it mean?"

"Well, I have just a vague knowledge of the word," Tom said. "It's a term from the Hindu religion. Cakras are supposed to be the psychic centers of the body."

"Hmm... And *penultimate,* of course, is supposed to be the greatest, or the best?" Gruber asked.

"That's actually a common misuse of the word."

"What do you mean?"

"It really means *next to the last*, or *almost the ultimate*," Tom said.

"Well, that's why I'm a detective, and not an English teacher." Gruber laughed.

"It's not exactly a word you need in your everyday life." Tom paused and studied the sentences again. "But Joni would have known better. Penultimate cakra... Almost the ultimate psychic center." He shook his head. "I can't say yet. I'll have to study this some more, I'm afraid."

"That's fine. You've been a lot of help already." Gruber sat forward as though he was about to leave.

"Inspector..."

"Yeah?"

"Do you know what the drugs were yet?" Tom asked.

"Just preliminary. Looks like heroin in the syringe. That's what killed her—a massive overdose. And the capsules probably contain some LSD. I don't know why she had those, unless to psyche her up for shooting the hard stuff."

Tom recalled finding the capsules in the English department office desk, and his meeting with Walt and Joe. *It only takes a tenth of a milligram to send you to the moon*, Joe had said.

"Inspector...the capsules..." Tom said. "What if..."

"What?"

But then Tom remembered Walt, spinning around in his chair, demanding, "I don't want anything said about drugs to anybody until we find out what we're talking about!" And they didn't know yet. They could be anything.

"What if *what?*" Gruber repeated.

"Nothing. Never mind."

"Okay. So is there anybody else I should talk to who could give me a line on Joni?"

"Anyone else..." Of course. Who else? She worked with her for four years. And Tom wouldn't have to say a thing. "Yes. You should talk to her regular English teacher—the one I'm subbing for."

"Who's that?"

"Bonnie Teague. But you'll have to see her in the hospital. She's recovering from an automobile accident."

"Teague..." Gruber's eyes narrowed and he smiled knowingly. "Yeah. I know about her. That's not my case, but yeah, I've heard."

Tom wondered for a moment if he'd given Gruber too much information. But Bonnie was the best contact, and getting information which might relate to Joni's death was more important now than protecting Bonnie from additional police questioning.

"Thanks, Mr. Kerzig," Gruber said as he stood up.

"Sure." Tom stood and shook hands with the inspector.

"Contact me when you find out about those *kakras*, or *sakras*, or *chakras*, or whatever," Gruber said as he headed toward the door.

"I sure will."

Gruber turned in the doorway and leaned against the frame. "Interesting thing about that Teague case."

"What's that?"

"Well, she got a pretty bad head injury, you know?"

"Right."

"Somehow she went through the *passenger* side of the windshield."

"What?"

With a shrug and a smile, Gruber walked out of the room.

10

The lingering chill of winter hung in the air and, even with the sun directly overhead, Tom found it more comfortable to place his hands in his pockets as he passed through the wide concrete archway leading to the cemetery. The landscaping outside the black fence was full and green, but inside, most of the trees were deciduous, their bare branches thrusting themselves upward in stark surrender to the elements. Even the ground was raked clean of all evidence of their life-bearing leaves. *No one should be buried in the winter time,* he thought. *Not here. There's too much death above the ground. But the trees will live again in the spring.*

A small gathering of people sat in closely arranged chairs twenty yards away, and Tom quickened his pace as he approached them. The memorial service had concluded an hour ago, and the Irvings had elected to have the burial immediately following—but no processional. Just a small gathering of family, close friends, and those who wanted one last chance to say goodbye. A few chairs sat empty in the back row. He sat down and the cold chill of the metal passed uncomfortably through his trousers. He leaned slightly to see through the heads of those in front of him. Lloyd and Sally Irving sat motionless in the front row. Beside them sat Pastor Bentley.

Tom heard a squeak and a dull noise from the chair beside him. He turned to see Walt sitting down. The principal smiled and patted him on the arm.

"Am I late?" Walt asked.

"No. They haven't started yet. I didn't see you at the memorial service."

Walt shook his head. "I knew there'd be a lot of people there. Coming here, I can be sure to see the parents." He paused and squinted across the top of his half-glasses. "What are their names?"

"Lloyd and Sally."

"That's right. Anyway, make sure they know the school people are here for them." Walt shifted his body and leaned back. "Were many of our people at the memorial?"

"Joe, Nita, and most of Joni's teachers."

"Good." Walt nodded and crossed his arms. "That's good."

Tom looked forward again. Through the heads in front of him he could see the form of the casket, hanging on its temporary stand, waiting to be lowered. A large spray of flowers sat on top of it, the bright colors a stark contrast to its drab gray. Pastor Bentley leaned over and whispered something in Sally's ear. Then he stood and stepped forward. He paused momentarily before the casket and then turned back to the gathering. He was a stocky, middle-aged man, with pronounced facial wrinkles and a large nose. The slight breeze sporadically shifted the pastor's heavy, loose-hanging hair. His lips were turned in a sad smile, and his hands were clasped before him around a small Bible.

"Lloyd and Sally wanted me to thank you all for coming," Pastor Bentley said. "Most of you, I believe, were at the memorial service. Some of you took the opportunity to share the many wonderful things you remember about Joni Irving. We are not here now to close the chapter on those memories, for they will last as long as there are loved ones, friends, and acquaintances to recall them. But there is a closing as there will be in all of our lives. And that is the purpose of this brief ceremony—a time for us to acknowledge that Joni has left the mortal trappings and passed into immortality."

Pastor Bentley raised the Bible and leafed slowly through its pages. He placed his hand on a page and looked up. "All of us remember Joni's quiet smile and willing nature. She is the perfect example of what Paul was talking about in his letter to the Philippians." He lowered his head and read:

> Do all things without murmuring and disputing, that you may become blameless and harmless, children of God without fault in the midst of a crooked and perverse generation, among whom you shine as lights in the world, holding fast the word of life, so that I may rejoice in the day of Christ that I have not run in vain or labored in vain.

Pastor Bentley looked up and smiled. "Oh, how Joni's light shone! And how blamelessly she stood in the midst of *her* perverse generation. Joni was truly a child of God. Joni was truly blameless." Pastor Bentley closed the Bible, squeezed his eyes shut, and lowered his chin into his hand. He stood motionless for a moment, as tears streamed from his tightly closed lids. Then he clumsily wiped his face. "Forgive me." He turned his head upward. "Forgive me, Lord." He opened the Bible again and nodded slowly. Then he looked up with a faint smile. "I'm supposed to be an example of strength here. And, of course, in the way that really counts, I can be. Joni is with the Lord! And we can praise God for that!"

A few whispers of "Yes," and "Thank you, Jesus," erupted silently from those gathered.

"She will rejoice in the day of Christ," Pastor Bentley continued. "But now *we* have a responsibility to see that she did not run in vain, or labor in vain. We have a responsibility to her memory, to hold it blameless, as she, in her life, became blameless through the grace of God." He placed his hand on the corner of the casket. "Goodbye, Joni. We will miss you. But we will see you again in the day of the Lord." Pastor Bentley turned back and spoke softly. "Please join me in prayer."

Tom closed his eyes and lowered his head. He felt Walt shift in his chair as Pastor Bentley began to pray.

"Dear Lord, we are not here to pray for Joni. For she is your child and she is with you now. But we miss her. And we want to do everything in our power to preserve her memory—unmarred. She stood wonderfully above the perversity about her. May we use her memory as a memorial to Your love and as a beacon to the truth of Your Word. In Jesus name we pray. Amen."

The people stood and whispered quietly. Lloyd and Sally walked up to either side of Pastor Bentley and he put his arms around them. The people formed a line and passed slowly by them, some saying a few words, others compassionately holding their hands or embracing them.

Walt took Tom by the arm and pulled him a few feet away from the gathering. "I'm going to wait until the others pass by."

"All right."

"Listen, I haven't had a chance to speak with you since Wednesday. How did...ah...how is everything going with the class?"

"Just fine." Tom paused and then added wryly, "They hardly skipped a beat."

"Wonderful. That's just wonderful." Walt seemed to miss the touch of bitterness in Tom's voice. "Nita did a great job of handling them. I must remember to thank her again."

"What I meant, Walt, was that the other kids are going on almost as though she never existed," Tom said. "They never even talk about her."

"Well, they've developed a wonderful ability to bounce back," Walt said. "That's the strength of the program. It builds tremendous emotional stability."

"I don't see it quite that way."

"Oh, look," Walt interrupted their discussion. "Most of the others have gone. Let's go up and give our respects."

Walt walked quickly up and stood behind the person now talking to the Irvings. Pastor Bentley stood a few feet away, talking to a small group of people. Tom shook his head and followed Walt. As he approached, Lloyd acknowledged him with a tight smile.

"Lloyd, Sally, I'm sure you've met Walt Josephson, the principal."

"Yes, of course," Sally said vaguely.

"I just want you to know how saddened I am by this tragic event." Walt shook Lloyd's hand and then Sally's. "Joni was a wonderful student and one of my favorite people."

"Thank you," Lloyd mumbled.

"If there is ever anything we, at the school, can do to help you through this time, please let us know."

"Yes, yes we will," Lloyd said.

Walt placed his hand on Tom's arm. "We need to place something in the bulletin, something nice. Why don't you see me on Monday and we'll put something together?"

"Sure."

Walt patted him on the arm, turned, and hurried off.

Tom was about to apologize to Lloyd and Sally for Walt's insensitive behavior when Lloyd raised his hand and shook his head slowly.

"It's all right, Tom. We know Walt. He's just...it's all right."

"Thank you for coming, Tom," Sally said. "Joni really

enjoyed the brief time..." She closed her eyes and turned away.

"I still can't believe it," Tom said.

"Neither can we," Lloyd said. "Not her death. But the way, the circumstances..." His face was contorted with disbelief. "Joni never used drugs, Tom."

"No, never!" Sally looked up with tear-filled eyes. "And she would never have taken her own life."

"No, of course not," Tom agreed. But he was just trying to reassure them. He truthfully didn't know what to think. He didn't want to believe it of Joni. But he remembered her composition...the foreboding language...the almost occult images. And there was the suicide note. And Gruber had told him that the parents always deny... Of course. Wouldn't he?

"We were wondering, Tom," Lloyd said. "That day you had asked to talk to us about Joni. Was there something wrong then?"

"No, nothing wrong," Tom replied impulsively. "I just wanted to have a chance to talk to the two of you and Joni."

"But you seemed so eager, Tom," Sally said. "Was there anything that made you think she was depressed, or... We have to know."

He wanted to tell them about Joni's composition and ask what thoughts might have been racing through her head to engender such strange images. How often, since her death, had he studied her final written words. He wanted to give them some assurance, but there were phrases: *A greater shadow...a silhouette vaguely painted in a pastel of gray against the gray of the night. It whisks by quickly, places a veil over my window... I will chase myself away from the presence of the light, like a vision, searching for the night....* Her words were almost searching for death, it seemed. How could he show this to them, at this time, when they were struggling so desperately to reject that possibility?

"We have to know," Sally repeated. "If there's anything you can tell us, please..."

"I just don't know," Tom said, evading the question. "I'd had the class for only two days." He struggled for something to say. Then some of Joni's words came to mind. "I do remember she told me there were a lot of things she didn't like about the program."

"You mean that special program she was in?" Lloyd asked.

"Yes."

"We knew that," Sally said. "We considered taking her out if it."

"But we were told that only certain parts of the program were...ah...controversial," Lloyd said. "So we studied what was offered in those parts and exempted her where we thought it was necessary."

"Did she ever seem to resent that?" Tom asked.

"Not at all," Lloyd said.

Tom wondered if this was true, or if Nita was correct in her assumption that Joni was repressed. But he wasn't the person to decide. And this was not the time or place to bring it up.

"If there's anything you can find out, Tom, please tell us," Sally said.

"Yes. Yes, of course. Of course I will."

Lloyd took Sally by the arm. "Your folks will be at the house, Sally. We should be going."

"Yes." She took Tom's hand and grasped it hard. "Thank you for coming."

"Yes, thank you, Tom," Lloyd echoed as he guided Sally toward the archway.

Tom started to leave the cemetery also, but he turned back as he heard Pastor Bentley calling to him.

"Tommy, wait a minute!" Pastor Bentley waved to the group of people he was talking with and walked quickly over to Tom. "I haven't seen you for a while, and I wanted to be sure to talk with you before you left."

"Yes, it has been a while." Tom held his hand out to him.

Pastor Bentley grasped Tom's hand and shook it firmly. "I'm sorry it has to be under these circumstances."

"Yeah."

"The last time we spoke was when you told me about Clair. And that was what...three months ago?"

"About that," Tom said.

"Has there been any change?"

"No. No change at all."

Pastor Bentley shook his head. "What gets into people? She had just finished her degree, hadn't she? Just gotten a good job?"

"Yes."

"That should have been a positive event. But sometimes success gives people a false sense of direction."

"Well, in her case, I think it was *no* sense of direction," Tom said.

"What do you mean?"

"She told me that her main reason for wanting to separate was that she needed time and space to *find herself*."

Pastor Bentley grimaced and shook his head. "Boy, have I heard that a lot!" He touched Tom on the chest. "Do you know what I call people who are trying to find themselves?"

"What?"

"Self-seekers," Pastor Bentley said, smiling.

Tom laughed. "I fell for that one, didn't I?"

"Well, the thing is, it's not a joke," Pastor Bentley said more seriously. "The good thing about it is she recognizes she's lost. We were *all* lost. That's why Christ came to earth—to save the lost sheep."

Tom shifted uncomfortably as a hot surge rose from his spine. He hoped Pastor Bentley would not become sanctimonious...not now. It was all so much more complicated than that. "I don't think that's what she meant," he muttered finally.

"Probably not," Pastor Bentley said. Then he continued softly, "Come back to church, Tommy, before staying away gets to be a habit."

Tom looked up. Those words sounded strangely familiar. And then he remembered...at the dance. "That's what Joni told me, too," he mumbled.

"She was a shining light."

"Yeah..."

"How about tomorrow?" asked Pastor Bentley.

"What?"

"Come to church tomorrow."

"Well..." Tom paused as he remembered the rest of the weekend's activities. "Oh, I'm picking up Jennifer this afternoon. I'll have her until tomorrow night."

"Perfect," Pastor Bentley said. "Bring her, too. You know, she and Clair haven't been to church since the separation, either. Remember how important church was when you were Jennifer's age."

He remembered. Pastor Bentley had been appointed pastor at the church when Tom was about Jennifer's age. He and Clair were married there. But then they had drifted away.

"I'll see, Pastor," Tom said and turned to walk away.

"Oh, there's one other thing," Pastor Bentley said. "Joni...Lloyd and Sally told me the police haven't come up with an official cause of death yet. They're so set on suicide they don't seem to be looking for anything else."

"I know."

"What about at school?" Pastor Bentley asked. "Does everyone just assume she overdosed on drugs and killed herself?"

"I'm afraid so."

Pastor Bentley clenched his teeth and pounded his fist into the palm of his hand. "They rush to judgment!"

Tom sighed. "What other explanation could there be?"

"When the obvious conclusion doesn't make any sense, people should look for another conclusion."

"Or try to understand why the obvious happened," Tom offered.

Pastor Bentley frowned, placed both hands on Tom's shoulders, and spoke intently. "There are so many strange things going on in the community. So many dark influences. We need help to bring them out...understand them. Will you help?"

"How?"

"Withhold judgment. Search for answers!"

"But aren't the police..."

"The police didn't know Joni," Pastor Bentley said.

"I didn't know her that well, either..."

A banging noise caused the two men to look toward the burial site. Two workers were beginning to fold the chairs. Pastor Bentley squeezed Tom's shoulders and walked over to them.

Tom remembered that he had to pick up Jennifer in a half hour, so he walked quickly toward the cemetery entrance. As he approached the large archway, he saw a figure standing behind the concrete pillar. It was Mark Banazech.

"What are you doing out here, Mark?" Tom asked.

"I didn't know if I should come in or not."

"Well...you were at the memorial service, weren't you?"

"Yes, all the student body officers were there," Mark answered. "And a lot of the other students, too."

"I'm sure it would have been all right, if you wanted to come to this ceremony," Tom said.

Mark looked toward the casket and his eyes narrowed. "It's so...final, isn't it?" Mark turned toward him and started to speak. But then he leaned against the pillar and looked down.

"What is it, Mark?"

Mark looked up. "You were at the dance last week. Something's been bothering me about that. Since Joni..." His voice trailed off.

"What?"

"Well, I was such a jerk...forcing her to dance like that. I mean, she was really upset. And then Monday and Tuesday she seemed so depressed."

"What are you getting at?" Tom asked.

"I just wondered if something I did made her feel so bad that, well...you know..."

"That it would make her commit suicide?"

Mark nodded.

Joe was right about Mark. He really was arrogant! To think that he actually believed his childish actions could drive *anyone* to suicide! Tom suppressed an urge to laugh in his face. "No, Mark. I'm sure that's not the case."

Mark sighed heavily and smiled. "I'm sure glad to hear you say that. It's really been bothering me."

"Well, you can forget about it."

"Thanks, Mr. Kerzig." Mark started to leave.

"Oh, Mark, you know that her death hasn't officially been ruled a suicide yet, don't you?"

Mark frowned. "Well, yes, but, I mean...everyone says..."

"We should wait until we get the official ruling," Tom said. "Don't you think that would be fair...to her parents, I mean?"

"Oh, sure!" Mark quickly agreed. "You're absolutely right."

"Joni wasn't exactly the picture of a typical drug user, anyway, was she?" Tom asked.

"Well..."

"Was she?"

"You're right, Mr. Kerzig. She's dead now. Why should anyone have to be judged after they're dead?"

"What..."

But the boy turned abruptly and ran off.

Tom looked back into the cemetery. The chairs were gone as well as the workers and Pastor Bentley. Only the casket remained—stark and gray against the closely shorn lawn. Soon it would descend and the earth would wrap it in the warmth of its darkness.

11

Tom climbed the four steps and stood on the familiar porch. He glanced to the right and saw something different about the swing that sat near the railing. Then he realized what it was. A brightly colored cushion rested where before had been bare wooden slats. He raised his hand slowly to ring the doorbell. He still couldn't get used to the feeling that he was coming as a stranger to his own home...their home. He pressed the black button, and a two-toned chime rang softly from inside the house. In a moment, he heard the sound of rapid footsteps. The door swung open and Jennifer stood before him, smiling.

"Hi, Dad!"

Tom couldn't remember exactly when Jennifer had shifted from "Daddy" to "Dad," but it was just after the separation. Clair had told him that Jennifer felt more mature now that she was in the third grade. He pulled open the screen door, stooped down, and hugged her.

"Hi, honey. Missed you."

Jennifer gave him a squeeze. Then she pushed herself back and took his hand. "Come in."

Tom stood up and let her pull him into the house. "Are you ready to go?"

"Is that you, Tom?" Clair's head appeared in the door leading to the kitchen. "No. She's not quite ready yet."

"All right." He stood there, holding Jennifer's hand,

looking at Clair. Her slim figure was silhouetted in the sun-light emanating from the kitchen and her short blond hair fell neatly about her face. He hated this—standing in their house, seeing the person who was once so much a part of him now a distant, rigid entity.

"Go back to your room and finish packing, Jennifer," Clair said.

Jennifer released Tom's hand and scurried down the hall to her room.

"She'll just be a few minutes," Clair said. "Want a cup of coffee?"

Tom sighed. "Sure...if it's not too much trouble."

"It's already made." She turned back into the kitchen and motioned for him to follow.

He walked slowly toward the doorway and entered the room he remembered so well. Clair had made a number of cosmetic changes through the rest of the house, but the kitchen looked the same as it did the day they separated. He stepped up to the high breakfast counter and sat on a stool.

"Do you still take it black?" Clair asked, picking up the glass coffee pot.

"Yeah." *We were married for ten years, Clair,* he thought, *and we've been separated for only four months. Why would you have to ask that?* "I see you bought a cushion for the swing."

"Hmm?" She looked up absently and then resumed pouring. "Oh, yes. The warm weather will be here soon and I thought it would be nicer."

"It looks...ah...very attractive," Tom said, fumbling for something to say.

"I think so. Jennifer likes it." She gave a cup of coffee to Tom and set another one on the counter. Then she pulled an adjacent stool out and sat beside him.

"Thanks." He raised the cup to his lips and sipped at the

hot coffee. Out of the corner of his eye, he could see her doing the same. For so many years, they had sat together here, comfortably talking. How quickly that had changed. "I thought you'd have been at the memorial service this morning," he said.

"For Joni Irving?"

"Yes."

"Well...I haven't had any contact with the Irvings for several months. I didn't really feel right about going. It was terrible about her, wasn't it?"

"Yeah."

"I guess I should admit... That's another reason I didn't feel good about going. I deal with negative things all the time at work."

"I thought you felt good about your work at the welfare department," Tom said.

"Oh, I have the opportunity to help people a lot, and that's good. But it really gets frustrating at times." She shook her head. "You were sure right about one thing."

Tom looked up hopefully. "What's that?"

"People are so helpless." She took another sip of coffee and continued talking to him without looking at him. "This afternoon I have to go meet with a family. The father is paralyzed. He gets around in a wheelchair. The mother works for minimum wage at the pharmacy. They have four kids. The oldest one is fifteen and she's just thrown her family into turmoil by having an abortion.

Tom remembered Nita mentioning on Tuesday about having to meet with Walt and some angry parents over a fifteen-year-old's abortion. "I think I know about that situation."

Clair looked at him in surprise. "She's not one of your students, is she? She's just a ninth grader."

"No. I heard about her from Nita Masters."

"Well, that's the one, then," Clair said. "Nita called me a couple of weeks ago to ask about the family."

"That was before the abortion."

"Yes, she told me the girl was pregnant, and she wanted to know how well-equipped I thought the family was to deal with it."

"Deal with it?"

"Yes. You know, financially, emotionally..."

"Why did she ask you, instead of the parents?" Tom asked.

"I work with the schools all the time on family problems," Clair said. "With people that are part of my case load, that is. That's one of my responsibilities."

Tom shook his head and muttered in disbelief, "But why you and not the parents?"

"The girl didn't want her parents to know. I'm an objective third party, representing an involved agency." Clair closed her eyes and took a long gulp of her coffee.

"And so the girl decided to have an abortion?"

Clair nodded slowly.

"Was that the right thing to do?"

"I don't know, Tom," she replied somewhat irritably. "I work for a public agency. I don't make value judgments in situations like this. I just provide information so that other people can make good decisions."

Tom paused and then spoke slowly. "Did this girl make a good decision?"

Clair looked blankly across the room and then responded dispassionately. "That's what I'm struggling with. There were complications...an infection. The parents found out about it and it's torn the family apart. Nita called me two days ago.

She asked me to meet with them, talk to them about their daughter's legal rights and the school's position."

"What are you going to tell them?" Tom asked.

"As I said, that's what I'm struggling with." Clair glanced at the clock on the wall. "I'll know in about two and a half hours."

"Mom..."

Tom turned around to see Jennifer run into the kitchen. He realized for the first time that her hair was cut in a different, stylish wave.

"Should I take my homework?" Jennifer asked.

Clair looked at Tom questioningly. "I don't know what your father is planning to do."

"Yes, bring it," Tom said. "You'll have plenty of time to work on it."

"Oh..." Jennifer scowled.

"Actually, you can probably work on it this afternoon," Tom said. "I'm going to stop at the library on the way home."

Jennifer's face lit up. "Oh, that'll be neat!" And she ran out of the room.

"Her hair is styled differently," Tom said as he watched her leave.

"Yes. A lot of the girls in her class are doing it."

Tom looked at her and held up six fingers. "Six years, Clair. In six years, Jennifer will be fifteen."

"What about it?"

"What if she gets into a situation like this?"

"She won't..."

"Oh?"

"I mean, I hope she won't." Then she scowled at him. "That's why it's so important what you teach your students."

"Our schools have been providing sex education for years," Tom said. "That didn't seem to help this girl."

"Things are different now. Kids are under a lot more influence, pressure." She shook her head. "Maybe you should start sooner."

Tom took another sip and gave her a sideward glance. "So, how soon do you think it should start?"

"As soon as possible," Clair said. "I mean, this girl was only in the ninth grade. There's no telling how long before..."

"Seventh grade?"

"Yes, certainly."

"Fifth grade?"

"Well, in some fashion...an awareness..."

"Third grade?" he persisted.

Clair glanced toward Jennifer's room and sat back. "I don't know."

"Suppose it still fails, Clair?" Tom asked. "And in six years, Jennifer becomes pregnant and doesn't want you or me to find out about it. So she goes to her school counselor..."

Clair shook her head and stood impulsively. "It's too soon, Tom. I don't even want to think about that now. It's too soon."

"I'm ready, Dad!"

Tom looked toward the doorway and laughed as he saw his daughter, suitcase in one hand and a school carrying case in the other. "Okay, young lady. Let's go." He stood and followed her to the front door.

"Have a good time, Jennifer," Clair called. "I'll see you tomorrow night."

Tom opened the door, but then he turned back, and gave Clair a quizzical look. "What did you mean, *I was right?*"

"What?"

"About people being helpless," he reminded her.

She shrugged. "It's just what you've always prided yourself on. You say people shouldn't rely on outside sources for
help if they can't learn to help themselves."

"But I didn't mean..." Tom raised his hand in a vague
gesture. Then he smiled, changed it into a wave, and followed
Jennifer to the car.

Very few changes had been made to the spacious community library since Tom's parents had brought him there as
a child. Tom had introduced Jennifer to the library when she
was four years old, and she enjoyed visiting it as much as he
did. Jennifer instinctively lowered her voice to a whisper as
they entered through the dark double doors, and pointed to a
large oak table near the back which was empty. Tom nodded
and they walked quietly to it. Jennifer set her carrying case on
the table and sat on one of the high-backed wooden chairs.
Tom leaned across the table.

"I'll be right back," he whispered. "I'm going to find
some books."

"Okay, Dad, I'll save your place." She pulled the chair
closer to the table. Then she crossed both legs under her on
the seat of the chair.

"Is that comfortable?" he asked.

Jennifer nodded. Then she leaned forward slightly,
crossed her arms on the table, and closed her eyes.

"Are you sure?"

Jennifer nodded slightly without opening her eyes.

"Okay." He chuckled softly at the sight of his daughter
sitting in such deep thought and walked quickly to the reference section.

This was the first opportunity Tom had had to do some

research since he had talked to Inspector Gruber on Wednesday. He had promised the inspector he would find more information about the term *cakra*. Based on the catalog reference descriptions, four books seemed to provide the most productive search. He gathered those from the shelves and headed back toward the study table. As he approached, he saw Jennifer's feet were now planted firmly on the floor. A book sat open on the table in front of her and a white sheet of paper and an opened box of crayons lay beside it. She was studying the book intently and holding a crayon loosely in her hand.

"Are you doing an art assignment?" He set his books on the table.

"No, it's science," she whispered without looking up.

"Oh."

Tom pulled the chair out carefully and sat across from Jennifer. He found the term *cakra* in the index of one of the books and turned to the page referenced. He confirmed first that what he had told Gruber was correct. Cakras are thought of in Hinduism and Buddhism as psychic centers of the body. He found that the term is used to conceptualize mental states arrived at through the practice of yoga. In Hinduism there are seven major levels, beginning at the base of the spine, and culminating at the top of the head. The psychic experience consists of attempts, through meditation, to rise from cakra to cakra until self-illumination is reached at the highest level—the *samadhi*. And yet, ironically, at that level, nothing external remains, and a person who is in that state for twenty-one days is dead!

But the suicide note had not referred to the *highest* level. Tom could find nothing in this book about the *penultimate*, or the next to the highest level. He searched through the next book without success. Then, in the third book, he found what he thought might be an important reference. The same movement from level to level was mentioned. It came from Tantric tradition, which visualizes a person's female nature-energy remaining dormant and coiled in the form of a serpent. It is awakened and rises through the cakras until it reaches the top. There, it merges with the male supreme being. But at the sixth stage—the penultimate level—a significant vision occurs. The form of God is seen, but a light veil covers the image. The light is there, but it is like the light in a lantern, which cannot be touched because of the intervening glass.

Tom closed his eyes and pressed his thumb and finger against the bridge of his nose as he attempted to recall the phrases that Joni had used in her composition. They came to mind: *scattered...a vision, searching for the night...a small window, bumping against my wish...a glimpse of what's outside...the light from my window cuts through the darkness...I push my wish aside so that I see.* Tom wondered if that was some desperate wish for death attainment of the samadhi. But if that were the case, why did the end of her paper refer to the window remaining intact. What was the phrase? *The rays from the distant star pierce the smallness of my window...my warring thoughts fall back and nestle quietly within the comforting of my mind.* Comforting? Then why such a drastic shift to self-destruction? And why would she relate death to the penultimate level, instead of the final level?

"Do you have a headache, Dad?"

"Hmm?" Tom looked up and saw Jennifer leaning across the table with a concerned look on her face. "Oh. No, honey, I'm just thinking really hard."

"Oh." She nodded and sat back. "I know. I do that, too."

Tom jotted down the page number for copying and closed the book.

"What are you thinking about?" Jennifer asked.

"What?"

"What are you studying in all those books?

"Oh, cakras," he said absently.

"Oh, I know about those!" she said excitedly. "We're studying about them in school. That's what my assignment is about."

Tom smiled and shook his head. "No, Jennifer. I don't think so."

"Mmm-hmm!" she insisted. "Look!" She moved her book aside and tapped her finger on her drawing, which was now complete. In the center was a small girl, sitting cross-legged, with her eyes closed, and her arms crossed before her. Behind her was a brightly differentiated rainbow, and above that were two people, standing back to back.

Tom leaned over the table and studied her drawing.

She pointed to the little girl. "This is me. I'm thinking really hard, just like you were. They're teaching us how to do that in school." She pointed to the lowest arc on the rainbow—a deep violet. It was situated directly behind the base of the girl's spine. "We start thinking here. And when we get better and better, we can understand a lot more things." She emphasized her words by tapping each succeeding level, until her finger reached a bright red band situated behind the girl's head. Tom let his eyes scan back downward over the arcs of the rainbow and a vague recollection from his early school years burst on his consciousness. ROY G. BIV. It must have been in science studies in the fourth or fifth grade, but now it bounced back unbelievably, as a speedy reminder of the seven major colors of the spectrum—red, orange, yellow, green, blue, indigo, violet. There they were in Jennifer's rainbow, beginning correctly at the bottom with the greatest angle of refraction, and proceeding to the least at the top. There they were, the seven colors, the seven levels.

These are the *cakras*. Jennifer moved her finger rhythmically up the bands of the rainbow again.

"Why are you studying this in science?" Tom mumbled.

"We're actually studying about light," Jennifer answered. "But our teacher told us the rainbow can help us understand things. So I'm learning to think really hard so I can understand."

Tom was numbed by the realization that Jennifer's teacher was using a Hindu spiritualist term in a discussion of light refraction. What could possibly be gained by that? Was there some deeper meaning behind this exercise? Or was it merely this generation's ROY G. BIV?

Tom reached his hand across the table and placed his finger at the base of the rainbow. "So as you go higher and higher through the rainbow, you understand more and more?"

"Mmm-hmm."

"And what happens when you get here?" He placed his finger on the top, red band.

"Then we can really understand a lot of things," she said confidently.

Tom sighed and looked again at the two figures, standing back to back. "Who are these?" He pointed to them.

"This is you," she answered, pointing to one. "And this is Mom," she continued, pointing to the other. She drew her hand away suddenly and began collecting the crayons. "I don't know if I'll ever get that good, though."

Tom sat back and silently watched his daughter efficiently box the crayons and place them, the drawing paper, and her book in her carrying case. The drawing was gone, but its image rebounded from his retina and mirrored itself grotesquely on the dark oak of the table. And scattered among the imagined spectrum were jumbled phrases from Joni's paper: *I am the master...follow me...seven colors about his head...they whirl crazily...our deity is unleashed...we will build a city...let the children come...let the children come...*

12

The late morning sun shone brightly behind the low spire of the church and cast a magnified shadow across the broad walkway leading to the auditorium. Tom grasped Jennifer's hand and they walked slowly past the crowd of people gathered outside. The congregation of Pastor Bentley's church was quite large, and when Tom had attended regularly, he was able to slip into a comfortable state of semi-anonymity.

During the first years of their marriage, he and Clair had found satisfaction here. They appreciated the help the church seemed to provide in raising Jennifer. But then, five years ago, things began to change. This was the period Tom had struggled to reconstruct in his attempt to understand Clair's request for a separation. She had begun college and he was busily involved in his career. He had once concluded that their lack of time had caused them to drift away from one another, but he realized now that this hadn't really been a factor. The cause stemmed from some of the courses Clair was taking. She was highly motivated. She would relate her new knowledge to Bentley's messages, and then question Tom about his beliefs. She became...demanding almost. She had asked for simple responses to questions that were so complex. That was the thing he remembered most—his inability to give her a simple response about his complex system of beliefs.

Tom and Clair had agreed to attend other churches, in search of a mutually satisfying religious experience. For over a year they had attended seven or eight different denominations. For a while they had even gone to Daniel Worley's Church of the Inner Spirit. Tom never felt comfortable there, however, because the messages always seemed directed toward an insipid state of self-satisfaction. Then, when Pastor Worley was elected to the school board, Tom decided that the combination of professional and spiritual authority created a deep feeling of discomfort. Until the time of the separation, then, they had returned periodically to Pastor Bentley's church, or, more often, stayed home.

Tom and Jennifer passed through the congestion of people and hurried toward the long classroom building. On the walkway adjacent to this was a table, bearing a large sign: *Sunday School Information.* Tom walked up to the table and was greeted warmly by a heavyset woman sitting behind it.

"Tom! It's good to see you again!" Marge Templeton reached across the table and took his hand firmly. "And hello to you, Jennifer." Marge ruffled Jennifer's hair.

"You remember Mrs. Templeton, don't you, Jennifer?" Tom asked.

"Yes," Jennifer answered politely, but pulled back slightly.

"I need to find the third-grade class," Tom said.

"That's room ten. The third room back."

"Thanks."

Tom led Jennifer quickly to the room where he found a sign-up sheet on a table outside the door. He bent over to enter Jennifer's name.

"Hello, Mr. Kerzig!"

Tom looked up and saw Charlie Shaeffer standing in the doorway. "Well, hi, Charlie!" Tom finished writing Jennifer's name and then stood up and shook Charlie's hand. "Are you bringing someone here? Your sister or..."

"No." Charlie smiled and patted himself on the chest. "I'm the teacher!"

"You are?" Tom asked, somewhat shocked. "Well, that's great!" He bent down and moved Jennifer toward him. "Jennifer, this is Charlie Shaeffer. He's one of my students at school, and he'll be your teacher here."

"Hello, Jennifer," Charlie said, warmly shaking her hand. "Why don't you go on in with the others? We'll be starting in a few minutes."

Jennifer looked at Tom with an expression of apprehension.

Charlie squatted down and folded his arms in an angular position. "There. Now we're the same size. Is that better?" he asked, making a face.

Jennifer giggled, waved goodbye to Tom, and entered the room.

Charlie bounced up to a standing position. "She'll be fine."

"I'm glad she's in your class. That should be quite an experience."

Charlie laughed and started to go into the room. Then he turned back and spoke softly. "That was a nice memorial service yesterday, wasn't it?"

"Yes, it was. Very nice." He never remembered Charlie looking this serious. He was always cracking jokes, making light of things that happened. "Charlie, what do you think about what happened to Joni?"

"It was terrible! I couldn't believe it." He stepped out of the doorway to allow a group of children to enter, then leaned against the registration table. "We did a lot of things together at church. And we were both members of the Christian Perspectives Club at school. I still can't believe it."

"Can something like this happen?" Tom asked. "I mean, you know what goes on at school, Charlie. Can a person be involved with drugs and hide it from everyone?"

"Oh, sure. It happens all the time. But Joni..." Charlie slid his hands into his pockets and studied his feet for a moment. Then he looked up slowly and gazed distantly over Tom's shoulder. "The only thing I can think of is the program." He shifted his eyes toward Tom. "Except for the club, I didn't really have much contact with Joni at school, because she was in the program. She had all her classes with the same people."

"Could that make a difference?" Tom asked.

"I don't know. Maybe." Charlie shrugged and turned to go into the classroom. Then he turned back. "Those kids are so different." He entered the classroom and closed the door behind him.

It was about time for the service to begin, so Tom hurried back to the auditorium and stepped inside the dimly lit foyer. An unfamiliar couple smiled and extended their hands to greet him as he entered. He did recognize the usher who met him, however, and the large, balding man raised his eyebrows and waved as he handed him a bulletin.

"Hi, Leonard," Tom greeted him. "Good to see you again."

"I think there's a spot down in the middle," Leonard said.

Tom glanced at the pews in the back, but they were full. "All right."

He let Leonard lead him down the aisle. They stopped about halfway, where an empty space remained at the end of a pew. Tom stepped in and sat quietly. As the organ began playing in soft, slowly melodious strains, he looked at the title of today's sermon, printed boldly on the front of the bulletin: FALLING DOWN FROM HIGH PLACES. Tom mused for a moment about what this might refer to, opened the stiff folded sheet, and read aimlessly through the announcements.

The sound from the organ abruptly increased in volume

and tempo, and Tom looked up to see that the choir had entered. Their voices joined the organ, loud and joyously: "A mighty fortress is our God..." Tom breathed in deeply and let the resounding tones fill his ears. The familiar rush of excitement tingled from his spine as the fullness of the voices reverberated from the walls of the auditorium. He closed his eyes and nestled back against the hard wood. He imagined for an instant that Clair was there, beside him like before. He resisted a sudden impulse to reach out his hand to touch her. "A bulwark never failing..." sang the choir. But somewhere, beyond the plaintive imaginings of this captive moment, a bulwark *had* failed. Clair was gone. A fifteen-year-old girl had destroyed her own child. And Joni was dead.

Pastor Bentley's sermon initially hit Tom with a vague sense of irrelevant images. He recalled that he had felt this way frequently as a youth, sitting beside his parents, straining to make sense of the foreign-sounding names and concepts. He remembered studying about this time in history, over three thousand years ago. And about the towers, and sacred pillars, thrusting the smell of incense toward some unseen idol that was worshiped by those who had rejected the simplicity of a single, omnipotent God. He had enjoyed learning of the events, but he had never found any relationship to modern-day existence. No such towers existed now; there was no incense burning to the idols of Baal.

Pastor Bentley's words flowed freely, if not persuasively. The "high places in our hearts," he called our "towers" and "idols." "We all struggle rebelliously against the simplicity of God's existence and reach vainly upward toward some shadowy idol of our own making. Material gain, personal acceptance, power, dignity—all those worldly things on which we so frequently rely to explain our existence. The high places will be torn down and we will all fall to oblivion or to our knees."

But there was something else. A specific reference of

Pastor Bentley's: "King Josiah did what was right in the sight of the Lord. He tore down the high places, east of Jerusalem, on the south of the Mount of Corruption." Something about this was so familiar. "High places for *Ashtoreth* the abomination of the Sidonians, for *Chemosh* the abomination of the Moabites, and for *Milcom* the abomination of the people of Ammon." Those names... They were in Joni's paper!

Tom pulled himself away from his contemplation as Pastor Bentley concluded the prayer at the end of his sermon. Heads all around him raised and people shifted in their places. But Pastor Bentley raised his arms and spoke into the microphone. "Just a moment, please. Lloyd Irving has asked to say a few words, and I'd like you to give him your attention before we dismiss."

The congregation directed their attention to the pulpit. Pastor Bentley stood to the side, and Lloyd walked slowly toward it. He leaned against the pulpit and spoke haltingly.

"Thank you, Pastor. Sally and I want to thank all of you for your prayers and your support. This has been a terrible time for us and, without you, well..." He shifted slightly and cleared his throat. "Our lives, our community...there are contrasts, you know. There are many wonderful things to share. But there are also many evil things happening. Things we just can't understand. Sally and I didn't think about those things much...before. But, now, many of you have come forward, and have told us about other things, concerns you have. Some are related to what goes on in the community, some even here in our church and many in the schools our children are attending."

Lloyd wiped the back of his hand across his eyes and continued, clutching the pulpit. "It's too late now for Joni. But maybe we can learn something—we can understand why. If there's anything we can do to prevent this kind of thing from happening again, we have to find it. Pastor Bentley has consented to our meeting here to talk about this, and that's what we're planning to do—next Sunday night, at seven o'clock, in the auditorium. If any of you have any answers, or even questions or thoughts, will you please join us here? Sally and I would really appreciate it." He nodded toward Pastor Bentley and walked back down the steps.

The line of people leaving the service moved slowly as they greeted Pastor Bentley on the way out of the auditorium. As Tom finally approached, the pastor looked up with a wide smile. He finished his conversation with the couple standing in front of him and reached forward for Tom's hand.

"Tommy, I'm glad you came!"

"I am, too. I enjoyed the service."

"Good...good!" Pastor Bentley gave Tom's hand a final shake and then pulled him back away from the line of departing people. "Listen, Lloyd and Sally told me you had asked to talk to them about Joni on Tuesday."

"Yes."

"They thought that, maybe, well, you might know more than you told them yesterday."

"I, ah, tried not to give that impression."

"Then there *is* something," Pastor Bentley said.

Tom glanced to the side and then turned his back to the line of people. "I don't want to get them upset without reason. Joni wrote a composition for the class I'm teaching. It was very dark, very... I would never use this word in front of Lloyd and Sally, but it seemed almost *satanic*."

"Oh, no..."

"That's why I didn't say any more," Tom said. "I could be completely off base about this."

Pastor Bentley pulled his lips into a frown. "Do you still have the composition?"

"Yes."

"Could I see it?" he asked. "You may need a second opinion."

"Of course! I'll bring a copy to you."

"Thanks. And Lloyd and Sally should eventually see it. They are so anxious to find out anything that might have caused this terrible thing to happen. Did you hear Lloyd's announcement about the meeting next week?"

"Yes."

"You know, it would really be nice if you could attend," Pastor Bentley said. "Since you teach in the school system, you'd have some valuable input."

Tom had always avoided gatherings of church members which were directed toward complaints about the schools. He believed he should remain neutral, objective in his view of how school activities might influence religious beliefs. Maybe that's what Nita meant when she said he was more "balanced" than the other members of the congregation. But this time, for some reason, he felt an urge to participate, listen to the concerns these people had with the system of which he was a small part.

"Yes," Tom said. "I can do that. But you know who should really attend?"

"Who?"

"One of the board members."

Pastor Bentley grimaced and tilted his head.

"All I can do is provide information," Tom said. "They're the ones who make the decisions."

"It's just that, well, this meeting is preliminary," Pastor Bentley said. "We aren't likely to come out with any well-defined arguments."

"That's probably better. Effective communication requires selection, of course, and clarity. But more than that, it requires an understanding of people's feelings. If I were a board member, I think I would rather listen to people in an informal setting before they came to me with a precise, well-organized argument."

Pastor Bentley smiled. "I think you're right. But *you* would listen. I'm not sure about the members of your board."

"You may be right about that."

"Who do you think would be the best one to ask?"

Tom lowered his head in thought. He hadn't attended many board meetings, but he had definitely formed opinions about its members from the few that he had. Daniel Worley was the flamboyant pastor of the Church of the Inner Spirit. His participation had always reminded Tom of Bonnie's department meetings, so he doubted that he would provide an objective ear. John Horning was a successful real estate broker. Horning's main motivation at each board meeting seemed to be to conclude as early as possible, and he would probably bring the same impatience to a gathering of church members. Marion Coleman was a housewife. She was always pleasant, but she never seemed willing to express an opinion without first testing whether it would be acceptable to the other members. There was Dr. Roland Lessa, the university professor. He was an influential board member and would be a good one to invite, but Tom still couldn't push past his feeling of irritation with Lessa for the influence he'd had on Clair. She had taken two courses from him during her last year, and the philosophical views she gained from them definitely influenced her decision to separate from Tom. No, none of these.

"Barbara Shannon," Tom said finally.

"The board president?"

"Yes."

Pastor Bentley smiled and shook his head. "Hmm...a member of the law firm of choice for A.C.L.U. cases— Zidon, Mueller, Shannon, and Bowarts. I don't think so,

Tom. Barbara Shannon represented the group that tried to prevent the manger scene from being placed in the park last Christmas."

"I know."

"Then why?"

"She's the best listener."

Pastor Bentley chuckled. "All right. I'll call her tomorrow. Say, Tommy, why don't you bring Clair to the meeting?"

Tom thought for a moment, then smiled and nodded. "Okay. I'll ask her, anyway."

Pastor Bentley gave Tom's hand a final squeeze, then turned to a small group of people who waited in the foyer to speak with him.

Tom left the auditorium and headed for the classroom complex. He was glad Pastor Bentley had suggested bringing Clair. He was constantly searching for something, anything that would give them an opportunity to relate on a normal, non-threatening basis.

By the time Tom reached the third-grade classroom, the children had been dismissed, and fifteen or twenty of them stood in a group outside the door, talking excitedly. Charlie stood in the doorway, ushering out the remaining few, and patting them on the head as they passed.

"Hi, Charlie," Tom said. "Is Jennifer still inside?"

Charlie turned into the classroom and called, "Jennifer, your father is here."

Jennifer's smiling face appeared, and she passed beneath Charlie's arm.

"Thank you for joining us today, Jennifer." Charlie extended his hand.

"Thanks, Charlie." Tom took Jennifer's hand and led her toward the parking lot. "Did you have a good time in class?"

"Mmm-hmm."

"What'd you do?"

"Charlie read us a story and then we talked about being honest. He told us God wants us to tell the truth *always*."

"Yes, that's a good rule," Tom said.

"Yeah, I guess. Except for some times."

"What?"

"Well, I learned in school that sometimes you can't tell the truth."

"What do you mean?"

"Like, if you're going to be hurt," she explained. "Or if you don't want to hurt somebody else." Jennifer shrugged. "I don't know. We just started learning about it. It's kinda complicated."

"Can you give me an example of what you're learning?" Tom asked.

"Oh, I remember!" Jennifer stopped walking and turned to him with an expression of discovery. "Sometimes parents don't tell the truth. That's one thing we learned about. Like Santa Claus. When parents tell their children about Santa Claus."

Tom chuckled. "I guess I never thought about that as lying. But you could look at it that way."

"So, there may be other times when it's okay not to tell the truth," Jennifer said.

"I don't think so, honey."

"But my teacher says there are some things people just *think* are true," she continued, disregarding his response. "One of my friends shared once in class that her parents told her God created the world."

"Right..."

"And she asked our teacher if that was a lie. Our teacher said that if they *knew* God didn't create the world, and said

He did, then it was a lie. But if they really thought He did, then it was just their opinion. So we have to know when we're lying and when we're just saying what we think."

"It shouldn't be that complicated, Jennifer," Tom said. "Charlie was right. You should remember always to tell the truth."

"*Did* God create the world?" Jennifer asked.

A hot surge rose from Tom's spine. "Yes, of course He did."

"Is that just what you *think*?"

Tom removed his hand momentarily from hers, wiped the perspiration from his palm, and then took her hand again. "No, that's what I believe," he said finally.

"Is believing like thinking?"

"Yes."

She walked with him silently for a few moments. Then she looked up and pulled on his hand. "Did you believe in Santa Claus, Dad?"

"Yes, when I was a child."

"When did you stop believing?"

He tried to remember the vague, wished-for image of the smiling, bearded man, dashing across the sky in his toy-laden sleigh. The period of belief was brief, as he recalled. "I think some of my older friends finally told me. And then I realized it was just sort of a fairy tale."

"One of my friends told the class he didn't think God created the world anymore," Jennifer said. "My teacher told him it was okay to think that, because it was kind of like not believing in Santa Claus anymore."

"No. It's different, Jennifer. It's *very* different. Santa Claus is just a fairy tale."

"Oh."

Tom sighed in relief as Jennifer appeared to drop the conversation. But he knew the discussion would arise again. He felt a sudden surge of discontent over his inability to respond adequately to Jennifer's questions. Belief could be complicated for adults, of course. But it shouldn't be that way for children.

Tom remembered sitting with Jennifer by the window on Christmas Eve years ago, searching the sky for a faint burst of star dust. He suddenly wished he had never told her there was a Santa Claus.

13

The porch light was not on, so Tom led Jennifer carefully up the stairs to the front porch. She swung the screen out, pushed open the front door, and walked inside the house. She then turned and motioned for Tom to follow.

"C'mon in, Dad."

"You'd better ask your mother first," Tom said.

Jennifer frowned lightly, then called toward the study. "Mom! Dad's coming in."

There was a moment of silence, then Clair called, "All right. I'll be there in a minute."

He stepped inside the house and closed the door as Clair appeared from the study and walked toward them.

"Hi, honey!" Clair bent down and gave Jennifer a hug. "Did you have a good weekend?"

"Yes," Jennifer said softly.

"Good." Clair stood up and looked questioningly at Tom. "Does she still have some things to bring in, or..."

"No, I, ah...I need to talk to you."

"Oh." Clair raised her eyebrows and sighed. "Well, all right. Jennifer, why don't you put your things away and get ready for bed?"

Tom squatted and took Jennifer in his arms. "You have a good week." Tom let his hands fall, but Jennifer still clung tightly to his neck. "I'll see you again soon. I love you."

"I love you, Dad." Jennifer picked up her carrying case and headed down the hallway.

"I'll be there in a minute, honey," Clair said and turned toward Tom, who was now standing again, directly in front of the doorway. "What's up?"

"It's Jennifer. I think she's learning some strange things at school."

"Strange things?"

"Yes. I just wondered if you noticed anything unusual lately about her class assignments."

Clair looked perplexed for moment. Then she smiled and nodded. "Oh...that. She's in that special class this semester, you know."

"You mean the LENA program?"

"Yes."

"There are some things I think you should be aware of."

"Why don't you call me tomorrow and we can talk about them."

"No!" Tom said intensely. Then he backed off again. "No, Clair. It's important that I talk to you tonight."

Clair sighed. "It's late, Tom. I don't want to disturb Jennifer."

"Okay. Let's go outside, then."

Clair nodded her head. "Let me just see that Jennifer gets to bed first."

"I'll wait for you outside."

Tom stepped onto the porch. The outline of the swing was visible in the near darkness. He walked over to it and sat on the thick cushion. The chain creaked against itself as he slowly pushed the swing back and forth. It had been a Christmas gift from his parents six years ago. His father had told him that when he and his mother were a young married couple, his parents had given them a swing. They had received a great deal of enjoyment from it—relaxing on the weekends, talking with their neighbors as they cared for their yards, waving to others as they passed by on leisurely afternoon strolls. Tom and Clair had used their swing a lot that first summer, especially when his parents had come to visit. But the neighbors were never working in their yards, and the afternoon travelers screeched noisily out of their driveways and disappeared down the road without speaking. And then, that November, his parents were killed in the automobile accident.

The outside light suddenly flooded the porch with illumination. The screen door swung open, and Clair stepped out onto the porch. She wore a long black coat and a silk scarf was wound heavily about her neck. She placed her hands in her pockets, walked stiffly over to the swing, and sat at the opposite end.

So...what is it that has you so worried about Jennifer's class work?" she asked.

"Well, yesterday afternoon, at the library, I was doing some research on cakras." He paused and looked at her. "Do you know what those are?"

Clair shook her head.

"They're psychic centers of the body. From Hindu spiritualism. Yoga."

"I've never heard of them."

"Well, the strange thing is, Jennifer knew all about them. She said she'd learned about them in school."

"Well..."

"She's learning how to access them through meditation," Tom said. "She even drew a picture of herself and explained how she's learning to pass upward through different levels. The levels were displayed in a rainbow."

"Oh, sure," Clair said. "The meditation exercises. I know

about them. They're just for concentration. They're designed to help the students with their studies."

"By sitting cross-legged, with their arms folded and their eyes closed? That's what Jennifer was doing in the library."

"Hmm, now that you mention it, I think I've seen her do that a couple of times. That does seem a little strange, doesn't it?" She pursed her lips and shook her head. "But it's just an exercise. I mean, they aren't being taught to be Hindus, or anything like that."

"It just seems like a strange activity."

"I'll keep an eye on her, but I don't think it's anything to worry about." Clair leaned forward. "Is there anything else?"

"Yes. This morning, in church..."

"You took her to church?"

"Yes."

"Bentley's?"

"Yes."

A faint smile appeared on Clair's lips. Then she nodded and sat back against the corner of the swing.

"Anyway, she went into a Sunday school class and the teacher presented a lesson on honesty. Afterward, Jennifer compared that with what she had learned in school."

"That's good," Clair said.

"Yes, but what she learned in school was, I don't know...strange. She exhibited an understanding about honesty that was almost situational."

"What do you mean?"

"Well, she said you should be honest unless you're going to be hurt or you'll hurt somebody else."

"You must have misunderstood her."

"No. She even followed it up with an example of how parents lie when they tell their kids about Santa Claus."

Clair laughed lightly. "Well, maybe Jennifer didn't understand what the teacher was saying. I'll talk to her teacher at the next open house and find out what that lesson was all about."

"You may have to go a little deeper than that," Tom said. "She's comparing belief in Santa Claus to belief in God."

Clair frowned and shook her head. "There must be some reasonable explanation."

"Why would that kind of question even come up?"

"When they moved Jennifer into the special program, they told me that the experiences would be more challenging," Clair said. "They're teaching the students to think more rationally and question things from an objective perspective. I'm sure that's what this exercise was directed toward." She folded her arms and leaned back again. "When they told me that, I was grateful. That is exactly what I was learning in my courses at the university."

Criticizing what she'd learned at the university would not have a favorable impact on this discussion. Tom held his tongue. "But that's the university. Do you think that type of values analysis should be expected of third graders?"

"No, of course not. It should be presented in a much more basic manner. But the sooner children develop these skills, the better prepared they will be to search for meaning in their lives as they grow older."

Forget the impact on the discussion! He couldn't resist. "How's *your* search coming, Clair? Your attempt to find yourself?"

"Oh, Tom, don't start on me."

"Have you had any success?" Tom was afraid he had asked the question almost flippantly. But he sincerely wanted a response.

"That's one of the things I hate about you being a

teacher," Clair said. "You treat our encounters like a mid-term exam."

"But I really want to know. I think I have a right to know."

Clair sat forward rigidly. "I don't understand you, Tom. Of all people, I'd think you'd be happy to see your daughter taught critical thinking skills."

"What?"

"And then you took her back to Pastor Bentley's church," she continued heatedly. "Of course there's conflict! Don't you remember what that did to us?"

Tom sat back, shocked by the intensity of Clair's response.

"I thought I had the right to know some things then, too," she continued. "Do you remember what you told me?"

"I remember the time..."

"You said, '*Life isn't true or false. It's multiple choice!*' "

He *had* forgotten. But now the words gushed into his memory as though he had spoken them yesterday. That was different, of course. And yet the intensity of Clair's recollection was so poignant, so meaningful.

"Clair, if we could just talk..."

Clair closed her eyes and raised her hand toward him. "Don't push me. Yesterday morning I might have been able to give you a quick answer. But not tonight."

Yesterday? Oh, yes. Clair had had to deal with that touchy family problem. "The fifteen-year-old and the abortion?"

Clair nodded. "I had a bad day yesterday." She folded her hands in front of her and pushed the swing gently.

Tom looked at Clair, sitting three feet from him. For the first time in months she appeared soft—no, *receptive*. "Tell me about it," he said.

"It's a confidential case, Tom."

Tom interrupted her with a raised hand. "It's all right. I know about it anyway, from Nita. Remember?"

"Still, it's my case, and..."

"Tell me about it," he pleaded softly.

She sighed. "I don't know where to start."

"At the beginning," he said. *Take your time...minutes... hours.* His heart wrenched at the possibility that she would communicate with something more than a rejection of his presence in her life. Even her face seemed different somehow. Her lips trembled slightly and her eyelids fell relaxed from their previously intense pose.

"It was a textbook case," she said finally. "It was almost exactly like a situation I studied about in Roland's class last spring. You remember the one—*Public Welfare and Public Policy.*"

"I remember you talking about it," Tom said.

"A family receiving aid," she continued. "Father disabled, several children, all minors, and the oldest one gets pregnant. We analyzed all possible solutions. Working with the parents, working outside the parents. Cooperating with the school, excluding the school from involvement. Aborting the fetus, allowing the child to be born. Raising the grandchild as part of the family, putting the child up for adoption."

"Multiple choice," Tom mumbled.

"Exactly! The concept of client privilege was an important concept in the decision. We discussed the fact that the school had an easier time of it, because they had only a single client—the girl. The welfare agency was placed in the position of a potential conflict of interest, because its client was the entire family. So we analyzed the situation from the perspective of the greatest good for the agency's client—both individually and collectively. And we allowed for complicating factors. If the girl and her family had come in one accord and demanded an abortion, the choice would have been simple, because the client would have been united in its perspective. But if the family were opposed to this solution and the girl desired it, or if the girl was simply confused and didn't want the family involved in the decision, then the situation became much more complex."

"Yes."

"The textbook case was exactly like this one. That's why it was so similar. The parents were presented as people who would be reluctant to allow the abortion and the girl just called for help...umm, direction."

"How was the textbook case resolved?" Tom asked.

"The family didn't have the resources to support another child. The girl was too young for marriage and had no long-term interest in the boy who had gotten her pregnant. And she didn't seem to have any major moral objections to terminating the pregnancy. The solution was quite clear. As long as the parents did not find out about it, abortion was better for the girl...better for the family."

"Better for society?"

"Yes. That was also a factor in the decision."

"What about the unborn child?"

"The textbook case assumed that the abortion occurred prior to the state of...what was the term...*viable life-formation.* So that wasn't a consideration."

"And everyone lived happily ever after?"

"There was no follow-up study beyond the first six months," Clair said. "But until that time, yes."

"So what about the real case?"

Clair sighed and shifted, and the swing moved slightly from side to side. "As you know, the parents found out. The girl didn't fare as well, either, because she developed an infection. It was fairly minor and the physical effects passed within two weeks. But not the emotional..." She rested her head back against the chain.

"Did you meet with the girl and her parents together?"

She grimaced and leaned forward. "Oh, yes. But there was a textbook case for that, too. A case where the parents found out. And the responsibility of the agency was to protect one party—the girl—from the wrath of the other party—the parents. It was very clear in the sample given. The girl was adamant in her right to have the abortion without parental consent, and the agency supported her in this legal right. The other party—the parents—though still enjoying client privileges, had to accede to the individual right and to the *greater good* concept."

"That's what you were prepared for yesterday," Tom said.

"Well, that's what I was *preparing* myself for yesterday. I didn't feel really comfortable about it, but I had my textbook in the car."

"So what happened?"

Clair pulled her feet up on the swing and leaned forward on her knees. "Even the setting was similar. A small, tattered dining room table, the parents, the girl, and the welfare representative..." Clair sat transfixed for a moment, her eyes gazing unresponsively beyond him. "But the girl didn't follow the book. She was crying...hysterically. *'I want my baby!'* she cried. *'I want my baby!'* So I had to change. I couldn't use protection of the girl's rights. But it had been her decision. We had studied cases like this, too. Once the decision is made, the responsible party is accountable." Without moving, she raised her eyes and looked at him. "I guess you've seen her, Tom. She's fifteen. Frail. Short, stringy hair. A few freckles on her forehead." She lowered her eyes again and spoke haltingly. "I can't believe what I did. I took her by the arm and said, 'You made the decision. You're accountable. You're accountable.' " She placed her fist against her lips and her eyelids closed over a burst of tears.

Tom reached out and placed his hand on hers. She remained motionless for a moment. Then her eyes opened abruptly and she sat up, pulling away from him.

"I'm sorry." She wiped her eyes quickly with both hands. "I didn't want to do that." She laughed nervously. "The textbook has one for that, too. Unsuccessful case remorse."

"No, don't be sorry. Don't reject your feelings. Forget the textbook!"

"Maybe. After I get this one resolved." She turned forward and placed her feet back on the floor.

"What are you going to do?"

"I'll work it out. If Nita asks, tell her not to worry. I'll work it out." She sighed deeply. "How did we get into this, anyway?"

"We were talking about searching. And Jennifer..."

"Oh, yes. And that didn't help, either," she said, turning toward him.

"What?"

"When you asked me what I would do if Jennifer ever got into a situation like that. I thought about that, too, until...well, I didn't get much sleep last night."

"It could happen."

Clair frowned at him and began to get up.

"Clair..." He reached out and touched her arm tenderly, stopping her motion. "You can get a lot more out of real people and their problems than you can out of textbook situations."

"Well, after I've worked for a few years, I'll have had the chance to be involved with more real people."

"But there are other ways. I mean, people have concerns that you can get some insight from."

"Sure. I know."

"Listen, next Sunday night, there's a group meeting at the church to talk about..."

"Pretty sneaky intro!"

"No, really. They'll be talking about current influences of society and how they affect our kids. The meeting's been called by Lloyd and Sally Irving."

"Oh."

"They need all the support they can get," he said.

"Yes, I'm sure they do." She stood and jammed her hands into her pockets. "Maybe. Call me Friday." She walked toward the door and opened the screen. "You're welcome to stay on the porch as long as you want. But I'm going in. Good night." She disappeared into the house.

He sat back in the corner of the swing and looked across to the other corner, where Clair had sat. He visualized her form, still there. He could hear her voice, pleading for answers, searching...as she had several times before. And how had he responded? Multiple choice.

The porch light suddenly went out. He stood impulsively, as though in an attempt to snatch a few lingering rays, but there were none. Before his eyes could accommodate to the darkness, he stumbled forward clumsily, clutched at the wooden railing, and stepped blindly down the stairs toward the road.

14

Tom had been teaching Bonnie's first-period class for over a week now, and everything had gone surprisingly well, especially considering the tragic interruption of Joni's death. But today's exercise seemed to meet with disapproval on the part of the students. He stepped slowly from the head of one row to the head of the next as he picked up the stacks of papers which had been passed forward. A few of the students frowned and whispered to one another. Tom collected the papers from the last row, straightened the stack, and placed it on the desk. He then turned and smiled at the grumbling students.

"I get the distinct impression some of you don't approve of today's lesson. Someone want to tell me why?" He looked slowly about the room, but no one volunteered. "I know you guys aren't shy about talking." Finally, a boy in the center of the room raised his hand reluctantly. "Frank."

"We don't think you should have given us a spelling test without giving us a chance to study for it."

"I see. I told you what type of test this was, didn't I?" He glanced around the room. "Who remembers the term? Yes, Mary Ann."

"A diagnostic test."

"That's right. A diagnostic test isn't used to issue you a grade, but to find out what you're having trouble with, so I'll know what to stress in the lessons." This explanation didn't help. They still sat with somber expressions. "I don't under-stand why you find that objectionable. Surely Miss Teague gave you diagnostic tests from time to time, didn't she?"

Several students shook their heads and a boy in the back raised his hand.

"Yes, Marshall?"

"Bonnie doesn't believe in diagnostic tests. A diagnostic test focuses on *weaknesses*. Bonnie says we should always focus on our *strengths*."

"I see. And how *do* you learn to spell?" He recognized a girl in the front of the class. "Beth, can you tell me?"

"We decide which words we want to learn to spell based on which words we want to use in our compositions. Most of us already know how to spell pretty well from all the reading we do. But sometimes there are special words, and if we hesi-tate using them because we don't know how they're spelled, then we really *want* to learn how to spell them."

"All right. Let's look at it this way. Do any of you like to work on cars?"

Several students nodded.

"Suppose you want to work on your car, but you're not sure if you have all the tools you need. So you take your tool-box to a mechanic. Now he can tell right away what tools you're missing and he gives them to you. Does that focus on your weaknesses or make you any less creative?" He waited a moment to let that sink in. "That's all I'm trying to do. Give you the tools you will need to increase your strengths—free you to be more creative." He paused and surveyed the stu-dents who now seemed more receptive. "You can't just decide to use any size or shape of tool to work on those cars, can you? There are standards. And when you're writing a compo-sition, you can't just use any combination of letters to make words. There are standards. There are rules."

"But English is a strange language," Marshall said.

"That's true. But that makes it all the more challenging for you creative people."

The students laughed lightly and Tom decided to continue.

"When you were in grade school, I'm sure you learned the saying, *i* before *e*, except after *c*. A lot of rules have exceptions, but there are still rules that you can follow." He stepped forward and pursued his point. "Example: You know that the letter *g* can have two sounds. It will help your spelling if you remember that when it has the soft sound, like a *j*, it won't be followed by an *a, o,* or *u*."

"Mr. Kerzig!" A boy in the back waved his hand wildly.

"Yes, Ed, what is it?"

"Margarine!" he exclaimed triumphantly.

"Excellent! You found the exception. And now you'll never forget the rule!"

Ed sat back with his hand still raised partially, a light smile crossing his face. Several members of the class turned to one another and laughed.

Tom glanced at the clock. "The period's almost over. Remember that I'll be gone the first three days of next week. I want you to finish reading the excerpts in the Anthology from Malreaux's novel, *Man's Fate,* by Friday. As you read, remember that each main character is used to display some way that man tries to fulfill himself, to escape the absurdity of life. We'll discuss these on Friday, and your assignment for next week will be based on our discussion."

The bell sounded and the students gathered their materials.

"You're dismissed. Have a good day!"

The students rose from their desks and filed out of the room. Tom picked up the spelling papers and tossed them into his open briefcase. He felt good about the turn the discussion had taken today. Now he was even more annoyed that he had to take three days from his classes next week to attend the LENA convention. But Walt had insisted. Tom closed his briefcase and looked up to see Ed passing by his desk.

"Thanks, Mr. Kerzig," he said and walked quickly out of the room.

Joe and Inspector Gruber peeked in the door. "Hi, Tom," Joe said. "Can we see you for a minute?"

"Sure."

Joe glanced into the corridor and started to close the door, but then stopped as Marla appeared in the doorway.

"Oh, I'm sorry." Marla held her hand to her lips. "I just wanted to see Tom for a minute. Tom, what's your schedule like today? Could you meet me in the cafeteria for lunch and help me with some of my plans?"

"Oh," Tom snapped his fingers. "We never did get around to that, did we? Sure, I'd be glad to."

"Thanks..."

"Say, Marla, could you watch Tom's second-period class for a few minutes?" Joe asked.

"Sure, Mr. Carter." She turned and headed toward Tom's room.

Gruber closed the door and he and Joe joined Tom at his desk.

"I told the inspector already," said Joe, "and I thought you would want to know. I got the results from the lab. The capsules you found contained LSD."

Tom sighed. "Oh, boy..."

"So did the ones we found with the dead girl," Gruber said. "I wish you people had told me about finding those sooner."

"That wasn't Tom's fault," Joe said. "It was just..." he

paused and looked at Tom, "a policy issue."

"I understand, Joe," Gruber said. "I'd like to see where you found them."

Tom walked to the door leading to the department office, took the key from his pocket, and unlocked the door.

"Is this door always locked?" Gruber asked.

"As far as I know." Tom pushed the door open and then remembered Marla's access. "Although the custodian opens it for people who need access to materials."

Gruber pushed by him and entered the small office. He glanced quickly over the shelves and placed his hand on the desk. "The capsules were in here, weren't they?"

"Yes," Tom said. "They were in the back of the middle drawer." He pulled out the drawer. It was completely empty. "There were some other things in here, some booklets, badges, rainbow stickers. And some crystals. Everything's gone now."

Gruber slid the drawer completely out and turned it over in his hands. "The capsules were in an envelope?"

"Yes, right here." Tom pointed to the crack at the rear of the drawer.

Gruber slid the drawer back in again. "How about the rest of these?" He pointed to the other drawers.

"Nothing unusual. The large bottom drawer is locked."

"Oh?" Gruber reached toward the drawer.

"Yes. And none of the keys I had fit, so—" He stopped suddenly as Gruber slid open the bottom drawer. It, too, was completely empty.

Gruber looked at Joe and raised his eyebrow. "Do you know anything about this?"

Joe frowned and shook his head. "This is English department stuff. I don't even think this desk is standard school issue."

Gruber closed the drawer, leaned against the desk, and crossed his arms. "I don't think I need to tell you...we may have a relationship here. Your teacher tested positive for the same chemical."

"Bonnie said there was a mistake, though," Tom said. "She said all she'd taken was some aspirin and a prescription for PMS."

Gruber smiled and shrugged. "Well, there was LSD in her blood stream. How it got there may still be up for discussion. And then there's the issue of her head and the windshield. I suppose, if she was high on LSD, she could have been driving the car from the passenger's seat, but..." He shrugged again.

Tom realized he still hadn't told anyone except Bonnie what Joni had said the Monday after the dance. "She may not have been alone," he said.

"That's what I think," Gruber said.

"I mean, that's what Joni said," Tom muttered. "She told me that on Monday. She said that Friday, when Bonnie left the dance, she wasn't alone."

"You didn't tell me this," Joe said.

"No, because her reference was so vague. And then I asked Bonnie about it, and she told me Joni was mistaken. So I didn't pursue it."

"Well, we can't ask Joni now, can we?" Gruber tilted his head and scowled. "You don't suppose she was the one who was with her, do you?"

"Joni? No."

"But think a minute, Tom," Joe said. "She left the dance at about the same time."

"Your teacher friend is facing a D.U.I. charge," Gruber said. "If this girl was with her, and driving instead of her, you'd think she'd say so. Especially now that the girl's dead."

"No, folks." Joe shook his head. "If Bonnie was distributing drugs to one of her students, she'd have a lot more to worry about than a D.U.I. charge."

"Hmmm..." Gruber passed his thumb slowly across his chin several times. "I think I'll pay Miss Teague another visit."

"She's been dismissed from the hospital," Joe said.

"I know."

"Do you need her address?" Joe asked.

"No, I have it. It's in my file."

"I thought you said that wasn't your case," Tom said.

"It is now." Gruber smiled.

"Oh, Inspector, I found some information on cakras." Tom reached into his briefcase and pulled out a clipped set of pages he had copied from the library references. "I have the specific sections highlighted."

Gruber took the pages and scanned them quickly. Then he looked up. "Do you know any more now than you did before?"

"No."

Gruber chuckled. "We'll work on it. Thanks." He waved and left the room.

Tom slid his tray up behind Marla's at the cashier's stand, but before he could remove his wallet, Marla had already paid for both of their lunches. He shook his finger at her, but she just smiled and tilted her head for him to follow her.

"Thank you." Tom pointed with his tray. "There's an empty table over in the corner."

They zig-zagged through noisy groups of staff members and set their trays on the table. Marla moved a stack of books from the tray to the table and sat, while Tom pulled out a chair and sat across from her.

"Cottage cheese and orange juice?" Tom said. "That's a pretty slim lunch."

Marla laughed. "That's the idea."

They cleared their trays to allow more room and set them on an empty chair.

"I'm sorry I didn't get together with you sooner," Tom said. "It's been a tough week."

"I'll say it has. It's all right. Things have gone pretty well. My main concern has to do with my general approach, I think."

"What do you mean?"

"Well...when I was a ninth grader, I think I was a lot more serious about my studies."

Tom laughed. "Well, you might have been. But I think we were all pretty squirrelly in the ninth grade."

"Maybe so. Anyway, most of my kids are very vocal and they seem to enjoy participating in discussion exercises. And they like the literature selections I've given them to read."

"Well, that's half the battle."

"It's the other half that's the problem. They don't write very well, and I like to spend at least two days a week on grammar and spelling."

"Sure."

"But they tell me it's boring," she complained.

Tom smiled. "I think they have you figured out. What do you do when they tell you they're bored?"

"I change activities to something they enjoy."

Tom laughed. "Yes, they definitely have you figured out."

"I know. I worry too much about what they think of me."

"Almost everyone does that the first year they teach."

Marla placed a large bite of cottage cheese in her mouth and motioned for him to wait until she swallowed. "It's just that, when I was in Bonnie's class, I remembered we always seemed to have a lot more fun."

"Well, that was the twelfth grade. And, of course, Bonnie's approach may be viewed as more enjoyable by students." He laughed lightly as he recalled this morning's interaction. "I know that I'm definitely not very popular with some of her first-period students."

"You're not? Why?"

"Don't you remember me being a terrible task master when you were in my eleventh-grade class?"

"No...I mean, yes, but..." She shook her head and laughed. "Now you have me confused. What I meant was, you were very demanding and we didn't always enjoy the things we did. But I always appreciated being in your class. I always thought we were learning."

"That's the most important thing," Tom said. "Just remember that and that you're in charge. Everything will go fine."

"Maybe so." She scraped up the remaining cottage cheese and placed it in her mouth. "Of course. There was another factor involved when I was in your class."

"What was that?"

"I had a terrible crush on you."

"Oh?" Tom laughed nervously.

"Mmm-hmm. So I wouldn't have traded being there for anything."

"Well, that's not uncommon with high school girls. Usually it just goes unnoticed, but sometimes... That's why it's important to retain a definite teacher-student relationship."

"You didn't notice it, then?" she asked, feigning disappointment.

"Nope."

"I remember I used to wish you weren't married. Isn't that awful?"

"Well..."

"But of course, now you're not, are you?"

"Well, actually, yes, I am. Clair and I are just separated, not divorced."

"Oh, of course. I just meant...in a manner of speaking." She sat back in her chair and slowly sipped her orange juice from a straw.

"Listen, I almost forgot," Tom said, changing the subject. "Thank you for watching my class this morning."

"Oh, sure." She finished the last gulp of juice and set the container on the table. "What did that policeman want, anyway?"

Tom looked up suddenly in response to her question. "How do you know he's with the police?"

"Well, I could say I have psychic powers." She closed her eyes and moved her arms slowly across the table. "But actually," she opened her eyes again, "I saw him last week when I visited Bonnie. He was just leaving her hospital room when I came in, and she told me who he was."

"Oh." Tom wondered why Bonnie had confided to Marla about Gruber. "Did she tell you why he was there?"

"He was looking into Joni's suicide." She rested her chin in her hand and shook her head. "Isn't it just terrible? Where do you suppose she got the drugs?"

"Joni, you mean?"

"Yes."

"That's what the inspector is trying to find out."

Marla slowly shook her head. Then she leaned up to the table and gathered her books together. A light gold chain swung out from her neck and a dark purple crystal dangling from it clicked as it landed on the table. Tom sat back startled as he looked at the oddly-shaped crystal. It was one of the ones in the desk drawer last Monday—the ones that had disappeared when they looked in the drawer this morning.

"Where did you get that?" Tom asked.

"What?"

"The crystal...on your chain."

"Oh, this?" Marla placed her finger behind the chain and raised the crystal into full view. "Isn't it lovely? Bonnie gave it to me."

"Bonnie?"

"Yes. When I visited her last week, she told me she needed the things out of the middle desk drawer in the department office. So I cleared it out and took them to her. There were several crystals in there and she said I could have one. I chose this one and put it on this chain." She laughed. "When I picked it out, Bonnie told me she wished she'd had it with her on Friday night"

"Why is that?"

"I don't know. Luck, I guess."

Tom smiled as he recalled the research he had done at the library on Saturday. *Not just luck, Marla,* he thought. *That's an amethyst. The ancient Greeks thought they prevented intoxication.*

"There were some other pretty ones there, too, but I liked this one the best."

"Did Bonnie have you clear out the bottom drawer, too?"

"No. Just the middle one. Why?"

"Someone got into it," he said.

"Oh." She stood and picked up her books. "Well, I'd better get ready for fifth period. I'm going to go practice being bossy." She laughed.

"Thanks for lunch."

"No problem." She turned and looked coyly back at him. "Now you owe me!"

15

Stu Welbourne had called a brief meeting of the LENA project teachers that afternoon. Tom didn't feel compelled to attend these meetings, since he was just substituting for Bonnie, but he thought it would give him an opportunity to talk with the other teachers about Joni. Even with Gruber working on the case, so many loose ends still remained. And he had promised Bentley he would help.

Every subject called for its unique environment, and Stu's room was replete with maps, political charts, and pictures of prominent historical figures. Stu had placed two tables in the shape of a long rectangle. Tom sat at the end of the table, nearest the door. At the other end, Stu leaned back in his chair, toying with his filled, unlit pipe. The other four teachers sat at the sides. Stu leaned forward and clicked the stem of his pipe on the table.

"I appreciate your coming today," Stu said. "This won't take long. I think we should start with some introductions. I'm sure we all know each other, but we may have forgotten what others are doing." He laughed lightly. "I'm sure you all know Tom Kerzig. He's taking Bonnie's twelfth graders while she's out, and he asked to sit in with us today."

The others greeted him cordially.

Stu pointed to the teachers on his left. "Chris Donnelly teaches science. Marilyn Peters has the health and personal values course." He turned to his right. "Susan Reed is our art teacher, and Ed Staley teaches music. Lee Wong has physical education. He would have joined us, but he has a seventh-period class." Stu set his pipe aside and leaned forward. "The main reason we're meeting today is to make sure we're all set for the convention next week."

"Las Vegas, here we come!" Susan shouted. She was a tall woman with large teeth and angular features. This outburst seemed somewhat uncharacteristic for her, but the others laughed without surprise, so it was probably not unexpected.

"Remember you're going there for art, Susan, not oral expression," Chris joked. He was a man of medium height with slick-backed dark hair and a stern expression on his face.

"I don't think I have to remind you, people, that we do have to be on our best behavior," Stu said. "We're going to an academic convention which just happens to be taking place in the fun-filled capital of the world."

"Don't worry, Stu," Marilyn said. "Susan and I are leaving on Saturday, so by the time you guys get there on Monday, we'll be ready for business." Marilyn Peters was a short, heavyset woman with tightly curled blond hair and a coarse voice. Tom had not yet officially met her.

"Ed, are you all set for the trip?" Stu asked.

"Oh, yes. And I, for one, don't need the external stimulation."

The other teachers exploded with hoots of disapproval. Ed adjusted his glasses on his long, thin nose and sat back quietly.

"All right. Now, Walt and Nita will be coming Wednesday with the student participants. They're bringing Mark Banazech, Beth Crawford, and Frank Ziderly. Anyone have any problems with those choices?"

The teachers looked at one another and shook their heads.

"Good." Stu paused and looked at Tom. "Tom has asked

for a few minutes of our time today. He'd like to find out a little more about Joni Irving."

The four teachers shifted in their chairs and glanced at Tom expectantly.

"I know this is an unpleasant subject," Stu said. "But I agreed because I think it's important that we try to find out what happened...why one of our project students would have taken this drastic step."

"Aren't the police working on this?" Marilyn asked.

"Yes," Tom spoke up. "But I've gotten information from other people that makes the whole thing seem a bit strange."

"But you knew her for only a couple of days," Marilyn said.

"In the program, yes, but—"

"That's why we need to give our input," Stu said. "She's been in our classes for over three years, and we surely know her better than the other teachers." He stood, walked to a chart holder behind him, and picked up a large piece of tag board. "I thought it might help if we looked at it in terms of the courses she's taken from us."

"Scope and sequence time, children," Donnelly joked.

Stu smiled. "Well, it doesn't do us any harm to review what we're supposed to be doing from time to time." He set the large chart on the holder and stepped aside so that all at the table could see it. The courses in each subject for all four high school years were printed in bold letters:

COURSE	Grade 9	Grade 10	Grade 11	Grade 12
MATHEMATICS	Algebra	Geometry	Intermediate Algebra & Trigonometry	Calculus
ENGLISH	Basic Literary Analysis	English Literature	American Literature	World Literature
SOCIAL SCIENCE	Geography	Anthropology & World History	American History & Government	Psychology
SCIENCE	Basic Scientific Analysis	Biology	Chemistry	Physics
PHYSICAL EDUCATION	Controlled Relaxation	Fitness	Focused Conditioning	Interactive Skills
HEALTH		Health & Personal Values		
ART			Experiences in Art	
MUSIC				Experiences in Music

"It never hurts to do a little fine tuning occasionally, either. I told you the other day, Tom, that our students all take a full course in Mathematics, but that this subject is not formally a part of the LENA course of study."

"Yes." Tom glanced at the other teachers, who seemed to be frowning in disapproval.

"And, of course, you're familiar with the English offerings," Stu went on. "And you've talked to Bonnie about Joni's work there."

"Yes, but there's a lot more involved than just literature." Tom recalled the strange experiences that had taken place in Bonnie's class. "A lot more."

"Of course," Stu said. "As there is in all of our classes. But these are placed here for major topical reference." He looked at the chart again and pointed to his own subjects. "I remember Joni as an outstanding student, in every case except..." his finger moved across the chart and stopped, "except psychology. This year, she seemed somewhat resistive. I don't know why. I noticed it especially when we began the unit on Freudian analysis. She *understood* all of the concepts, but she seemed to reject their importance."

"That's the pattern I recall," Chris said. "Joni was extremely bright, but spotty in her excellence. I noticed it first in the tenth grade. She had an exemplary grasp of the biological structure of living organisms. But she had a negative attitude toward basic principles of evolution."

"Yes, I think I recall a paper you showed me that Joni had done two years ago," Stu said. "It was a detailed scientific argument against the concept of evolution."

"Yes, it was a remarkable work," Chris said. "It was difficult to dispute, except, of course, that it totally ignored the fact of evolution."

"Was that the only problem area?" Stu asked.

"No. She had some trouble this year, too," Chris said. "In my physics course, I include a unit on Psi Phenomena."

"What's that?" Tom asked.

"We take a scientific look at extrasensory perception, psychic phenomena, and recorded out-of-body experiences," he explained. "There's a wealth of material out there on this subject, but Joni again seemed to reject its validity."

"Hmm..." Stu glanced at the chart again. "Lee isn't here to talk about her experiences in Phys Ed."

"I'll see him later," Tom said.

"Marilyn, how about you?" Stu asked.

"I can't say anything," Marilyn said. "Joni was exempted from my class, remember?"

"Yes, that's right."

"But that's very significant in itself, isn't it?" she asked. "The very things she had trouble with in your classes would have been introduced in mine. She would have been prepared." She sat back and crossed her arms. "I really get angry when Walt allows students to exempt out of my course. It's basic to everything else they learn!"

"Well, Marilyn, I take exception to your attributing more value to your one-year course than to my entire four-year curriculum," Chris chided.

"Wait until our next meeting, when I present the results of my study," Marilyn said. "You'll see!"

"Well, let's go on," Stu said. "Susan, how did Joni do in art?"

"She did an adequate job on the traditional," Susan said. "But in my classes I stress, of course, the broad, free exploration into color and design. Joni was always a little hampered by this."

"That was the same problem she had in music," Ed said. "She was an extremely capable pianist. But that both added to, and detracted from her more creative abilities."

"Why is that?" Tom asked.

"Well, in November, I began a study of the fifty-three-tone musical scale," he explained. "We have the electronic technology to support it, and there's a great deal of interest in this world-wide." He leaned forward, pushed his glasses up on his nose, and frowned at Stu. "Of course, quite a few of my students have had trouble with this concept. And I just want to go on record that my students would do a lot better if we had total curricular support."

"Oh, Ed, don't start that again," Marilyn said.

"Well, here's an excellent example of the need," Ed said.

"I'm sorry. I don't understand," Tom said.

"This is a little academic discussion that's been going on for...oh, about six years," Stu said. "Ed is upset that the math strand isn't included in the LENA program at the high school."

"The students need the support from a related math program to allow for a full analytical base in music," Staley said. "There's nothing mysterious about that. Mike just needs to accept it."

"Mike Underwood is the mathematics department chair," Stu told Tom.

"Yes, I know."

"He and the other teachers were unwilling to..." He shook his head. "No, that's too strong. They're not ready to change the math curriculum to match the program objectives."

"I liked *unwilling* better," Ed said.

"Nevertheless, we're not going to solve that issue here, are we?" Stu looked around the table. "Does anyone have any more information about Joni?" When no one responded, Stu took the chart off the rack and set it on the floor. He then picked up his pipe and waved it toward the group. "All right. Make good plans for your substitutes for next week. I'll see you at the convention."

The four teachers rose quickly and left the room. Stu walked toward Tom and sat in a chair next to him.

"I don't know if that was of any help or not," he said.

"It may have been. I just need to take time to piece things together."

"Sure." He sat back and gestured aimlessly toward the empty chairs. "These are good people, Tom. They're just very individualistic. But that's what the program fosters, isn't it?" He leaned forward and spoke intensely. "And they are very dedicated to the program."

"Yes. I can see that."

Stu glanced at his watch. "Lee is still in class. Maybe you can catch him."

"Yes, I think I will." Tom rose and headed toward the door. "Thanks for your help."

"Any time."

Tom turned back and looked at Stu. "What do you think? "About Joni, I mean?"

Stu placed the stem of his pipe on his lip and pushed it down lightly. "I think Joni Irving had a great deal more to offer than any of us ever imagined. I will miss her, Tom."

Tom raised his hand momentarily in a vague gesture of agreement, then left the room.

Lee Wong's class was held in an exercise room adjacent to the gymnasium. As Tom approached the door, he heard a muffled, rhythmic sound of speaking. He swung the door open and entered the room. At one end, Wong sat on a large mat, cross-legged, his arms held crossed before him, eyes closed. Facing him, seated in the same position, were fifteen or sixteen students. Wong spoke in terse sentences and the students repeated what he said.

"I have feelings, but I am their master," Wong chanted.

"I have feelings, but I am their master," the students echoed in unison.

"I may have emotions, but not be subject to my emotions."

"I may have emotions, but not be subject to my emotions."

"I may have anger, but it does not control me."

"I may have anger, but it does not control me."

"I may use my anger as a tool for my survival."

"I may use my anger as a tool for my survival."

"I am ready," Wong chanted, slowly emphasizing each word.

"I am ready," the students responded.

Wong and the students then rose to their feet. The students placed their hands at their sides and lowered their heads. Wong looked over to Tom and nodded.

"Very well, we will do some three-on-one," Wong said to the class. "Mark, you begin."

Mark Banazech stepped forward and stood in the center of the mat, his head lowered.

Wong moved off the mat and looked at the other students. "Who?" Silently, first one, then two, and finally three students stepped forward and joined Mark on the mat.

"Very well."

Mark raised his head and placed his arms in a combative posture. The students surrounding him did the same.

"Begin!" Wong barked.

The three students paused slightly, then quickly turned to attack the single figure in their midst. Before they could lay a hand on him, Mark spun around. His foot landed in the stomach of one assailant, and his knuckles struck another in the forehead. Then he grasped the third by the nape of the neck and thrust him to the ground. The three stood, bowed lightly and returned to their places. Mark returned his hands to his sides and lowered his head.

"What do you think?" Wong asked as he approached Tom.

"Very impressive. Does anyone ever get hurt?"

"No." He looked at Mark. "He's in complete control. I teach my students to stop a fraction of an inch before the deadly blow." He smiled and illustrated by thrusting his fist to within a hair of the palm of his hand. "One moment, please." Wong spoke to the class, "Continue the exercise. If any of you lands a hand on Mark, you take his place." He turned back. "Now, what can I do for you, Tom?"

"Oh, I was just at the project meeting."

"Oh, yes. Preparations for the big convention."

"Yes, that. And I also wanted to talk to the project teachers about Joni Irving."

"Yes. Very unfortunate."

"Her parents are friends of mine," Tom said. "I'm trying to get a lead on why she died."

"I was very shocked also."

Tom glanced at the group of students. "I notice there are some girls in the group. Was Joni in this class?"

"No. About half of my students elect the combative course. "The others have advanced conditioning. Joni was in that class."

"Can you tell me anything about her?"

Mark had subdued another group and all were standing silently in anticipation of a third assault.

"It's important that we attain inner peace." Wong pointed to the quietly standing students. "Joni always told me she had found her inner peace, but she never participated in the focusing exercises. These techniques are critical to success. I'm afraid she didn't have a true understanding of what I was trying to help her accomplish. If she had," he raised his hands questioningly, "who knows?"

"I see." Tom put his hand on the knob of the door and turned it slightly. "But you said you were shocked."

"I can't explain it. Even without the exercise, she did seem to carry an air of composure...contentment." He nodded. "Yes. I was shocked."

"Thank you." Tom opened the door and glanced back at the group of students. Mark still stood, undefeated, on the mat.

The things Tom heard that day raised more questions than they resolved. Perhaps Nita could help him sort out the information. He went quickly from the gymnasium to the office. As he walked by Walt's office, he noticed that Marilyn Peters was there. She stood just inside, near the door. He couldn't see Walt, but he assumed he was there, because Marilyn was speaking loudly and waving her arms frantically. Walt's secretary looked up as Tom approached. She stood quickly, walked to Walt's office, and pulled the door closed.

Tom waved at the secretary as he passed and headed toward Nita's office. She sat behind her desk, reading a large book, but when Tom entered, she looked up immediately, smiled, and placed the book aside.

"Hello, Tom. Come in."

Tom walked toward her desk, but she put a hand up to stop him. "No, over there." She pointed to the pair of uphol-stered chairs in the corner. She followed him there, and they sat.

"Looks like I interrupted some heavy reading," he said.

Nita shook her head. Then she cupped her hand to her lips, leaned forward, and whispered, "It's a novel!" She laughed and leaned back again. "What can I do for you?"

"I've been talking with the project teachers."

"Oh, that's right. Stu had a meeting, didn't he?"

"Yes. I'm trying to find out some things."

"About the program?" she asked, smiling broadly.

He shook his head. "Joni. I'm still trying to understand."

The smile left her face and she brought her legs up on the chair beside her and passed her fingers slowly down a thin gold chain which hung from her neck. "Maybe you should put it away, Tom."

"Why?"

"Worrying about things like this can get you down without accomplishing anything. Sometimes we just have to put them away." Her finger rested at the bottom of the chain.

"Is that what you do?" he asked.

"Yes, Tom, I— Oh, no!" Her finger had pressed so hard that the gold chain broke. It slid off her neck and she let it fall into the palm of her hand.

"Sorry." He waited a moment, then, "I can't drop it, Nita. Not yet, anyway. Everything I hear about Joni makes me more confused. I thought maybe you could help me."

She clenched her fist over the chain and set her feet back on the floor. "Maybe later. I don't really have time right now."

Tom glanced over at the novel sitting on her desk. "Sure, that's all right. I should talk to some more people first, anyway. I need to know what she was like in the first two years of the program. I'm going to see her junior high school teachers."

"Do you know them?"

"No." He stood up abruptly. "But I'll introduce myself."

"Wait." Nita stood and crossed to her desk. "You don't want to go in like a bull in a china shop." She picked up her phone and pressed a single button. "Karen, get me Brenda at Eastside Middle School, will you please?" She covered the mouthpiece with her hand and spoke to Tom, "Brenda Calloway. She's the project counselor for grades seven and eight. She should be able to help you." She removed her hand and spoke into the telephone again. "Brenda? Hi, this is Nita....Yes, yes, I'm fine. Listen, I have a favor to ask of you. One of our teachers wants to talk to you about one of the project students. She was with you in the seventh and eighth grades. She is...she was a senior. Joni Irving... Yes, I thought you would... Yes. The teacher's name is Tom Kerzig." She looked at Tom and winked. "He's a neat guy, so give him all the help you can... What?... Oh." She covered the mouthpiece again and looked up. "Tomorrow afternoon all right, Tom? Four o'clock?"

"Sure, that's fine."

"That's good, Brenda," Nita said into the telephone. "Thank you... Yes. Goodbye." She hung up the phone.

"Thanks, Nita."

She felt absently for her missing chain. Then she smiled and nodded.

Tom left Nita's office and headed toward the front of the building. He was intercepted by Walt, who had just stepped out of his doorway.

"Tom, can I see you for a minute?"

Tom stopped. "Sure, Walt. In your office?"

"No, I'll walk with you."

They left the building and strode across the cracked sidewalk leading toward Tom's classroom.

"I just spent a few minutes with Marilyn Peters," Walt began. "She tells me you were at the project meeting. That's good. That will help you get into the swing of things." He chuckled nervously. "But, she said you brought up this Joni issue. Got the teachers a little on edge."

"I didn't intend to." Tom stopped and turned to Walt. "No, Walt. It didn't get them on edge."

"Well, actually she was probably reacting to the way Stu handled it, giving the impression that something in the program might have contributed...you know."

"No, I don't think he gave that impression at all."

"Well, Marilyn got that impression," Walt said. "And maybe others did, too. These people are sensitive, anxious to know that they're giving their kids the very best. This kind of thing can tear them apart. It wasn't their fault. And it's certainly not the program's fault."

"And yet, maybe the program's not right for *everybody*," Tom said.

Walt shook his head and grasped Tom by the arm. "Now, you see, that's the kind of suggestions that make these people very...well...sensitive." He released Tom's arm and laughed nervously. "But I understand that you mean well, Tom. You just haven't had enough experience in the program. That's why I'm having you attend the convention with the others. You'll get a good grounding there. And you'll see. The program *is* for everybody. It really is. In the meantime," he patted Tom's arm, "let's not worry them about Joni." He tipped his head down slightly and raised his eyes across the top of his half-glasses. "All right?"

Tom frowned and raised his hand to his chin.

"Fine!" Walt said, patting Tom's arm again. "That'll be just fine!" He turned and walked back toward the office.

16

Tom pressed his brakes momentarily and leaned on the steering wheel as he realized he had just bypassed the freeway on-ramp. He had taken that way home for so many years that turning there had become habitual. So why, today? No matter. He would just take the longer route. There was no hurry. He knew why he had missed the turn-off, of course. His mind was reeling with conflicting information. Nita was probably right. He should just put Joni's death out of his mind and let the police handle the investigation. Still, Pastor Bentley had asked for his help. But why? Tom hadn't known Joni that well and he'd had her as a student for only two days. But the recognition of that fact only increased his feeling of confusion. A casual acquaintance with her at church and two brief days in the classroom—yet he couldn't get her out of his mind. The paradox was too great. The bright, confident girl, and the lifeless form, victim of a deadly dose of heroin.

Talking with the teachers hadn't resolved anything. She wasn't totally with the program, but what of that? Tom saw that has a healthy sign, not as an internal conflict that would lead her on a road to self-destruction. Don't worry them about Joni, Walt had demanded. But she was their student. For three and a half years they had nurtured her, trained her, led her in the ways of the academically gifted. Why shouldn't they be worried that one of their bright leaders of the new age had chosen self-annihilation? Why shouldn't they care?

Tom stopped at a red light and noticed that the

crossroad looked familiar. He glanced at the sign and realized he was near Bonnie's house. She had invited the English department teachers to her place for a holiday party during the winter break. He remembered that she had told everyone she was giving proper respect to the season as she was wearing gold jewelry and myrrh-scented perfume and burning frankincense. He had stayed long enough to bid everyone a merry Christmas, and then left. But now he felt a sudden urge to speak with Bonnie. More than anyone else, she should have some insight into Joni's life...and death.

A horn beeped and Tom realized the signal had changed. He quickly activated his left blinker, waved his hand apologetically above his head, and turned onto the crossroad. After he had driven only four blocks, he recognized Bonnie's street, and turned onto it. She lived only a block and a half away. Her condominium complex contained identical-looking units, but he remembered that she had painted the black iron gateway leading to her entrance pink, so that people could find it easily. He pulled the car to the curb in front of the distinctive entrance and turned off the engine. Dusk had fallen, and in the approaching darkness, the light in her window was barely visible. Tom left the car, walked quickly through the brightly painted gate, and stepped onto her narrow porch. He rang the doorbell and waited. Shortly, the large entry door swung back slightly and Bonnie's face appeared. She still had several light bruises and areas of puffiness about her face, but the bandages were gone.

Bonnie squinted at him. "Tom?"

"Hi, Bonnie."

"I wasn't expecting you." She opened the door wider. "Come in."

Tom stepped inside and Bonnie closed the door. The interior entry seemed nearly as dark as it was outside, and as Tom glanced into the spacious living room, the mauve walls and brightly contrasting trim that he remembered blended into nondescript color. He looked at Bonnie. Something was different. She usually wore her hair short, in close curls, but now it hung straight and long, below her shoulders.

"You like my new look?" She held her arms up and spun slowly in a circle.

"Sure. It's different."

"It's temporary. They shaved my head in the hospital, so I'm wearing this until my hair grows out."

"Oh. So how are you feeling?"

"I'm getting by." She raised her eyebrows slightly and gestured toward the living room. "Can I get you something to drink?"

"No thanks."

Tom followed her into the large room. Something had changed since the time of the party. One entire end of the room was covered with a huge mural which depicted a forest scene. Standing before that was a long aquarium with several exotic fish swimming in it.

"That's new, isn't it?" Tom pointed to the mural.

"Yes. That was my Christmas present to myself. The aquarium was in my bedroom, but I moved it out here because I thought it would blend in with the forest."

Tom nodded. She was right. The base of the mural showed a cool mountain stream, and the fish in the aquarium seemed to be an underwater extension of the peaceful scene.

"Sit down." Bonnie pointed to one end of the plush couch.

Tom sat and Bonnie collapsed at the other end. In front of the couch stood a heavy table and in the center of the table was a large glowing pyramid with three sections. The sections spun slowly about, soft colors radiating out from them into the dimly lighted room.

"You sure I can't get you something to drink?" Bonnie asked.

"No, thank you." Tom realized Bonnie was holding a drink which she sipped slowly as she sat quietly in the corner of the couch. "Are you okay, Bonnie?" he asked. "You seem a little depressed."

"I guess you might say that." Bonnie raised her glass to her lips, tipped her head back, and drained it. She dropped her head forward again, shook it twice, and placed the empty glass on the table. "His majesty, Mr. Inspector Gruber, told me he had a nice little chat with you and Joe this morning."

Tom leaned back as he recalled the meeting. Was that just this morning? He remembered Gruber said he was going to pay Bonnie a visit. "Yes, that's right."

"So, I would think you might ask me first if you had a question about something you found in *my desk*."

"Not when it comes to drugs, Bonnie."

Bonnie shot forward. "It wasn't drugs!"

"Joe had them analyzed."

"Lighten up and listen to me, will you? The point is, you told Gruber about them, and now he's decided to take my case because of the—" Bonnie made a gesture with her fingers to indicate quotation marks. "Similarities with Joni's case."

"Well, you have to admit..."

"What's similar?" she interrupted. "I didn't kill myself! I didn't shoot heroin into my arm!"

"The capsules. He found some of those with Joni, too. The capsules containing the LSD."

"Ahh..." Bonnie waved her hand downward in a gesture of disgust. Then she pulled her legs up on the couch and placed her chin on her knees. "I told them I was all right. I just lost control of the car on the curve. But now this Gruber has made it his personal challenge. Why can't he just believe me?"

"Because the drug was in your system."

"Tom..." Bonnie shook her head slowly.

"You can't deny that, Bonnie." Tom paused as he recalled another possibility Gruber had mentioned. "Unless, of course, someone gave it to you without your knowing it."

Bonnie raised her head from her knees and spoke in a sudden, hard tone. "No, that's not what happened."

"Then...what?"

"I...I took it myself," she mumbled.

"So why did you deny it?"

"I denied that I took *drugs*. And I still deny that." She curled her legs beneath her and fluffed a cushion as she sat back again in the corner of the couch. "LSD is not a drug, not in the way you're referring to it. It's a mind-expanding formula for..."

"Oh, Bonnie..."

"Do your homework before casting stones," she said. "It's non-addicting. It's not harmful to the body in any way."

"Anything that alters your mind like that is harmful."

"Oh, you're so naive!" She reached over and picked up her glass from the table. "This alters your mind, too, doesn't it?"

"Sure it does."

"But Gruber wouldn't be involved if you found a pint of whiskey in the desk, would he?"

"He would if it were illegal."

"Ah, yes... The legality issue."

"And if you'd been under the influence of liquor while driving, you'd be in just as much trouble."

"That's why I never drink and drive," Bonnie said.

"Alcohol dulls the senses, slows the responses. LSD makes you *more* alert...*more* responsive."

"I can't accept that."

"It's just a matter of time. People will realize how beneficial it can be to the self-awareness process. The laws will change."

"I hope you're wrong."

"Of course you do, because you have a narrow view."

"When it comes to drugs, you bet I do! The kids in our schools have enough trouble resisting as it is."

"Exactly!" Bonnie sat forward and spoke heatedly. "And why is that? Kids want what they can't have, don't they? That's what the whole legality thing has done, don't you see?"

"What are you saying? That drugs be made legal?"

"No, not *drugs.*" Bonnie emphasized the last word. "But why do kids take drugs?"

"There are many reasons."

"Yes, but isn't it, ultimately, to feel good about themselves? To experience sensations that the world inhibits? To expand their awareness?"

"Sometimes."

"Those desires aren't bad. What they need is an acceptable, safe way to achieve them."

"Are you saying that kids should be *encouraged* to take mind-expanding drugs?" he asked.

"Well, it's still much too early in the flow of the world's time-table to think that's going to occur right away." She nodded slowly. "But it's coming."

"I think you're way off base on this, Bonnie. LSD is not safe." Then he remembered the reason he came. "It was definitely not safe for Joni, was it?"

Bonnie frowned and shook her head. "Joni didn't die

from LSD. She died from heroin."

"Both were found with her."

Bonnie raised her eyebrows and pointed at him. "If she'd had instruction on how to safely achieve her awareness goals, she'd be alive today."

"No. No...no." Tom realized that this discussion wouldn't be productive. But Bonnie must have some insights into Joni's death, even with her weird ideas. Perhaps *because* of her weird ideas. "Bonnie, why did Joni die?"

"She killed herself," Bonnie spoke quickly.

Tom raised his hand to stop her. "*Why?*" he asked pointedly.

"I'm not a psychiatrist."

"Why do you *think?*" he persisted.

Bonnie sighed deeply, pulled a cushion down in front of her, and rubbed her hand lightly over it. "Joni was a strange girl. I think I told you before that she really wasn't with the program."

"I've heard that a lot lately."

"Well, it's true. If she had been more accepting, she could have dealt with her own problems more adequately."

"Didn't you have any clue, any warning in her behavior?"

"No. It's not always that simple."

"Nothing in her class activities? In the things she wrote?" Then he remembered that Nita had given Bonnie a copy of Joni's composition. "You got a copy of her last composition, didn't you?"

"Yes, and that illustrates what I'm talking about," Bonnie said. "It's so dark, destructive..." She gestured aimlessly. "I give my students the tools for *joyful* self-exploration. Joni's paper was the antithesis of that." Bonnie pushed the cushion back and sat forward. "I mean, I certainly don't teach my students anything about some *dark master.*"

"Yes..." That term. It haunted him. "What do you think she meant by that?"

"The only thing I can think of is that it's a symbol of her fundamentalist religious upbringing. The narrow spiritual persuasion of her parents drawing her away from her true search for self-realization."

"Do you really believe that?"

Bonnie leaned forward. "I sensed it from the beginning. Many students come into the program with similar backgrounds, but I can always wean them away...gently...lead them toward productive self-awareness. But Joni resisted me. I worked with her to free her from her inhibiting environment."

"How did you do that? Can you tell me?"

"Well, through the class work, of course," she said. "The values clarification and external awareness exercises are usually sufficient. But Joni required much more. So this year, I met with her after school every week or two."

"I didn't know that."

"Yes. I told her I was interested in learning more about her religious beliefs. That turned out to be an excellent strategy, because she was eager to talk. She told me it gave her a chance to—what did she say—witness to me. Often, our encounters sounded like a broken record. I would tell her how much I wanted to free her from her restrictive controls, and lead her into the joy of the knowledge of her own divinity..." Bonnie's voice trailed off and she stared toward the mural.

"And what was Joni's response?" Tom asked finally.

"Oh..." She turned her head and focused on him again. "She always said she *was* free, that she knew a joy beyond all understanding." She placed her fist against her cheek and her eyes narrowed. "But most importantly, she always said she wasn't afraid to die." Bonnie placed her hand across her eyes and drew it slowly downward. "I never could break the barrier. It's my greatest guilt that I failed to free her from her bondage." She looked blankly toward the mural again.

"But you met with her frequently?"

"Yes."

"The night of the dance, the Valentine's Day dance. Did you meet with her then?"

"No."

"Did she go with you after the dance? Was she with you when you had the accident?"

"What?" Bonnie suddenly snapped her head back and spoke harshly. "Is that what this is all about?"

"Was she with you?"

"First the inspector and now you. You're intent on proving that someone was with me the night of the accident! I told him, and I'll tell you...for the last time. I don't know how the right side of the windshield got cracked. When the car missed the turn, I probably moved over to avoid hitting the steering wheel."

"Okay, Bonnie."

"It's my head! It's my car! It's my D.U.I., you know! Don't you think I've gone through enough?"

"Okay, let's drop it."

Bonnie rose abruptly, took the glass from the table, and walked over to a bar separating the living area from the dining area. She grasped a bottle from the bar and filled the glass. Sipping from it, she turned and walked slowly back to the couch. "Next week is the convention. It's just killing me that I can't go."

"Walt asked me to go in your place, you know."

"Yes, and that's good. You need the experience." She took another sip from the glass and spoke excitedly, "It will be so stimulating. You'll see. It could change your life!"

"We'll see."

"I just hate it that I can't go!" She took a longer drink. "I told Walt I'd even pay my own way, meet everyone there. But he told me it wouldn't be in the best interest of the program."

"I think he's right."

"Of course he's right," she interrupted. "But that doesn't change the way I feel." She paused. "Will you do something for me?"

"If I can."

"There are two presenters I really wanted to see—Helene Farris and Kurt Quinlan. Will you attend their sessions, take good notes, and bring back whatever materials they have?"

"Farris and Quinlan," he muttered. "All right. I'll do that."

"Good." She finished the drink and placed the glass on the table. Then she walked over to the aquarium and studied the fish. "I suppose these fish aren't afraid to die, even though they're held captive in this terrible glass prison. But I can see them so easily, understand their movements. I could never quite see Joni." She grasped the edge of the aquarium, and it moved slightly as she leaned against it. "Why wouldn't she let me save her?" She stared at the simulated path which appeared to wind into infinity in the painted forest, but which was in reality only twelve inches from her head. "And why did she feel so free?" Bonnie turned around suddenly, a broad smile on her face. She stepped to the side of the aquarium, and backed into the mural. "What do you think? I bought this mural, because I thought it complemented my psyche the best." She turned around and ran her hand over portions of the mural as she spoke. "The forest...so quiet...so deep. And even when the trees die, their fruits replenish themselves like the phoenix. Whitman loved the forest, too, remember? '*I bequeath myself to the dirt, to grow from the grass I love. If you want me again, look for me under your bootsoles.*'

I tried to get Joni to love Whitman. She always told me the dirt could have her body, but her soul would be in heaven. Like I said, she was never quite with the program. And it's my guilt that I couldn't save her."

She leaned hard against the mural, her head turned to the side, and her arms positioned like an ancient Egyptian painting. "What do you think? Am I not an integral part of the grandeur of this forest?"

She was transfixed, her eyes squinting, and her mouth open in a wide smile. Her head seemed to merge with the branches of a mammoth redwood, and her tightly opened palm was flattened against the path, pointing to some unseen destination beyond the wall.

"Sure, Bonnie," Tom said. "You are what you think."

17

By the time Tom dismissed his sixth-period class and prepared his materials for the next day it was after 3:30. He hurried out of the building and sped across the lawn toward the faculty parking lot. When he reached the lot, he heard a voice.

"Whoa there! You're breaking the speed limit."

Tom stopped abruptly and turned around. He had run right past Mike Underwood, the mathematics department chairman. He was a short muscular man with a crew cut and a broad smile.

"Oh, hi, Mike. I'm sorry I didn't recognize you. I'm on my way to a meeting and I guess I have a one-track focus."

"Don't let me stop you."

"No, actually, I'm glad you hollered. I've been wanting to talk with you."

"Oh? What about?"

"The LENA program."

Mike hunched over and rubbed his hands together rapidly. "Ahh...my favorite topic!"

"So I hear." Tom smiled. "I attended a project meeting yesterday. There seems to be quite a breach between your department and the others regarding the program."

"That's putting it mildly."

"Can you tell me why you elected not to participate?"

"Elected?" Mike tilted his head and raised an eyebrow. "How much time do you have?"

Tom glanced at his watch.

"Where's your car? Let's walk and talk."

"Sure," Tom said and the two of them headed slowly across the parking lot.

"When the program was adopted five years ago, I called a department meeting," Mike began. "The teachers reviewed the goals of the program, and we decided they weren't compatible with our subject. Mathematics is based on absolutes. And the LENA program is the antithesis of absolutes."

"Simple versus complex," Tom mumbled.

"Well, those terms are not necessarily antithetical. Mathematics is a highly complex study. And yet it's simple also, in the fact that there is a right way to arrive at conclusions. There is a correct answer. So it contains the complexity of content *and* the simplicity of absolutes."

"And you thought the LENA program would have a negative impact on your courses?"

"That was the decision the math teachers made," Mike said. "And it wasn't easily arrived at. We had no argument with the general focus of the program—teaching students to be more analytical, to question the events influencing them, rather than just blindly accepting them. But we concluded that the questioning was being carried to ridiculous extremes. The model lessons called for students to challenge things where challenge was simply not called for. For example—this is an exaggeration, but it will give you an idea—*Two plus two equals four. What do you think about that, Johnny? Does that seem reasonable? How does it coincide with your view of life?*"

Tom laughed. "You're right. That must be an exaggeration."

"But..." Mike stopped and took Tom by the arm. "How

about this one? *The area of a circle may be determined by the product of pi and the square of the radius. Consider the circle as the life force surrounding you. Your energy radiates from the center. It duplicates itself by its own force, and merges with the mysterious universal relationship to create a new sense of being.*"

"You're kidding."

Mike shook his head. "That's right out of one of the suggested textbooks—*Geometry for the New Generation.* 'Relational motivation,' they called it. It's supposed to give the students a feeling of oneness with their studies. The math teachers didn't see it that way. We thought the approach would be counterproductive."

"I can see why," Tom said, as they resumed their slow pace toward his car. "So Walt agreed to your non-participation?"

Mike laughed and shook his head. "Let's just say he decided not to fight that battle yet. We know that if push comes to shove, we'll have to comply or go somewhere else to teach."

They stopped beside Tom's car, and Tom reached out and shook Mike's hand. "Thank you. That was helpful."

"Anytime. You know, Tom, in mathematics the distinction is pretty easy to state. But there are other absolutes, too...other concepts that shouldn't be challenged just for the sake of the challenge."

"I know." Tom placed his hand on the roof of his car and the cold metal pierced the warmth of his palm. He waved and watched the short man turn and walk away.

Tom walked up the neatly bordered sidewalk leading to the administration building of Eastside Middle School. A number of students mingled about on the lawn, apparently waiting for the late bus or a ride from their parents. When he went to school, these were called "junior high schools," but then the term "middle school" became the norm. Apparently a transitional connotation was considered more favorable than one that suggested a lower relative value. But the kids were the same. The small group on the lawn displayed an amazing array of shapes and sizes. "Middle school" really was a better term. These students were definitely in transition.

The office was still bustling with activity, and as Tom entered, the buzz of conversation filled his ears. But one sound rose loudly above the others—raucous, high-pitched laughter. Tom leaned toward the young, smiling receptionist behind the information counter.

"Brenda Calloway?"

Her smile broadened, and she turned and pointed in the direction of the laughter.

"Thanks."

Tom walked down a narrow passageway toward an open office. As he approached, the sound of the laughter became louder. He stopped at the doorway and peered inside. A huge woman stood beside a desk, a telephone pressed snugly against her flabby face. She looked up at Tom and raised her hand in recognition.

"Listen, I've gotta go, Martha," she said loudly. "I'll see you for dinner tomorrow night.... Okay. Bye." She hung up the phone and stepped strenuously toward the door. She held out her hand. "I'll bet you're Tom."

"Yes," Tom said, allowing his hand to be engulfed by hers. "I'm glad to meet you, Brenda."

"Come in, and please excuse the mess." She roughly gathered some papers from a small table and placed them on her desk. Then she pointed toward a chair on one side of the table. "That's yours."

"Thanks." Tom sat slowly and leaned against the table.

Brenda pulled a rolling swivel chair out on the opposite

side, supported her weight with the table, and sat. The chair disappeared beneath her massive form. "Tom... I don't remember meeting you at any of the project gatherings."

"No. I've just been in it for a couple of weeks. I'm taking Bonnie Teague's seniors while she's out."

"Oh, yes, Bonnie. How's she doing?"

"Better. She's out of the hospital."

"Good. I'll bet she's going to hate missing the convention."

"Her exact words," Tom said.

Brenda smiled. "Are you going in her place?"

"Yes."

"You high school teachers are lucky. You get all the perks. Our teachers didn't get invited. The district says we'll learn from you. The trickle-down principle, you know." She laughed. "I get to be there for the last day, though, to watch the cross-age tutoring presentations. So I guess I shouldn't complain. Now, what can I do for you?"

"I want to find out any information you might have about one of my students. She was here in the seventh and eighth grades."

"Oh, that's right. Joni Irving. Of course. Nita told me." Her jowls fell into a frown. "Very sad."

"Yes. Her parents are friends of mine, and I'm just trying to sort through some things, see if can find any explanation."

Brenda raised and lowered her body in a deep sigh. "I can't even believe it. Of course, I was just hired here three years ago myself, so I never knew Joni. But I do have all her records in the archives." She pushed her chair back from the table and turned toward a large lateral file. "Let's see, five years ago, I guess."

"Yes. Five and a half."

She opened a drawer just above the level of her lap and

studied the tabs on the tightly packed folders. "Ah, here we are!" She pulled out a folder and closed the drawer. Then she turned the chair back and forced it into a slow creep until she was again close to the table. "We track students by exception here. Anytime a teacher notes any atypical behavior related to an assignment, he or she fills out a pink referral slip, attaches it to the student specimen, and brings it to this office. So if a folder is skinny, it means the student behaved fairly normally." She held Joni's folder out before her. It was filled with papers. "As you can see, Joni was not a typical student."

"I wouldn't have thought she was," Tom said.

Brenda set the folder flat on the table and opened it. "All the students have the first few pages. They contain standardized test scores and semester grades." She squinted and passed her large hand over the information presented on the left and then on the right. Then she raised her eyebrows, turned the page, and repeated the process. "Well," she shook her head, "these are exceptionally good. High test scores and almost all A's in her courses. Why would she have so many exceptions?"

"That's what I'm here to find out."

Brenda pulled the file closer to her. Then she flipped to a segregated section. "Let's look at the seventh grade first." She pulled out a single sheet of paper with a heavily noted pink slip stapled to it. "Oh, sure," she said, reading the notation. "*If I Were God of the Universe.*"

"What?"

"*If I Were God of the Universe,*" she repeated. "It's a projective, goal-setting exercise. Students are supposed to imagine themselves as all-knowing, all-powerful gods, and list things they would do. Then the class shares what everyone has written. It's a great values-clarification tool."

"Why is it in there?"

"Well, let's see what Joni wrote." She flipped back the pink slip and read from the paper beneath. "In response to this assignment, Joni said, 'There is already a God of the universe and He is perfect.' "

"There are absolutes," Tom mumbled. "Concepts that shouldn't be challenged, just for the sake of the challenge."

"What?"

"Nothing."

"Well, that response definitely would not advance the exercise, would it? That's why the teacher sent it in. Joni was considered a non-participant. Let's see... What's this?" She glanced at the next notation. "Oh. This is just a reminder that Joni was exempted from the seventh-grade health and sex education course."

"She was exempted from the one in grade ten, also."

"Really? She must have had a real problem relating. Sexually, I mean."

Tom remembered, even from his brief encounter, her poise, her confident interaction, and the way she handled Mark at the dance. "I don't think so."

"They can sometimes hide it pretty well." Brenda paused for a moment and then turned her attention to the next document. "Well, this isn't anything Joni wrote. It's just a three-page note from her physical education teacher." She squinted again and read through the document, speaking as she read. "Yes. The teacher assigns a focusing exercise—you know, for meditation. A lot of seventh graders have difficulty understanding what she's getting at, so she asks them to imagine that they have a spirit guide that leads them into...what did she call it...the enchanted land of thought. Sometimes she has a picture of a pyramid they concentrate on. That helps, too. I've seen this demonstrated. It's really a great exercise."

"And..."

"Well, the teacher says here that Joni claimed God was her spirit guide and that she didn't need to concentrate to follow Him."

"And the teacher didn't like that, I guess."

"Well, no. Joni missed the whole point of the exercise. It wasn't supposed to be a religious experience. God is irrelevant. The students are just supposed to meditate, to help bring out their inner power." Brenda pulled out another document, read the notation, and laughed lightly. "Oh, yes. C & C."

"C & C?"

"This was during the time that a big stink was being raised over D & D...you know, Dungeons and Dragons."

"Oh, yes."

"So our teachers came up with an alternative—C & C—Caves and Creatures. It was basically the same game but with the different letter tag, the parents didn't get upset...for a while. Eventually, they had to move the whole activity into the health and sex education course, so people could exempt out of it if they wanted to."

"But Joni wasn't fooled, I guess," Tom said.

"Well, she certainly didn't like the activity," Brenda said, reading the document. "She said it brought out too many evil thoughts. The teacher tried to explain to her that the whole idea of the exercise was to show that good and evil are relative, depending on the situation. But Joni refused to play the game."

"That doesn't surprise me."

"Let's look at some eighth-grade notes." She turned to another section and pulled out a document. "This one's from her science teacher. He had given the class an assignment to identify similar body parts in apes and humans, as a proof of evolution. Oh, there is a paper from Joni with this one. It's a real one-line zinger! She wrote: 'Physical similarities do not prove sequential lineage.' "

Tom shook his head and laughed lightly.

"I detect from that," Brenda said, "that you're not surprised by this response, either."

"Not really. In the tenth grade, she wrote a paper on creation theory that confounded her science teacher."

"Oh?" She shrugged. "Well, she was a very bright girl. There's no doubt about that. It's just that she was...disjointed." Brenda pulled out another paper. "Here's one from her social science teacher. Oh, yes, this is a great exercise. I've used it with students a lot myself."

"What is it?"

"It's called 'The Tyranny of Should.' The teacher asks the students to list all of the possible 'shoulds' they get from their parents that are destructive to their own psychological development—their own value system. You know, *you should wear this...you should talk this way...you should associate with these people*, and so forth. And then the class discusses the lists."

"What's the purpose of that exercise?"

"Most people's hang-ups come from trying to follow a value system imposed by their parents," Brenda said. "The sooner they can break away...in a positive manner, of course...the more well-adjusted they will be in later life. But Joni didn't participate. She just said that the *shoulds* she got from her parents weren't destructive to her psychological development."

"Maybe they weren't."

"Well, everybody has some," Brenda insisted. "And that's the whole purpose of the class discussion afterward...to bring out the subtleties. The kids begin to realize that damaging statements were made by their parents that they hadn't even recognized before."

Tom sat back and mentally reviewed the examples Brenda had shared. He realized that the reason he was not surprised by any of Joni's reactions was because he would have reacted in exactly the same way. But so many educators had analyzed these exercises and given them their stamps of approval. Was Joni overreacting? And was he himself that much out of sync with the times?

"Oh, now this one is really far out!" Brenda said. "This was an exercise designed to help students become aware of each other's physical attributes. Boys draw pictures of girls and girls draw pictures of boys—all without clothes on, of course. They then label the body parts and afterward discuss what they've drawn. They learn so much better this way. It defuses the sensational impact of sexuality, and—"

"Wait a minute," Tom interrupted. "I thought Joni was exempted from the health and sex education course."

"Oh, she was. This exercise was done in art."

"Art?"

"Well, to begin with. But then the students take them to their English class, and under the labels of the body parts, they list all the slang expressions they can think of."

"Why?"

"It's a great awareness exercise. It lets the students see that all the silly words they use on the playground are not so secret, after all. And they aren't as inclined to waste their efforts pursuing that activity."

"Is there any scientific backing for that theory?"

"Oh, I think so," Brenda said. "But look what Joni did in response to this assignment!"

Brenda removed a paper from the folder, folded back the attached pink slip, and handed it to Tom. It was a detailed drawing. In the foreground, at the right, a girl knelt, looking out a small window. Beyond that, a narrow road wound to the left, into a dark grove containing a smattering of gnarled trees, their leafless branches reaching into obscurity. Along the road were a few small figures...children...running. Above the tops of the trees, almost hidden in the shadows of the sky, was an evil-looking figure, with eyes glowing red against a dark face. It's arm was extended, but the hand was bent... gently beckoning.

18

The students seemed unusually restless this morning. It may have been because it was Friday, but Tom imagined that more significant than that was the fact that he would be gone for three days next week, and they were anticipating a let down in his absence. It was time to remind them of their assignment.

"All right. Who remembers the assignment for today?" he asked.

The students looked at him blankly. Finally, a single hand was raised.

"Yes, Andrew," said Tom.

"We were supposed to read the excerpts from *Man's Fate* in the anthology and look for ways that each main character tries to fulfill himself."

"Right. Malreaux used the setting of the Chinese Revolution and the predominately atheistic view of life to show how people create their own meaning for life," Tom explained. "They were all trying to find their... What word did he use for it? Anyone remember? Yes, Mark."

"Freedom."

"Right." Tom walked to the board and picked up a piece of chalk. "For the assignment, we'll concentrate on six characters. The introduction to the excerpts listed their unique ways to achieve freedom. See if you can find them as I write their names." Tom turned to the board and continued speaking as he wrote. "The first one is Ch'en." He wrote the name and a dash, then stood poised, waiting for a response from the class.

"Terrorism," one student said.

"Yes." Tom wrote that word and continued below with the next. "Kyo."

"Dignity," another student responded.

"Gisors."

"Drugs. Opium.

"Clappique."

"Gambling."

"Vologin."

"Obedience."

"And Ferrall," Tom concluded.

"Power."

Tom set the chalk down and turned back to the students. "I don't know who will be teaching the class while I'm gone, but I plan to set up a specific series of activities, so you'll know exactly what to do."

A burst of good-natured moans rose from the class.

Tom smiled. "On Monday, you'll break up into six groups—one for each character—and list as many examples from the text that you can find that illustrate that character's way to freedom. On Tuesday, you'll have a class discussion on what each group found. And then, on Wednesday, I want each of you to choose two characters, and write a composition which shows how their ways to achieve freedom could lead them into conflict with one another." He smiled and shrugged. "Doesn't that sound easy?"

Beth Crawford raised her hand.

"Yes, Beth?"

"Frank, Mark, and I will be at the convention on Wednesday. Does that mean we don't have to do the composition?"

"I don't think that would be quite fair," Tom said. "You can do it as a homework assignment."

Mark and Frank sat up suddenly in disapproval.

"We can't have the three of you being rewarded twice, can we?" Tom asked.

The other members of the class clapped and sneered at the three students.

"All right," Tom said. "Any other questions about the exercise?"

Most of the class seemed to understand the assignment, but a few mumbled in a tone of bewilderment.

"Let's do a few together to give you an idea of what's expected," Tom suggested. "We'll start with Ch'en. His freedom was terrorism. Who can think of an example from the text that illustrates this?" A few hands rose. "Andrew."

"In one place, somebody said that the most effective man is a man who's decided to die."

"Yes, that's a good example. Frank."

"I like the part where he said that murder is an ecstasy toward *downward.*" Frank emphasized the last word. "Like, heavy metal, man!"

The class laughed.

"All right. That may be a very appropriate correspondence. I want you to remember it as you read what happens to Ch'en." He glanced at the board. "How about Kyo? Dignity? Yes, Mark."

"He said dignity is the opposite of humility."

"Ahh, actually, that's not the right word," Tom said. "Who remembers?" He waited and then pointed. "Yes, Mary Ann."

"Dignity is the opposite of *humiliation.*"

"Yes. And while you're at it, consider the difference

between *humility* and *humiliation*. It can have a significant impact on your understanding of the story." He looked at the board again. "Who's next? Oh, yes, Gisors...opium. Who wants to... Yes, Jason."

Jason cleared his throat and responded in his high, resonant voice. "I could really understand Gisors. It was a lot like the meditation exercises Bonnie has us do." He flipped through several pages and read from the anthology. " 'His eyes shut, carried by great motionless wings, Gisors contemplated his solitude: a desolation that joined the divine, while at the same time, the wave of serenity that gently covered the depths of death widened to infinity.' " Jason closed the book. "It sounds like he had a real mind-expanding experience."

Several members of the class mumbled in agreement. Tom recalled Bonnie, standing in her darkened living room before the massive mural. "Just a mind-expanding formula," she had said, "and just a matter of time. Still too early in the flow of the world's time-table, but one day...feel good about themselves...experience sensations they have been inhibited from by the world...expand their awareness."

Tom's thoughts were interrupted by the sound of the door opening. He looked up to see Walt standing in the doorway. The principal raised his eyebrows and beckoned to him.

"Excuse me for a moment," Tom said to the students and walked over to Walt. "Morning. What's up?"

"I just got a call from the district office. Dr. McCray wants to see you this afternoon at 3:30."

"What for?"

"I just got the message from his secretary."

"My sixth period class isn't over until 3:00," Tom said. "And then I have a lot of preparations to make for the substitute next week. I don't know if I can—"

"Three-thirty," Walt interrupted emphatically. "Be sure

to be there." He turned away and let the door close behind him.

Tom sat back in the plush couch and drummed his feet nervously against the thick carpet. He stared impatiently at the closed door leading to the superintendent's office. It was 3:50, and he'd been waiting since 3:25. Occasionally he'd look questioningly at the gray-haired secretary sitting behind her desk, but she would just smile and return to her typing. Finally her intercom line buzzed. She picked up the receiver, spoke quietly, and replaced it. She caught Tom's eye.

"Dr. McCray will see you now, Mr. Kerzig," she told him.

Tom rose from the couch, stretched inconspicuously to remove the stiffness, and walked to the door. As he entered, Carson McCray walked briskly toward him, his hand out-stretched. Dr. McCray was a tall, slender man. He was totally bald and wore frameless glasses.

"Mr. Kerzig..." Dr. McCray shook Tom's hand warmly. "Thank you for coming on such short notice. Come, let's sit down."

Dr. McCray had a massive mahogany desk with a huge comfortable-looking chair behind it, but he pointed instead to a large round conference table. They sat in adjacent chairs and turned to face one another. Tom chuckled inwardly as he remembered that Walt always used his desk in meetings as a symbol of power. Dr. McCray didn't need the symbol. He *had* the power.

"Walter's told me good things about you, Mr. Kerzig. You've been with the district...what...six—"

"Eight."

"Eight years. Yes. And he tells me you're an excellent planner, extremely good in the classroom, and popular with the students. Are you thinking of going into administration one day?"

"I don't know," Tom said. "I don't think so."

"All my principals tell me that the kind of teacher they appreciate the most is one who goes about quietly, doing a competent job—one they don't have to think about." Dr. McCray shifted slightly in his chair and folded his hands on his lap. "That may seem a rather shallow evaluative statement, but I think it has a great deal of validity. As administrators, we are limited in our time, and if we have to devote heavy supervision to more than a few people... Well, the system breaks down. And that's why Walter is so positive about your contributions."

"Thank you." Tom wished Dr. McCray would get to the point and stop uttering platitudes.

"Beyond that, you've now taken on an additional assignment, I understand," Dr. McCray continued. "A LENA class."

"Yes. I'm taking Bonnie Teague's seniors while she's out."

"It's unfortunate about her accident." He paused for a moment, placed his hand on the table, and moved his thumb slowly up and down. "What do you think of them?"

"The kids?"

"Yes."

"They're challenging."

Dr. McCray laughed lightly. "Yes, of course. The seniors have been in the program since its beginning. I guess you might say they're the elite, the first graduating class that's received the entire secondary offering."

"They do seem very well versed."

"Unfortunately, though, one of the students didn't make it through," Dr. McCray said slowly.

"You mean Joni Irving."

Dr. McCray nodded. "Such a tragic situation."

"Yes."

"Walter tells me you're a friend of the family."

"Yes. Well, I've known them for several years."

"And that's why you're having such a hard time accepting her suicide?"

"Partially," Tom said. "And partially because of my brief experience with her in the class."

"Yes. Walter tells me you've begun a little investigation of sorts at the school."

"I wouldn't call it that."

"Probing into her academic history with the teachers who have worked with her?"

"Well, yes..."

"Walter is somewhat concerned that the teachers might feel, well...more disturbed than they should, if there's a suggestion that somehow the program contributed to her state of mind."

"I know he feels that way, but I don't believe—"

Dr. McCray raised his hand from the table in a silencing gesture. "My initial reaction was the same as yours. I didn't believe that anything you said could possibly make them question the value of what they're doing. In fact, I told him you should be commended for your actions. This was a terrible event, after all, and it's important that we discover all we can about this girl."

"I'm not looking to be commended, Dr. McCray," Tom said. "I just want to find out what happened."

"Of course. And I'm sure the other teachers do also. And that's a small enough group. What are there? About six of them I believe."

"Yes."

"A small enough group of teachers that any concerns can be worked out among the members." Dr. McCray placed his hand on the table again and brushed his palm to the side. "But yesterday I received a call from Calvin Weiser, the principal at Eastside Middle School. It seems you paid the counselor there a visit and asked some of the same questions."

"Yes."

"Well, Mr. Kerzig, I'm afraid I share Walter's concern when it comes to action beyond your own academic group."

"Why is that?"

"Your coming down from the high school and conducting an investigation there places a kind of unnatural urgency on the matter, don't you think?

"No, I don't," Tom said. "But I do admit to a feeling of personal urgency to find out what happened."

"Of course."

"And maybe..." Tom sighed and sat forward in his chair. "Maybe I do have some concerns about activities in the program that might have affected Joni's frame of mind."

"Ah, yes, you see. That's what I meant. And my fear is that you're reacting from a somewhat skewed frame of reference." Dr. McCray glanced from side to side. Then he leaned forward and folded his hands on his lap. "Let me be very candid with you, Mr. Kerzig. I'm risking violating my professionalism when I tell you this, but I think it's important for you to know. And I'm sure you will keep our conversation in total confidence."

"Yes."

"The person whose class you took... Walter tells me she went beyond the goals of the program in many instances. If she returns, it will be with a different understanding, you can be sure." He leaned closer and spoke intensely. "I assure you, Mr. Kerzig, the activities in the LENA program had nothing to do with Joni Irving's suicide."

"But it's not just Bonnie's class," Tom said. "I have questions about things in the other classes, too. And at the middle school."

Dr. McCray sat back, folded his arms in front of him, and sighed deeply. "Just a moment." He stood, walked to his desk, picked up the telephone receiver, and pressed the intercom button. A faint buzz sounded outside the office. "Louise, have Dr. Hernandez come in, please. Yes, right away." He replaced the receiver and walked back toward Tom. "You know Victor Hernandez, don't you?"

"Yes. The assistant superintendent for curriculum."

"I'd like you to talk to Victor. He knows a great deal more about the particulars of the program than I do. I'm sure he'll be able to answer any questions you might have. But, come to think of it, you're going to the convention next week, aren't you?"

"Yes."

"Splendid!" McCray clapped his hands together. "That'll be the perfect opportunity. Victor will be there all three days as well. I understand the presentations are outstanding. You'll come back with a much different view, I assure you."

The door opened and Victor Hernandez stepped quickly into the room. He was a short, heavy-set man, with black hair and a thin mustache.

"You wanted to see me?"

"Yes. Come in, Victor." Dr. McCray took him by the arm and presented him to Tom. "This is Tom Kerzig, Victor. He teaches English at the high school, and he's taking Bonnie Teague's senior class."

Tom rose and extended his hand. "Hello, Dr. Hernandez."

"Mr. Kerzig," he said, shaking Tom's hand. "Yeah, I think we've met a couple of times."

"I want you to talk to Mr. Kerzig about the goals of the program, Victor," McCray said. "But you'll both be at the convention, and I think that would be a splendid opportunity for you to answer his questions."

"Self-esteem is the big concept," Victor said. "When the state specs on this program came out six years ago, I jumped at it. It had everything our kids needed, especially the minorities."

"Of course, I keep reminding Victor this is not an equal opportunity program." Dr. McCray laughed.

"And it really hasn't been so far," Victor said. "But it will be, once we get the expansion beyond the pilot approved."

"Yes, there's that, too," Dr. McCray said. "You are aware, aren't you, Mr. Kerzig, of the board meeting two weeks from now?"

"Yes."

"Naturally, we don't want the board members to be unnecessarily diverted from their decision by...well, uninformed criticism."

Victor looked at Tom and frowned. "You aren't here to criticize the program, are you?"

"He has questions, Victor," Dr. McCray said. "Mr. Kerzig has questions, that's all. Now I want you to be sure to give him special attention next week. You know the presenters. Be sure he gets into sessions that will help him understand the positive aspects of the program."

"That'll be easy." Victor laughed and patted Tom's arm. "You should attend them all!"

Dr. McCray held out his hand toward Tom. "Thank you so much for coming this afternoon, Mr. Kerzig." He took Tom's hand and held it firmly but motionlessly. "Have a wonderful time at the convention. And in the meantime, just put this Joni Irving matter out of your mind. I assure you, the program had nothing to do with her death."

Tom started to pull his hand back, but Dr. McCray held it tightly. The tall man's head was tilted back slightly, and he looked at Tom through the bottom of his rimless glasses. His teeth gleamed through a wide smile. Tom recalled what Nita had told him the other day: *"Put it away, Tom...worrying about things like this can get you down...without accomplishing anything. Put it away..."* Victor's stout body jerked with erratic laughter behind Dr. McCray as the superintendent's words floated through his recollection. *"Nothing to do with her death...nothing...nothing..."*

19

The doors to the church auditorium were closed, but a large sign hung there, stating: *MEETING IN FELLOWSHIP HALL*, with an arrow pointing to the right. Pastor Bentley apparently thought an informal setting would work better for this gathering. The hall was in the adjacent building; lights shone brightly from the windows and open doors. Tom walked slowly toward the hall. He had waited at the church entryway for fifteen minutes, but Clair had not yet arrived. He had offered to bring her with him, but she'd insisted that she drive herself and meet him there. Maybe she had decided not to come after all.

A few people stood outside the building, but most gathered in small groups inside the hall, talking and drinking coffee. There appeared to be about a hundred people, and many of them Tom had never seen before. He saw Pastor Bentley and the Irvings at the front, and he was glad to see Barbara Shannon with them. He quickened his pace and joined them.

Pastor Bentley waved and took Tom's hand warmly. "Hi, Tommy. Thanks for coming. You know Lloyd and Sally..."

Tom greeted them. They still looked somber, but much less haggard than the last time he saw them.

"And you should know Barbara Shannon," Pastor Bentley continued.

Barbara Shannon was a tall, impeccably dressed woman, with a few light streaks of gray crossing through her neatly set hair. Tom had always thought she would make a perfect ambassador. "Of course." Tom reached out and shook her hand.

"Yes, Tom was..." Barbara stopped and looked at Pastor Bentley. "Is it *Tommy?*"

"Only from Pastor Bentley," Tom interrupted quickly, and they all laughed.

"Well, anyway, I've known Tom for some time," Barbara said. "I don't know if you remember, but my daughter was in your English class seven years ago."

"Of course. Her name is Irene." He recalled that particular class especially well. Irene was in the same class with Marla Vedder. He believed that Irene had also gone into Bonnie's twelfth-grade LENA class the next year.

"She really enjoyed having you as a teacher," Barbara went on. "And I've heard many other good comments about you since I became a board member."

"Tommy's the reason you're here tonight," Pastor Bentley said. "He said you were the best listener on the board."

"Oh? Well, perhaps I won't argue with that." She laughed.

"I don't recognize a lot of the people here," Tom said to Pastor Bentley.

"Well, over half are members of the church. But many of them asked other friends to attend, also." Pastor Bentley turned to Barbara. "There are more than I expected. I hope they don't generate too much hostility."

She smiled. "I'm used to that."

"I've talked to some of the people during the week and tonight, and I think you'll find that most of their concerns center around the special program in the schools."

"I expected that, of course," Barbara said. "That will be fine."

"Well..." Pastor Bentley glanced at his watch. "I think we'd best get started."

Lloyd Irving directed Sally toward a chair in the front row, and then he and Barbara walked toward a single table, which rested on a raised platform at the front of the hall.

"Didn't Clair come with you, Tommy?" Pastor Bentley asked.

"No, not with me. She may be here, though. I expect her."

"I hope so." Pastor Bentley smiled and pointed toward the front of the room. "You want to come up with us?"

"No," Tom said quickly.

"I may ask you to say something, though."

"Sure. That's all right." But he didn't have the slightest idea what he would say if Pastor Bentley called on him.

Pastor Bentley stepped to the center of the room and spoke loudly. "Will you please take your seats? We're about to begin." He stepped up on the platform and sat behind the table between Lloyd and Shannon.

The clusters of people quickly separated and headed toward the neatly placed folding chairs. Tom walked back to the entrance and looked outside in hopes of seeing Clair, but the sidewalk leading to the parking lot was empty. He turned back to the hall and spotted two chairs about halfway up on the outside. He sat in the second one and saved the one on the aisle for Clair.

Pastor Bentley tapped a microphone on the table, and a dull thump resounded from the speakers which hung from the ceiling in the front corners of the hall. "Thank you all for coming," he began. "For those of you who are joining us for the first time tonight, I'm William Bentley, the pastor here. I think most of you know Lloyd Irving." He nodded to his left, then pointed to Barbara. "And this is Barbara Shannon, the president of the school board. She has graciously consented to sit with us and respond to any questions you might have about the schools." Pastor Bentley lowered his head momentarily and then raised it. "Now, you all know what happened to Lloyd and Sally's daughter, Joni. That's why they suggested we have this meeting, to try to get some concerns out in the open." He turned toward Lloyd. "Why don't you start things off, Lloyd?"

"Thank you, Pastor," Lloyd said. "At first, after we suggested this meeting, we began to think maybe we were trying to make too general a problem out of our very specific case. But Sally and I have spoken with a lot of you over the last week or so, and we've learned that most of you feel the way we do. Joni...Joni was a warm and loving child, and..." Lloyd sat back momentarily and closed his eyes. Then he sighed and continued. "And she always shared with us her hopes, her fears... But even so, we felt over the last few years a kind of drifting away. Many of you have expressed the same feeling with your children. We know society in general is working against the traditional family, but we also have concerns that our public agencies—especially the schools—are contributing to this. We parents want to get back in the picture. We want to have more control over the events that influence our children. And I guess that's why we're here tonight."

"Thank you, Lloyd," Pastor Bentley said. "I'm glad you reminded us that we have concerns about the ways things are going in society in general. But tonight we will be focusing on the schools, because...well, we hope that there we can accomplish something." He turned toward Barbara. "Mrs. Shannon, you and the other members of the board literally hold the lives of our children in your hands. We're asking for your help."

"We're very much aware of that, Pastor Bentley." Barbara's voice, when addressing the people, seemed to be turned up a notch in delivery, and the dulcet tones filled the hall. "And it's an awesome responsibility. We very definitely solicit, and cherish, your input. Tell me..." She gestured toward the crowd. "How many of you have children attending our school system?"

Almost all of those in attendance raised their hands.

"Oh, my!" She turned toward Pastor Bentley. "This really is a constituency, then, isn't it?"

Pastor Bentley nodded.

"All right, then, the other question I have is, how many of you have children in the LENA program?"

About a third of the people raised their hands. Tom at first did not respond, but then remembered that Jennifer had just been placed in the program, and raised his hand also.

"Thank you," Barbara said. "I'd like to begin by saying that our schools are always open to any of you who have questions or suggestions. And the child privacy regulations guarantee that you have the right to review any of our materials that you might have a concern about."

"Mrs. Shannon." A large man in the center of the hall stood and raised his hand.

Barbara sat back, somewhat surprised, then smiled and recognized him. "Yes, sir?"

"I know that's what the law says," he began, "but it doesn't always work that way. I have a daughter in the seventh grade, and she came home one day and told me she was learning some things in her science class that...well, seemed rather mystical. So I went to the school to look at the materials the teacher was using."

"You had that right," Barbara told him.

"Yes, but you see, the principal just took me to a big room with thousands of books in it. He said, *Everything the teachers use is in here. Find the material you object to, and then we'll talk about it.*"

A number of people in the room mumbled in acknowledgment that they had had similar experiences.

"Well, that practice does fulfill the *letter* of the law, but certainly not its *intent*, does it?" Barbara responded. "Why don't you see me after the meeting, give me the particulars, and I'll look into it."

Pastor Bentley looked over the heads of the people toward the back of the hall and motioned with his arm. "Please come right in. We've just started."

Tom turned toward the back and saw a small, haggard-looking woman pushing a man in a wheelchair. And walking beside them was Clair! He stood impulsively, waved, and motioned for her to join him. She found a place for the man and woman and sat beside Tom.

"I was afraid you wouldn't make it," Tom said.

"It took a little longer because I picked up the Graingers."

The Graingers. Of course. They were Clair's case. Misty Grainger was the fifteen-year-old who'd had the abortion. "I didn't know you were bringing them," he said.

"Neither did I. During my weekly visit yesterday I told them I might be coming to this meeting tonight. They begged me to bring them. I thought..." She shrugged and sighed. "I don't know."

Tom sat back, and as their shoulders touched, he felt a rare wholeness that had been missing for so long. But he knew it was only temporary. He looked toward the front of the hall again and attended to Barbara's voice. She was addressing another man in the audience.

"...and since you mentioned having the same experience as the first gentleman who spoke, we may indeed have a problem," she said. "Why don't you both see me afterward?"

"Let me suggest something," Pastor Bentley said. "Our main purpose here tonight is to get as many concerns aired as possible. Mrs. Shannon can't possibly respond to all of them, but I'm sure she wants to hear them."

"Absolutely," Barbara said.

"Why don't you just stand as you feel led," Pastor Bentley suggested, "express your concern, and then let another follow? I think that will be much more productive."

And so it began. One by one, people stood, most individually, but some in pairs, and spoke of things happening in the schools that gave them cause to worry. The parent of a second grader complained about a values clarification exercise called the secret circle, in which students sat on the floor, holding hands, and divulged personal information about their thoughts, feelings, and beliefs. They were forced into moral dilemmas involving the rightness or wrongness of stealing. Tom recalled Jennifer's similar experience with the issue of lying.

A parent of an eleventh grader protested the use of what she considered an inappropriate exercise in a science class. Tom wondered if she was referring to Chris Donnelly's class, and realized she must have been, since she described the exploration into psychic experiences such as extrasensory perception, psychokinesis, and astro-projection.

The parent of a sixth-grade girl complained about her daughter being asked to participate in role-playing situations in which she took the part of a warlock, an exorcist, and a haunting spirit. And a widow wept as she told of her fifth-grade son being required to stand in front of the class and tell how he "dealt with" his feelings after the death of his father.

The parent of a sixth grader referred to an objectionable guidance practice in which her son was asked to describe his feelings about personal family matters. Another who had a first-grade child asked why the children were involved in an exercise in which dreams were discussed as a means to explore experiences outside their bodies. One child described to the class how she dreamed while floating on the ceiling and watching her body on the bed, and the teacher encouraged the others to try to achieve the same experience. Tom had a fleeting recollection of Jennifer, sitting cross-legged in the library, and her rainbow...and the cakras...

A reference to an eleventh-grade English class assignment recaptured his attention. The teacher had given a writing assignment using the following model paragraph: "The typical teenager has three main characteristics: he is affluent, he is educated, and he is casual about sex." The parent was concerned about the possible influence of the matter-of-fact reference. That must have been from Bonnie's class. And for Bonnie, that one was mild.

A low laughter arose from the crowd as a parent described the experience of her Kindergarten child in an activity called *Transactional Analysis for Tots*. But the laughter ceased as she told how the children were taught that parents are responsible for bad feelings that they have about themselves, and that they should go to the school psychologist if they are afraid to talk to their parents. And the parent of a tenth-grader bemoaned the fact that his daughter's modern dance teacher was using an obscene rap selection as the background for a dance routine.

No other persons were standing to be recognized, so Pastor Bentley turned toward Barbara and raised his hands in a questioning gesture.

"You have raised many valid questions," Barbara said. "I'm tempted to respond to some of them specifically, but I keep reminding myself that these are, of course, isolated instances. And I don't know how indicative they might be of a general problem."

"Excuse me." Pastor Bentley leaned forward. "I think this might be a good time for..." He searched the audience and his eyes fell on Tom. "We have one of the district's teachers with us tonight, and he said he wouldn't mind... Mr. Kerzig, would you give us your thoughts on this?"

Tom's stomach churned. He hoped Pastor Bentley would forget, but, of course, he didn't. He stood and quietly acknowledged the persons seated around him. "I'm an English teacher, as many of you know. I've taught many of your children over the last eight years. The things you've said tonight are disturbing, I agree. I...ah," he glanced at Clair, "have a child, too. A third grader. And she has told me about some activities that I question, too. But I have to remind myself that I often say things in class that might be misinterpreted or blown out of proportion. And yet..." He recalled the many disturbing incidents he'd uncovered in just the short time he had begun looking into Joni's history. "And yet there are so many things that *can* happen. A teacher is, in many ways, an isolated, self-governing agent. And it's almost impossible to know for sure all the things that go on behind the closed door of the classroom. As parents, we have to be alert to the things our children say. We need to become involved with our schools. Visit the teachers. Ask to see the materials they're using. I know I would welcome that kind of interest on the part of my parents. Most teachers would, I'm sure." Tom paused and looked at Bentley. "I guess that's all I'd have to say." He sat down.

Pastor Bentley smiled and nodded and then recognized someone over Tom's shoulder. Tom heard a slight creaking, and turned to see Mrs. Grainger wheeling her husband to the front of the hall. He felt the muscles in Clair's shoulder twitch as they passed by.

"Excuse me, ma'am," Mrs. Grainger said. "My husband would like to say something."

"Of course. Go right ahead, sir."

Grainger leaned forward in his wheelchair and his body bobbed slightly. He didn't have complete control of his arms and his speech was loud, but slurred. "It's not just the class-room and it's not just the schools. I'm a parent. I have four children. My wife has to work real hard to help keep us in clothes and food. We need more help from public agencies than most of you, prob'ly. But we're all parents and the school is a public agency, too. They just sometimes forget...parents are important. And, you know, parents are usually right about things."

Tom glanced at Clair. Her eyes were closed, her thumb and forefinger pressed against the bridge of her nose.

"One of my daughters," Grainger continued. "She's fif-teen. Just a little girl. And she got in trouble. You know—got pregnant. Now, I'm not blaming the school for that. It was her fault and prob'ly ours for... But, you see, we never knew about it." His body jerked momentarily and he pushed him-self up to a straighter sitting position. "The school knew. Our social worker knew. But we never knew! I don't know why our daughter didn't come to us for help, but she didn't. She went to the school and she got help. They showed her who to go to and they took her baby. And now she's sorry. And we never knew. We never knew! I know you have to do a lot of things in school to help the kids get by. And I know it's hard, because our kids aren't perfect...and we aren't perfect. But we're the parents, ma'am. We have to know. *We have to know.*" His body jerked again and he motioned clumsily. His wife rolled the wheelchair back to the side of the room and sat on a chair beside it.

Tom looked at Clair again. Her eyes were open now but red and glassy. "Are you all right?"

Clair nodded. "I thought they might say something. I'm...ah...actually, I'm glad."

Barbara was visibly moved by this last presentation. "Thank you. Thank you, sir." She seemed for the first time to be at a loss for words. "The...uh...situation you described is, of course, very rare. But in this state, the child has the right, under the law, to an abortion without parental consent or knowledge. There are times when this is probably a good law. There are others in which...well, it may not be. The school's role is in one way the *legal agent* of the child, and in another way the child's *guardian*. We stand in loco parentis—in the place of the parent. This is one of the awesome responsibilities that I mentioned. I wish I could say that the advisory action taken by the school in this instance was the right one. I simply do not know that. All I know is that it was legally permissible. And the laws were made for the greater good."

"The greater good," Clair mumbled.

"We must stand for the majority," Barbara continued. "And that relates also to many of the concerns expressed tonight about the academic program in the schools. There are currently about five hundred students in the district participating in the LENA program. Your students are, perhaps, twenty-five of them. I have to say that the comments I've received about the program before tonight have been overwhelmingly positive. So, you see, that places me in a dilemma, doesn't it? I will promise you, however, that I will investigate your claims and that I will be much more alert in the future to possible abuses."

"We appreciate that," Pastor Bentley said.

"As a church group, however," Barbara said, "you should be glad that your religious interests are being represented by a minister who is one of our board members."

A sudden round of laughter rose from the audience. Barbara sat back and stared at them with a perplexed look.

Pastor Bentley quieted the audience and placed his hand on Barbara's shoulder. "Please forgive the outburst. That was not polite."

"I don't understand," Barbara said. "What did I say?"

Bentley smiled, sighed, and spoke haltingly. "Daniel

Worley is not considered by most of these people to be...well...a strong spokesman for traditional values."

"Oh?"

"His Church of the Inner Spirit is more in tune with the New Age than the New Testament," Pastor Bentley continued.

"But don't you consider *any* religious representative better than none at all?"

He squeezed her arm and released it. "Another time, Mrs. Shannon. Another time." He turned to the audience. "And I have to be careful...we all have to be careful not to place too much condemnation on the churches on the fringes. There are so many other churches *within* the traditional framework, even ours at times, that have become lax and have fallen away from the insistence on adherence to biblical principles. If this meeting accomplishes nothing else, I pray that it will convince us to renew our commitment to bring traditional values back into all phases of society. Let's leave tonight with that promise on our hearts."

The people took this as a signal for dismissal. They stood quietly and began to leave the hall. A few headed toward the platform. Clair and Tom stood, and he followed her to the side of the aisle, away from those leaving. Pastor Bentley stepped through the line of people in the aisle and joined them.

"Clair, I'm so glad you came tonight," Pastor Bentley said. "How is your job going?"

"Oh..." She held her hand out flat and rocked it back and forth.

"Since you came in with the Graingers, I assume you were the case worker he referred to," Pastor Bentley said.

"Yes."

Pastor Bentley held his lips tight and nodded slowly. "It's

a tough world, Clair. We need all the help we can get. And sometimes the laws just don't provide it."

"I'll do all right," Clair mumbled.

"Of course, but..." He pointed quickly to her and then to Tom several times. "And this is another example of needing more than the law can provide."

Tom raised his hand. "Pastor..."

"No, you aren't going to stop me," Pastor Bentley said. "You and Tommy ought to be back together again, Clair. There's no sense to it. God blessed your marriage and He can bless it again."

"It's all right," Tom muttered.

"Excuse me." Clair smiled faintly, turned away, and walked toward the Graingers.

"I'm sorry, Tommy," Pastor Bentley said. "I guess I shouldn't have shot my mouth off like that."

"That's all right." Tom placed his hand on his chest and felt something in his inside coat pocket. "Oh, I almost forgot..." He reached in and pulled out a folded set of papers. "Here's the copy of Joni's composition I said I'd bring you."

"Oh, good. I'm anxious to read it." Pastor Bentley took the composition and placed it in his pocket.

Barbara Shannon walked up to them with a questioning look on her face. "Well, gentlemen, what do you think?"

"Mrs. Shannon, I really appreciate your coming tonight," Pastor Bentley said.

"It was my pleasure. These people are very sincere. Tom..." Barbara turned to him and squinted. "Don't you teach in the LENA program?"

"I'm just filling in with one class for a couple of weeks," Tom said. "I'm taking Bonnie Teague's seniors."

"Ohh... For some reason I thought... You said you had some concerns, too. What do you think?"

Tom shrugged. "The jury's still out."

Pastor Bentley laughed and looked at Barbara. "Now, you had that one coming."

"Agreed!" Barbara laughed. "Are you going to the convention tomorrow, Tom?"

"Yes."

"Good. Oh, Pastor Bentley, I should have told you...but your people probably already know."

"What?"

"The board meets in two weeks to consider expanding the program to all students."

"Yes, we know. And, of course, we're worried."

"You're welcome to come to the meeting."

"We'll be there," Pastor Bentley said.

"You also, Tom," Barbara said. "I liked what you said tonight. We really don't know what goes on behind closed doors, do we?"

"No, we don't."

She rubbed her fingers lightly across her chin. Then she pointed at Tom. "But you keep peeking, Tom." She smiled. "And let me know what you find." She waved and joined the remnant of the crowd making its way slowly out of the hall.

Tom looked back and saw Mrs. Grainger wheeling her husband toward the exit. Clair was walking beside them. His emotions welled up suddenly, and he stepped forward impulsively and touched her arm.

"Look, I'd really like to talk to you about all this, Clair," he said. "Can we go out for a cup of coffee or something?"

"I can't," Clair replied. "I have to take the Graingers home."

"No need for that," Tom heard Pastor Bentley say from behind him. The pastor had a broad smile on his face. "The

Graingers live near me. I'd be happy to take them home."

"That won't be nec—" Clair began.

Mrs. Grainger looked up at Pastor Bentley and said, "Oh, we'd like that, Pastor!"

Pastor Bentley nudged Mrs. Grainger aside gently and took the handles of the wheelchair. "My van's right outside the door."

"Thank you for bringing us, Mrs. Kerzig," Mrs. Grainger said and stepped up beside her husband.

"Well, of course," Clair muttered.

Pastor Bentley winked at them and pushed the chair toward the back of the hall.

"So..." Tom smiled at Clair. "How about that cup of coffee?"

Clair frowned. "Did you two have this set up?"

Tom raised both hands. "I swear!"

Clair sighed and shook her head. "All right. Just for a few minutes."

"Thanks!" Tom stepped up beside her and they walked toward the exit. It had been so long. He wasn't sure he'd even know how to treat her. But he felt...complete.

20

Tom leaned forward from the cool leather seat and placed his hands around the cup of coffee before him. Clair sat across from him, sipping slowly from her cup. They had taken separate cars to this quaint restaurant which had been a favorite spot before their separation. Of course, in those days Clair had always scooted around to the center of the booth and sat next to him. Tonight she remained at the edge. It was clear she intended to make this a brief meeting. She had declined his offer for dessert, so the table between them was starkly set with just their two cups of coffee.

"I appreciate your coming tonight," Tom began self-consciously.

Clair shrugged.

"I mean, to the meeting," he clarified.

"Oh."

Tom hated this—the struggle to make conversation with his own wife, to have to choose his words so carefully. "You hadn't arrived yet when Lloyd Irving spoke, had you?" he asked.

She shook her head.

"He thinks the direction society is going is the problem, you know, that it's working against the traditional family."

Clair raised an eyebrow. "You wouldn't be over-generalizing because of our situation, would you?"

"No, it's not that," he replied. "It's not just what Lloyd

said. The other parents, Clair...the things that are happening to their kids. You know what we talked about with Jennifer. I have some concerns, too."

"'Jennifer knows what's right. And she can adapt to her experiences.'"

"But since I've taken over Bonnie's class, I've realized how badly some kids have adapted."

"It doesn't have to be that way," Clair replied. "I'll watch out for her."

"You can't do it alone. It takes two parents!"

"Don't try to use Jennifer to get to me, Tom."

"I'm not. I wouldn't, if only..." Tom suddenly found himself grasping for words. He thought for a moment it was because of the artificially strained situation between them. But he quickly realized that Clair was right. He *had* used his concern about Jennifer as a tool to break through her resistance. But was that so wrong? He sat back and brushed his hand aimlessly across the table. "I just need to understand, Clair. What happened between us that was so terrible?"

"I never said it was *terrible*, Tom," Clair said irritably.

"Then what?"

"We were married too young," she continued mechanically. Then she nodded purposefully. "I really want to prevent Jennifer from doing that if possible."

"Now who's over-generalizing?"

"At least Jennifer seems to be establishing her own identity. That's one thing I never had accomplished."

"How can you say that? You never seemed to be having an identity crisis of any kind."

"That was because I just...accepted things," she responded. "My identity was all tied up in you and Jennifer."

"What's wrong with that?"

"That would be enough for some people, I suppose. But I began to realize there was more to me than just...just that."

Tom nodded. "And you realized that when you started your graduate work at the university."

She shrugged. "I suppose you're right. So are you suggesting that I shouldn't have pursued my education?"

"No! I just don't understand why that should have made any difference between us!"

Clair began to respond, but then turned her head away and sat back against the booth.

"Clair..." Tom slid his coffee cup to the side and leaned across the table. "We had so many good experiences...*wonderful* experiences together."

"I've never denied that," she said without turning back.

"Even tonight was..." Tom glanced up briefly and recalled the setting—sitting together, if for no other reason. "I don't know... Maybe we should have kept going to Pastor Bentley's church."

Clair sighed, raised and lowered her eyebrows, and crossed her arms before her.

"It just seems we were happier then," he added quickly.

"As long as it was just a social thing."

"Well, yes. A chance to be with people, raise Jennifer in a healthy environment."

"But I needed more than that, Tom." She relaxed her arms slightly. "And the church had more to offer than that. I wanted to *study*, learn what our lives were all about."

"It was a *church*, Clair, not a philosophy course!" he replied somewhat sarcastically.

She smiled and shook her head. "Well, that was because you didn't need the same things I did, I guess. That was the problem, Tom. You didn't need *anything*. You had your life all figured out."

"No, not *all* figured out. But I've tried to focus on goals...and relationships. Your identity question, Clair...I understand. I'd like to help."

Clair sat forward and tossed her hands in the air. "You can be so self-righteous!"

"What?" Tom sat back suddenly at the intensity of her response. Then he laughed self-consciously. "Well, that's one you've never used!"

"Because I never realized it before. But it's true!"

"Clair, why—"

"Life is bigger than that, Tom," she continued intently. "It's bigger than your own personal ideas about what's right and wrong."

"I...I never said it wasn't, Clair," he stammered. "I just..." He was grasping again. He sat forward and continued softly, "Look, whatever it takes. If you want to study, we could do that..."

"Clair!"

Tom turned suddenly at the sound of the strange voice. He looked up to see a man with thick wavy hair and a neatly trimmed beard. It was Roland Lessa—one of the board members and Clair's university professor.

Clair smiled. "Roland! What a surprise!"

"I was just stopping in to have a cocktail with some friends, and I saw you sitting here," Lessa said brightly. "So I thought I'd come over and say hello."

"I'm glad you did." Clair was clearly relieved that their intense discussion had been interrupted. "You know Tom, of course."

Lessa cocked his head and slowly extended his hand. "I'm not sure..."

"My...my husband. He teaches at the high school."

"Oh!" Lessa laughed and grasped Tom's hand. "Of

course!" He shook his hand vigorously. "There are so many teachers in the district, I sometimes have trouble remembering."

"That's understandable," Tom acknowledged.

"Listen, it's really providential that I saw you tonight, Clair, because..." Lessa motioned toward the booth. "Do you mind?"

"No. No, of course not." Clair scooted over next to Tom, and Lessa sat down beside her.

"I read your paper on that divorced mother of five," Lessa continued. "You made some extremely important points."

"Really?" Clair beamed.

Tom leaned forward. "Paper?"

"A class assignment," Lessa said.

"I thought that course ended last spring," he said.

"Oh, that was the one on *Public Welfare and Public Policy*," Clair said. "This semester I'm taking another one."

"Oh..."

"*Reshaping the Dysfunctional Personality*," Lessa added in an aside to Tom. Then he turned back excitedly to Clair. "Anyway, my lecture tomorrow is closely related to the topic you developed, and I wondered if you'd mind reading a portion of your paper to the class."

"I'd..." Clair appeared flustered. "I'd be glad to!"

"Good! Some of the members of the class are overly pessimistic about the prospects for children who are raised by single mothers," Lessa said. "I think a success story might help remedy that."

"Well..." Clair looked nervously toward Tom.

"You know," Lessa gestured vaguely toward both of them, "I thought you two were..."

"Separated. We are." Clair shifted in the booth. "We just went to a meeting tonight. And I took one of my clients."

"Meeting?"

"At Pastor Bentley's church," Tom replied. "Some parents wanted to get together to express some concerns about the LENA program."

"Oh." Lessa frowned. "The Christian Crazies at it again?" He shook his head. "They really have a skewed perspective. And I'm sure Bentley didn't have anybody there to present the rational side of things."

"Barbara Shannon was there," Tom said.

Lessa looked shocked. "Really?" He shrugged. "Well, maybe our position was well represented, then."

"We have..." Clair glanced at Tom and then back at Lessa. "Tom has some concerns about the program, too, Roland. You know that our daughter Jennifer was placed in it recently."

"Yes. That's marvelous!"

"Tom's a little skeptical about some of the things that are going on," she continued.

Lessa leaned toward Tom. "It's hard for a person outside the flow to get a full understanding of..."

"I'm not outside the flow," Tom interrupted. "I took over Bonnie Teague's LENA class after her accident."

"Oh!" Lessa snapped his fingers. "That's right! Walt did mention that."

"And I've seen some things I'm having a hard time accepting."

"For instance?"

"Well...values clarification...psychic discussions...out-of-body experiences..."

Lessa chuckled. "Yes. I heard about that out-of-body thing. That's the exception. But values clarification is an extremely significant part of the program, as it should be. That's what we're discovering even in the university courses. Isn't that right, Clair?" He turned toward her and smiled.

"Yes. Extremely."

He looked at Tom. "Why, it's only in the last few weeks that Clair and the other students have begun to realize how poorly trained *they* are in this skill."

"The exercises just don't seem to be based on any kind of standards," Tom said. "At least, that's the impression I received from our daughter's description."

"Standards are fluid in a fluid society," Lessa replied. "We have to learn how to mold our own inner values to the multifaceted challenges before us. And that takes training and time to be alone in the silence of our own psyches." He looked at Clair and smiled. "Clair is a prime example. Haven't you become stronger and more aware of your potential since you began applying what you've learned?"

"Oh, yes. Yes."

"Well..." Lessa stood up. "My party's waiting."

"Thank you for stopping by," Clair said.

Lessa smiled and nodded. Then he struck a pensive look and pointed toward Tom. "Oh, Tom...tomorrow..."

"What?"

"The LENA convention in Vegas starts tomorrow, doesn't it? You're going, aren't you?"

"Yes. I'll be there."

Lessa nodded. "Good. That will assuage most of your concerns, I'm certain." He bent over and patted Clair on the hand. "I'll see *you* in class!" He waved broadly and walked away.

Tom looked at Clair, who was still sitting beside him. "You didn't tell me you were taking another course with Lessa."

"I guess I haven't mentioned it."

Tom tried to get Clair to look at him. "He seems to be...very personal with you."

"Personal?"

"More so than a standard professor-student relationship," Tom ventured slowly.

"Oh." Clair shook her head. "I've had a few individual counseling sessions with him."

"Counseling?"

"To help me get a handle on my identity formulation," Clair replied defensively.

Anger suddenly flared up from the pit of Tom's stomach. "You never asked to be counseled by *me!*" Clair raised her hand quickly between them.

"Don't start that, Tom, please!" She took a quick sip of coffee and stood up. "Thanks for the coffee." She turned to leave.

"Wait a minute!" Tom reached out and grasped her hand. His anger was still seething, but he swallowed hard, and spoke slowly. "Look, I'm sorry..."

She tried to pull away.

He held her hand firmly. "There are still a lot of questions I have about Jennifer's class work."

Clair shrugged. "I'll try to get some information on..."

"No, I want us to speak with her teacher...*together*," Tom insisted.

Clair sighed. "Whatever."

"Soon," Tom added.

"You'll be gone this week won't you?"

"Three days," he replied. "Suppose I set up an appointment for Friday? Will you meet me there?"

"Sure," she responded nonchalantly. "Just leave the time on my voice mail."

"All right." He squeezed her hand and then released it.

"Anything else?"

He shook his head. "No, that's all."

Clair looked at him for a moment and walked away.

Tom watched Clair's retreating figure and resisted the urge to run after her and take her in his arms. He thought he was getting through to her. And then Lessa had arrived. He clenched his fist and pounded it on the table. If only she hadn't enrolled in that other course of his. A wave of frustration swept across his body. He wanted to go to war...win Clair back. But he didn't know who, or what, was his enemy. He had tried so hard, even capitulated. And why? It wasn't *his* problem. It was *hers!*

Tom lifted his cup and took a large swallow of coffee. Then he grimaced and set the cup down firmly. It was cold.

"Perfect..." he mumbled.

He stood up, removed has wallet, and tossed a five-dollar bill on the table. Then he thrust his hands into his pockets and shuffled toward the door.

21

Tom had been to Las Vegas several times. He remembered it as unbelievably bright, luxurious, and flourishing with activity. But that must have been the nighttime image. As they entered the town in the airport van at mid-morning, the almost nondescript buildings rose starkly against a bleak sky. No trees or lush vegetation signaled the appearance of a welcome oasis; only the asphalt, square structures, and miles of now invisible neon tubing, waiting impatiently to exude its splendor in the darkness.

Victor Hernandez had gathered them together at the airport and arranged for the van to transport them to the hotel. Tom, Stu Welbourne, Ed Staley, and Chris Donnelly rode with him. Marilyn Peters and Susan Reed were already there.

The van pulled to a stop at the hotel entrance, and the five of them got out and retrieved their luggage. As the van pulled away, they were met by a group of Hare Krishna solicitors. The white-robed figures danced about them to the beat of tambourines, and their shaved heads bobbed weirdly from side to side as they reached out for donations. Victor pushed one of the dancers roughly aside, and the five of them headed toward the front door of the hotel.

Tom paused momentarily to look at a colorful sign propped on a three-legged stand. Bold letters proclaimed: *LAS VEGAS WELCOMES THE LENA CONVENTION.* But the design of the sign is what captured his attention. It contained gaudy representations of ancient Greek festivals.

Clusters of grapes, silver, tipping goblets, fat laughing men, and partially clad women against a backdrop of purple, black, and marble. He realized the correspondence for the first time. The Lenaea was one of the major Dionysian festivals in ancient Greece. That must have been why the framers of the special program settled on the non-definitive acronym. In the corner of the sign, above the figure of a rotund, inebriated Greek with a goblet lying loosely across his chest, was the explanatory phrase: *LEaders of the New Age.*

"C'mon, Kerzig. We gotta register."

Tom looked up to see Victor impatiently holding the door open for him. Tom followed him inside, and as the smoked glass of the door closed behind them, the dreary ambiance of the desert morning was immediately overridden by the opulence of the hotel's interior. Here, the external light had no dominion and the cool darkness of the lobby allowed a full view of the bright, colorful activity. People crowded about tables and machines—some intent on their gambling, some laughing giddily, and others standing idly about with drinks in their hands and glassy-eyed stares.

"You guys get registered," Victor said. "I'll try to find Marilyn and Susan. I've arranged for a table for all of us for lunch and the opening session. I'll meet you there at 12:45."

"Welcome to Las Vegas," Stu said.

"It's another world," Tom mumbled as they headed toward the registration desk. "Another world."

After Tom and Stu checked into their shared room, they signed in at the long table in the lobby and received all of their convention materials. The first session was planned during lunch as a motivation for attendance. The strategy worked, for the huge meeting hall was filled with round tables, all crowded with people. Victor had succeeded at finding Marilyn and Susan, and during lunch they gushed

ceaselessly about the gaming, shows, and acquaintances they
had enjoyed during the preceding two days.

Tom shoved his empty plate toward the center of the
table and set his convention materials out before him. He
skimmed through the list of presenters and found that the
two presentations Bonnie had asked him to see—by Kurt
Quinlan and Helene Farris—were not scheduled until tomorrow and Wednesday. Then a presentation this afternoon
caught his attention: *"Psychological Inroads to the Minds of
Tomorrow"—Frederick Banazech*. Tom nudged Stu and
pointed to the entry.

"Look at this."

Stu glanced at the entry and nodded.

"Is that—"

"Yeah, Mark's father. I thought you knew."

"Well, I knew he was a prominent psychiatrist," Tom
said. "But I didn't know he had any connection to the program."

"Well, there *isn't* really a connection. He's just done a lot
of research and writing on the psychological aspects of learning, and he was sought out as a presenter. He's been at the
last four conventions. He'll be presenting all three days this
year." Stu leaned over and whispered, "And that's why Mark
is in the program."

"What do you mean?"

"Well, his academic history wasn't all that outstanding,"
Stu explained. "And he wasn't recommended for participation
in the seventh and eighth grades. But when he got into high
school, Walt insisted we reevaluate his qualifications. There
wasn't much to reevaluate, of course. But when Walt reminded us that Frederick Banazech was his father...well, most
of the others agreed that Mark qualified for the high school
pilot, after all."

"That explains a lot. He's done only mediocre work in the class since I've taken it over for Bonnie. I thought I just wasn't tuning into his particular academic wave length."

"No, you've seen the real Mark," Stu said. "Oh, he'll do fine. He's popular, of course, and he has the ability to con his way into anything. I guess that's a good survival skill. It's worked so far. With the help of his father, he talked his way into a great scholarship."

Everyone in the room suddenly began to applaud. Tom looked up to see that someone at the long, raised head table had just made an introduction. He leaned over to Victor. "Who is she?"

"Katie Howard," Victor said. "She's the state LENA coordinator."

The tall, neatly dressed woman stood behind the small podium and nodded. The applause subsided.

"Thank you," Katie said. "I'm really excited to see all of you here this year. I don't want to take too much of your time, but I thought it would be helpful for you to know how we organized the presentations this year. There are three days available to us, and we thought that this number—three—was peculiarly representative of the wonderful developmental process in the LENA educational approach. There are really three phases to the program, and they apply to all of us working in the program as well as the students. The first phase, we have termed 'self-awareness.' As a child, of any age, emerges into the world, he searches, explores, probes into the mysteries that confront him. This is what we see as our first responsibility—to provide rich, varied experiences for our students—experiences that will lead them into realms of thought and feeling that they wouldn't gain from an unaided view." She paused for a moment and smiled. "Our term for the second phase may surprise you somewhat—'self-denial.' "

She was right about the surprise. Several people in the

room whispered to one another and Victor sat forward suddenly with a perplexed frown on his face.

Katie laughed lightly and continued, "I told you it would surprise you. Because we're committed to building up the self, aren't we, not tearing it down? But let me explain. As we travel through the awareness phase, we are constantly bombarded with restrictions—limitations placed on our consciousness by traditional views, by the mores of our families, and by the influence of those about us. I like to think of it as the three P's—past, parents, and peers."

The room resounded in approving laughter. Victor, obviously eased, smiled and sat back again.

"Past, parents, and peers," Katie repeated. "They are constantly flinging obstacles in our paths, obstacles which are so real to us that they become a part of us. That is why the concept of self-denial is so important. Through our self-awareness, we should be led to recognize those things which are detrimental to the development of our personal sense of being. And we should be encouraged to cast them aside—eliminate them, eradicate them from our personality and outlook. And that is what the second phase of our program is directed toward."

Katie raised a glass of water and sipped lightly from it. She leaned on the podium. "And then, of course, we may arrive, unencumbered, at the longed-for third phase, which we have termed 'self-renewal.' We are aware of all the wonders that await us, we have denied—cast aside—all the meaningless restraints, and now we may be reborn. Our spirits are reawakened, we may regenerate our internal flow of power, and rebuild our lives toward the promise of life before us in a world of our creation. This is the message we ask you to carry back with you as you leave in three days—we and our students alike must realize true self-fulfillment. And we *know* that we can accomplish this goal."

Victor sat forward again and began to applaud. Others in the room joined him.

Katie smiled and backed away from the podium slightly. "So, today is the beginning—the awareness phase. We have arranged many experiences for you. Please take advantage of them. Think of the afternoon as a magic journey. Explore and investigate. The wonders of the world await your search!"

Approximately twenty booths, set up in a large hall directly across from the dining area, were situated in a way that required people to pass by them on their way to the presentations. The hall was crowded with people and the scene reminded Tom of a carnival atmosphere. A huge milky-white shell stood before him. In its center was a purple-hued, three-dimensional pyramid, and above that hung a sign: MEDITATION CAPSULE. Over a stream of soft music blared dulcet female syllables: "You are the sea... Your essence becomes one with the forces of nature..."

Ahead of him, laser shafts, circling white spots, and prismatic projections converged on a suspended screen. Below that, a group of people were gathered around a small table and a woman dressed as a fortune teller helped them manipulate a Ouija board. Ed Staley stood in a tiny booth, listening intently, and Tom could hear the presenter call, as he passed: "You select the mood, the belief, the urge, and we'll find the sound to match it." All around were books and pamphlets with exotic covers: *ESP Games for the Elementary School; Yes! Your Child May Be Psychic; Retrocognition: Lead Your Kids Through the Past; Space Talk—Right around the Corner; The Outer Experience for the Inner Soul; They Will Tell Your Future.* Just as he was about to pass from the crowd, a kind-looking gray-haired woman handed him a sheet of paper with bold print: "Sexual Awareness Surveys: Are Your Students Ready for the Pitfalls of Modern Society?"

As he left the large display room, the noise level diminished considerably, and he sighed in relief. He walked slowly down the broad hall and stopped momentarily before a door labeled: *Poseidon Room.* This was where Dr. Banazech was speaking. He glanced at his watch. The presentation was more than half over by now. Still, he was curious. He opened the door and stepped quietly inside.

The room held perhaps a hundred people and was about two-thirds full. Dr. Banazech stood behind a brightly lit lectern. He was a slight man, with long gray hair, a mustache, and a short goatee. He spoke into a microphone, but his voice was low, so Tom walked forward and sat in an aisle chair near the front of the room. He studied Dr. Banazech's features and wondered how he could be the father of such a large and muscular boy as Mark. He imagined that Mark's mother must be a large woman.

Tom looked around to see if anyone was holding a handout of any kind. Since he saw none, he listened to Dr. Banazech and tried to piece together the part he had missed from his narrative.

"And that is, of course, the folly of legislation," Dr. Banazech was saying. "The year prior to its enactment, we were using hallucinogenic drugs as an adjunct to psychotherapy with remarkably positive results. Naturally, some of these drugs found their way into nontherapeutic markets, which was to be expected. And, of course, if we were talking about harmful drugs—barbiturates or amphetamines—naturally, there would be a reason. But these drugs—d-lysergic acid diethylamide-25, N-N-dimethyltryptamine, and their derivatives—resulted in absolutely no harmful reactions or side effects. So we had a legally-induced hysteria which placed the drugs beyond the reach of serious practitioners, like myself, who could use them to mold healthy minds.

"In parts of Europe, of course, it is quite a different story. My son has a successful practice in Switzerland, where there is considerably less fear about these somewhat non-traditional techniques. And, of course, the seminar I recently attended in Prague was a testimony to the advantages of a chemically enhanced therapeutic investigation. Now..." Dr. Banazech raised his finger for emphasis. "Why is all this important to you people? You are like me. You are molders of minds. Any tool which will help you mold these minds toward excellence should be made available to you. Naturally, something as technically demanding as chemical ingestion must not be provided haphazardly. But I envision the day when a psychiatric technician is available on every school campus to provide that tool, when called for, to open the doors of imagination and inspiration and heretofore unseen insight into the meaning of life. But unless we professionals can reinstate our work, which was nipped in the bud, and continue to perfect the methods we have developed thus far, this wonderfully promising advancement in the exploration of the mind will remain where it is now—in the crime-ridden gutters of our cities. You can help! You are educators. You have the power to influence the future voters of our country. Make the next generation the recipient of this gateway to their inner consciousness!"

Dr. Banazech stepped back, removed a handkerchief from his coat pocket, and wiped his forehead. A few in the audience applauded lightly, and soon, everyone gave him polite acknowledgment. It seemed that the onlookers were more bewildered than supportive. A few toward the back of the room rose quietly and left.

"There is time for a few questions, I believe," Dr. Banazech said.

A woman across from Tom raised her hand and was recognized. "Dr. Banazech, this is a very controversial topic."

"Of course," he agreed.

"Are you recommending that we raise a generation of addicts?"

"No!" he said emphatically. "That's more legal propaganda. No! In all the studies conducted, there is not a single case of physical addiction to LSD."

"But what about *psychological* addiction?"

Dr. Banazech smiled. "Do you exercise?"

"Yes."

"How?"

"I play tennis every week," she said.

"Would you say that practice has become...habitual?"

"Yes, I think so."

"Could we say you are psychologically addicted to playing tennis?" he asked.

"Well..."

A man in the front row raised his hand. "Dr. Banazech?"

"Yes?"

"Aren't there other dangers? I mean, what about flashbacks?"

"Ahh, the famous flashbacks!" Dr. Banazech said. "Do you know what the studies show these to be? Mild, pleasant recollections of experiences encountered during the inducement. Yes?" He cocked his head and motioned as if for assistance. "But, of course, you are teachers. Tell me, was it not Marcel Proust...*A la recherche du temps perdu,*" he uttered in perfect French. "*Remembrance of Things Past?* Yes, past experience can be recaptured. The moments are recoverable—transcendent."

Yes, Tom thought, *but for Proust they were also the result of forfeited innocence, vain endeavor, perverse experience, and a life of despair. Look beyond the moments to the meaning.*

"What about the studies relating LSD to chromosome damage?" asked a woman in the back.

"That's just what they are—studies," Dr. Banazech

answered. "Nothing definitive has been discovered from them and I doubt it ever will be."

"But surely people engage in some very unusual, perhaps dangerous behavior while under the influence?" asked a man behind Tom.

"Yes," Dr. Banazech agreed. "And that's precisely the reason the close supervision of a trained technician, or at least an experienced user, is essential. Shall we not take a lesson from the Indians in their Peyote rituals? The benefits are enhanced and the hazards diminished by the method. Everyone stays together and socializes until the effects of the drug have worn off. They assign what they call a "road man" to look after people who become too withdrawn. Sort of a *designated driver*, if you will."

Several in the audience laughed. But Tom allowed his mind to linger on the last illustration Dr. Banazech had used. He visualized the stooped bodies, sitting around the fire, allowing their emotions to be led...where? Beyond the fire? Into the darkness? Above the gnarled branches of the trees? He recalled Joni's composition and her picture of the dark master beckoning to the children...and her lifeless form lying beside a handful of capsules. He sat forward impulsively and raised his hand.

"Yes?" Dr. Banazech said.

"Dr. Banazech, has any link been suggested between LSD use and suicide?"

"No. Except in cases where the drug was used as an adjunct to psychotherapy. In these cases, the occasion of suicide was no greater than statistically anticipated without its use. So my answer is, no. If a suicide occurs, and the person has been using LSD, then we may say without equivocation that the suicide was the result of an external, or a previous disposition." He directed his attention to the audience in general. "We may say that in all cases, the effects of the drug are related to the *expectation* of the user. Therefore if the user expects something negative—or something self-destructive, as in the case of the suicide example—the drug will *enhance* the inner motivation. But—and this is the most exciting part—if the expectation is positive, then the enhancement will bring the user to a positive experience beyond description!" He lifted a watch from the lectern. "I'm afraid our time has come to an end. Thank you for your attention."

The audience applauded lightly, stood, and began to leave the room. Tom started to join them, but then decided to introduce himself to Dr. Banazech. He walked forward, waited for another person to ask a question, and then extended his hand. "Dr. Banazech, I'm Tom Kerzig," he said.

"Yes?"

"I'm Mark's English teacher," he said.

Dr. Banazech squinted. "But I thought... Oh, yes. Miss Teague was in that unfortunate accident."

"Yes."

"I'm afraid I don't get involved much with school business. My practice keeps me very busy and I spend as much time as I can with my son in Switzerland. I believe I mentioned him."

"Yes, you did," Tom said. "But I hope to see you some time to talk to you about Mark's work."

"Yes, of course. But soon he will graduate and leave for the university. And Miss Teague seemed to think he was doing fine."

"Well, I still like to have time to meet with all the parents."

"Of course." Dr. Banazech raised an eyebrow. "You're the one who asked the question about the suicide, aren't you?"

"That's right."

"And that would be in reference to one of Mark's class-mates, I believe."

"Yes."

"Preexistent psychosis," Dr. Banazech said. "You may be sure of that."

Tom wanted to pursue the matter, but Dr. Banazech abruptly turned, tossed some notes in his briefcase, and walked past Tom toward the door. Tom turned and watched the slight, gray-haired man walk briskly down the aisle. How could he be so sure? He should at least have seen Joni's paper—looked at her drawing. What was her preexistent psychosis? The dark master? Or a frustrated, chaotic existence at the penultimate cakra—just a step away from the realization of truth...and beauty...and life.

22

The next morning, Tom joined a small group of people waiting for the presentation by Kurt Quinlan to begin. People kept coming, and the crowd soon blocked the hallway. Tom felt a slight shoving, and smelled the odor of extinguished tobacco. He turned to see Stu standing beside him, his pipe sticking out of his top coat pocket.

"Did you make it to the breakfast session?" Stu asked.

"Yeah."

"I've seen Gar Moritz several times, so I skipped this one. What was his topic this year?"

Tom gestured dramatically. "*Humanism and the Search for Excellence!*"

Stu smiled and nodded. "His latest book.

"Which you can purchase at a special price for two days only!"

They laughed.

"How did you happen to choose this presentation?" Stu asked. "It's directed more toward social science teachers."

"Bonnie told me not to miss it."

"Oh." Stu laughed. "I always suspected Bonnie was more a social scientist than a grammarian at heart."

"That's for sure!"

The double doors leading to the conference room swung open, and the crowd began to push forward instinctively.

Tom and Stu were propelled slowly down the aisle.

"Do you want to go up front?" Tom asked.

Stu shook his head and pulled Tom with him into a row about two-thirds of the way back. "Not with Quinlan."

"Why?"

"You'll understand later."

The room quickly filled. Within a few minutes the viewers were seated and quietly awaiting the beginning of the session. At the front of the room was a raised platform. At one end of the platform ten chairs were set up facing the other end. A slim man rose from the front row, bent over, and whispered something to the person sitting beside him. Then he jumped energetically onto the platform. His face was pock-marked, and a large larynx protruded from his thin neck. He glanced jerkily at the crowd and thrust his hands into his pockets.

"Hi! I'm Kurt Quinlan. How many of you know me?"

Most of those in the room raised their hands.

"Good. Saves introductions. The title of this presentation is *Teaching Students to Deal with Dilemmas.* Everybody in the right place?" He paused for a moment. "Okay, let's get started. What is a dilemma, anyway? Webster says it's a situation requiring a choice between equally unfavorable or disagreeable alternatives. Now isn't that the story of our lives!"

Everyone laughed and Quinlan smiled for the first time. "So how do we deal with dilemmas? And how do we teach our students to deal with them? It comes down to a matter of values, doesn't it? And the theme of this convention—of the whole *LENA* program—is that a person should be led in his choice by his own values, and not by the values of others. Sound simple? Hmph! We know better, don't we? We know our kids. They've been led down the primrose path of life, willy-nilly, following the pack or parents or tradition, no matter what they really want, and have never allowed themselves to make those hard choices. I mean, a dilemma for too many of our kids is...*Shall I have strawberry or chocolate?* And when they get out in the real world, where their very purpose for existence depends on their ability to make deep, crucial choices, they fall back trembling. Well, we're here to change all that. That's what we're being paid for."

Quinlan suddenly jumped off the stage and stood in the aisle at the front row. "Most of you know me. So you know what to expect." He began pointing and tapping people on the shoulders, first on one side, and then the other. "You...you...you...you..." he chanted, as he identified them. He continued until he had selected ten people. "Come with me." He turned abruptly and jumped on the platform again.

The persons chosen laughed nervously and stood. Then they slowly walked up the aisle and climbed the two steps leading to the platform.

"I see what you mean," Tom said. "Thanks."

Stu nodded knowingly.

"Okay," said Quinlan to those on the platform. "Sit down."

The persons mumbled and sat in the ten chairs. Quinlan moved to the side of the platform opposite the chairs.

"A lot of what we're talking about has to do with a feeling of risk," Quinlan continued. "If our comfort level in stepping forward in our self-realization process is too low, we won't take the step. So one of the things we have to do with our students is to raise their comfort level—make them more willing to engage in risk-filled behavior, if that behavior is compatible with their values. But a lot of what people term as risky behavior is clouded by their perceptions. Again, tradition and the influence of parents. We have to strip that away and get them to view the action itself, in its raw form. And often they'll see that it's not as risky as they once thought."

Quinlan turned back to the group of ten and addressed

them. "You're high school students, all right? I'm going to give you some situations, and I want you to think about whether they pose a high risk or not. If you think they are high-risk situations, I want you to stand up. All right? Number one—jumping off the Empire State Building."

All ten people immediately stood, looked at one another, and laughed. Quinlan motioned to them and they sat again.

"Playing cards with your friends."

One man stood halfway. "I always lose," he mumbled and sat back down.

Quinlan waited for the laughter to diminish and then presented another situation. "Swimming nude at a private beach with friends of the same sex."

Three people stood, looked self-consciously at one another, and then sat at Quinlan's command.

"Swimming nude at a private beach with friends of both sexes."

Seven people stood. One of them glanced at the three sitting and slipped back into his seat.

Quinlan continued with the rapid presentation of situations. Each time that the number of people standing was only six or seven, one or two people inevitably changed their minds and sat again. The situations appeared at first to be selected randomly, because the high- and low-risk behaviors seemed mixed. But a pattern emerged—a spiraling of incidents from a generally low to a generally high state of risk. And the participants in the exercise seemed not to be aware of the shift.

Then Quinlan presented them with the same situation he had given them before. "Swimming nude at a private beach with friends of both sexes," he said pointedly.

Only two people stood this time. One of them, a man, looked around quickly, laughed, and sat back down. The other, a woman, hunched over and smiled self-consciously, but remained standing.

"What we've seen here is an example of clouded perceptions of risk being stripped away in the search for true judgment based on personal values," Quinlan said.

Tom leaned over to Stu and whispered, "What we've seen here is an illustration of peer pressure."

Stu nodded.

"The choices made by your students will determine the extent to which they realize their human potential," Quinlan went on. "You can help them with these choices."

The woman still stood, but now leaned with one hand on the back of her chair. Her smile had changed to a frown. She watched Quinlan for the direction to sit, but none was forthcoming. She slowly, without purpose, sank back into her chair, into the obscurity of the other sitting participants...and a faint smile reappeared on her face.

Tom and Stu both wanted some time to talk, away from the confusion of the crowd, so they walked to the other end of the massive convention center and had an early lunch in a small lounge. After they finished, Stu pushed his plate aside, sat back in the corner of the booth, and lit his pipe. A curl of white smoke rose from the bowl, while Stu shook the match and tossed it onto his plate.

"You should have insisted we sit in a non-smoking section," Stu said. "Now see what you're up against."

"I don't mind." And he didn't. As the rich smell of burning tobacco entered his nostrils, Tom recalled his boyhood...his father, sitting in the overstuffed rocker, reading the newspaper, puffing peacefully from his pipe...

"Well, what do you think of the convention so far?" Stu asked.

"I don't know. I think it's about what I expected. I can sure understand why Bonnie enjoys them!"

"Yes."

"But I've seen a lot of examples of things that concern me," Tom added.

"Like..."

"Well, like at the breakfast session. Instead of an educational presentation, it seemed more an attack on traditional religious values."

"Well, that's Gar," Stu said. "He's a Humanist to the core. Everyone knows it and everyone expects him to come across like that. We have to take a lot of what he says with a grain of salt. But you're right. He is abrasive."

"And Quinlan's exercise... It was pure psychological manipulation. I don't think we should be doing that in the classroom."

"Of course, we were looking at a drastically shortened illustration of a behavioral change which might take place over...say...an entire year."

"But it's still a behavioral change," Tom said.

"That's the business we're in, isn't it?"

"But changing toward..." Tom was suddenly unable to express the exact nature of his concern. "Quinlan's exercises...they were more an example of a forced value direction...using peer pressure for..."

"Desensitization," Stu prompted. "And I agree. That aspect of the program troubles me to a certain degree. In fact, the LENA conventions themselves are a good illustration. The first one, six years ago, was like playing cards with friends. But this year's is more like swimming nude at a private beach with friends of both sexes." He laughed lightly and clicked the stem of his pipe against his teeth. "But who's to decide, if not we? I mean we are in the business of allowing for the development of a high-potential human nature."

"Allowing for it or *creating* it?" Tom asked.

Stu puffed slowly on his pipe and exhaled, a cloud of smoke issuing from his mouth and gradually dissipating. "The program places heavy emphasis on the future. We're preparing for the emergence of the universal man for the New Age."

"Quinlan's presentations were directed more toward social science teachers, you said."

"Yes."

"Is he really in line with the direction your studies have taken?"

"Well, social science covers the gamut, you know," Stu said. "But a few names do stand out peculiarly."

"Who?"

"Well, John Stuart Mill, of course. He envisioned an emerging moral theory based on Utilitarianism. Gar's Humanism takes this concept a few notches further."

"Yes."

"My son is fully grown, now, so I haven't perhaps experienced it personally, but I have seen a movement away from family influence that brings to my mind the writings of Marx. He insisted that the bourgeois family would vanish as a matter of course."

"But the LENA program certainly can't be equated with the goals of communism, can it?"

"No. In many ways, it's the absolute antitheses," Stu said. "But it's the similarity of the *byproducts* that interests me. Marx reveled in the notion that his utopian society would prevent the exploitation of children by their parents by replacing the family structure with socially determined values."

"And what we're promoting is an internal self-described

force, instead of an external, social force," Tom suggested.

"I'd always viewed them as opposites, but then the haunting words of Tocqueville wander through my deliberations."

"The tyranny of the majority."

Stu removed the pipe from his mouth and shook his head slowly. "You have aspirations to be a social scientist, too?"

"Absolutely not. But Tocqueville's views of the American Republic provide an insightful backdrop for the study of American literature."

"You're right," Stu said. "And that's the precise term that enters my mind whenever I see Quinlan's exercise."

"Because of the use of peer pressure."

"Yes, but on a much larger scale. Tocqueville recognized it as a tyranny based on a general expectation of the rewards of individual freedom.'"

"Because as soon as people believe they can personally resolve all of the problems life puts before them..." Tom began.

"They fall to denying what they cannot comprehend," Stu interrupted, quoting from Tocqueville, "which leaves them but little faith for whatever is extraordinary, and an almost insurmountable distaste for whatever is supernatural."

Tom glanced at his watch.

"Yes, we should probably be heading back for the afternoon presentations," Stu said.

Tom and Stu stood and walked out of the small lounge. The scene before them was a blur of activity—people at gaming tables and slot machines; others waiting at the doors leading to the hotel's extravagant array of shows.

Tom stopped for a moment and pulled out the brochure which listed the day's presentations. "Let's see if we can find something a little more traditional for our enlightenment this afternoon."

"Good idea."

"Let's see..." Tom chuckled as he read the names of the available afternoon presentations: "Getting Around Parents," "Big Lie/Little Lie," "The Unproductive Morality," "Discover Your Worst Blocks to Sexual Freedom," "Making the Most Out of Bad Advice," and "Who Says You're Not Perfect?"

"Flip a coin?" Stu suggested. "Oh, look. There's Victor. Maybe we should talk to him for a minute—see if he doesn't think things are a little past the edge this year."

"Good idea." Tom folded the brochure and slipped it back into his packet of materials.

"Ah, never mind," Stu said.

"What?"

"I'm not sure the good Dr. Hernandez will be completely responsive to our concerns at this particular time." Stu pointed across the room.

Tom looked in the direction that Stu was pointing. Victor was there, though he apparently hadn't seen either of them. The assistant superintendent looked furtively from side to side and then stepped quickly inside a pair of pink doors. Beside the doors was a large billboard which announced in blazing letters: *TODAY'S SIZZLING MATINEE—GIRLS GALORE!!*

23

People were crammed into the hallway outside the large meeting room the next morning, waiting for the doors to open to the last day's breakfast session. Tom knew Walt and the others had arrived, because he and Stu had received an early-morning phone message, reminding them to be at the cross-age tutoring demonstration this afternoon. With the mass of people pressing around him, though, he was unable to see anyone he knew. But then, behind him, he heard a familiar loud, raucous laugh. It could only be Brenda Calloway, the middle school counselor. He pushed his way backward through the crowd in the direction of the laughter, and saw her huge body, shaking with glee. Nita Masters was with her. Tom excused himself as he pushed through the last group of persons separating them and greeted the two counselors.

"Good morning, ladies."

"Oh, wonderful! A friendly face!" Brenda squealed.

"Hi, Tom," Nita said.

"You must have really taken an early flight this morning," Tom said.

"You've heard of the early-bird flight? We took the owl express!" Brenda boomed. "The next time your principal invites me to one of these things, I'm going to ask him to send me the night before."

"Are the others here?" Tom asked.

"Yes, they're around somewhere," Nita answered. "But with this crowd, I have no idea where." She stood on her toes and glanced from side to side. "Do they always make everyone wait outside like this for the plenary sessions?"

"No, the doors are usually open so that people can enter as they arrive. I don't know what the problem is this morning."

He had no sooner said that when the four sets of double doors swung open.

"Here we go!" Brenda said.

The crowd shoved forward in a single mass and flowed into the room. When they got inside, Tom saw that there were no tables or chairs set up, and no long, food-filled buffet awaited them, as was true yesterday morning. The people stood about on the empty floor, laughing and whispering to one another. The last of the crowd entered the room, and uniformed hotel workers closed the doors. Tom looked toward the speakers' platform and realized there was no podium there today—just a heavy, felt-covered table. No one sat on the platform, but as the doors closed, Katie Howard appeared from the side and walked to the table. She held a lapel microphone near her mouth as she greeted them.

"Good morning, all!" Katie spoke cheerfully.

"Good morning," a few people in the crowd responded.

"I'm sure you're wondering why you're standing here in an empty room, with no breakfast, right?"

"Right!"

"Well, yesterday, hopefully, you discovered strategies to strip away all those negative, restrictive feelings and influences that hamper your journey toward excellence. Today is the awakening—the time for self-renewal. Your spirits have been purged. And now you stand as empty vessels, waiting to be filled with the truth of your potential. The program planners thought we could best begin today's sessions by being uncluttered—even with such a mundane element as food!"

A few hushed mutterings arose from the crowd. Brenda groaned.

"But don't worry," Katie went on. "By the time we've completed this session, you'll feel completely satiated. Trust me."

Katie turned toward the side of the platform and motioned for someone to join her. A short, thin, dark-skinned man walked quickly to the center of the platform and stood beside her. He wore a poorly-fitted suit and a mismatched bow tie.

"I would like to introduce you to our speaker for this morning." Katie placed her hand on the man's shoulder. "He is a world-renowned expert in the field of creative meditation, and we are grateful that he was willing to make the long flight from India to join us at this year's convention. Please welcome him...Vishnadi Kalundi!"

The crowd responded with spirited applause. Katie handed Vishnadi the lapel microphone and walked off the platform. Vishnadi carefully clipped the microphone to his jacket, nodded several times, and waited for the applause to cease. He stepped in front of the large, felt-covered table, and in a single motion pulled himself on top of it and sat cross-legged, his hands resting on his knees.

"We must begin with the proper position," Vishnadi said with a heavy accent. "Please be seated, according as you see me now."

A number of quiet whispers and chuckles rose from the crowd as the people shuffled toward positions where they could comfortably sit.

"The morning awakens with a hush, and likewise should we also," Vishnadi said. "Please...with silence, take your places."

Tom and Nita positioned themselves on either side of

Brenda and helped her down. She collapsed with a loud grunt and forcefully pulled her legs into a crossed position.

"You'll need a crane to get me up from here!" Brenda laughed loudly, then stopped abruptly and placed her hand over her mouth.

Tom watched while Nita sat. Most of those in the room had now assumed the position. He chuckled as he considered remaining standing, like the woman in Quinlan's presentation yesterday. But then he thought better of it and became a member of the seated crowd. As he rested his hands on his knees, he felt a hand on his shoulder. He turned to see that Marla Vedder was sitting directly beside him.

"What are you doing here?" he whispered.

She smiled and leaned toward him. "Walt let me come today as an in-service bonus for new teachers."

"Really?"

"No, just kidding. I'll be working with the cross-age tutoring program, so Walt thought it would be good for me to come today and take part in the demonstration."

"The hush of morning," Kalundi urged. "The hush...the hush..."

The few remaining murmurs ceased and the large room became filled with absolute silence.

"Meditation is essential for the proper development of the intellect," Kalundi said without moving. "Some of you are already engaging your students in this practice, but it is important to learn the proper steps and terms. Otherwise the exercise may be ineffective or counterproductive. We begin with the proper position, as you now have—seated on the floor, legs crossed before you, hands resting gently on your knees. But some of you are not allowing for the full flow of relaxation. Place your shoulders back. Yes."

About half of those in the room had been slumped

forward, and now they pulled themselves to a rigidly straight position.

"You will find comfort in discipline. You will see. Now we must not take our breathing for granted. For as we learn to control our inhalation of breath, we also learn to control our *Prana*—our *vital* breath, our soul energy that emanates from our life force. Breathe with me...slowly, deeply."

The chests of the spectators rose and fell as they breathed in rhythmic obedience to the direction. After about the tenth inhalation, Tom began to feel somewhat light-headed from the increased oxygen, but he continued as the unison breathing continued twenty times.

"Now take a large breath," Kalundi instructed. "And as you let it out, speak the syllable, *Om*...and let the final letter murmur through your nasal passages. Observe..." He demonstrated by breathing deeply and then humming, "Ommmm... Together, now." He breathed deeply and the people followed suit. And as he spoke the sound, they did also, and the room was filled with the brief vowel and then the trailing hum between their closed lips. Kalundi repeated the exercise five times, and each time, the trailing hum became longer. "Practice as often as you need to. The Mantra will cleanse you of residual fears and inhibitions of thought. It will allow you to become finely attuned to the psychic, creative energy within you. This is Shakti. She is at the base of your spine. She is restless and struggles to be free. Think of her as you meditate. Make a path for her to follow, up your spine. She will pass willingly through your cakras, the psychic centers of your body."

Tom abruptly stopped his breathing as he heard the word *cakra*, and he again imagined the figure of Jennifer in the library beside her picture of the rainbow. What was she learning?

"It requires concentration," Kalundi continued. "But as

Shakti passes through each level, the energy increases, and her struggle becomes powerful. And now, at the neck...so close, and yet the image of perfection is shielded. A veil falls across the energy flow. And beyond the veil, Shiva awaits. He is the pinnacle of your intellect, but he cannot be fulfilled without the vital breath. The veil must be burst, yes. Shakti strips it away...and she and Shiva are joined in glorious, psycho-sensual union!"

Tom thought he felt a slight breath on his face. He turned and Marla's eyes pierced his. She smiled coyly and turned away.

The cross-age tutoring presentation was held after lunch in the Minotaur Room. Walt had asked for this room because it had a larger capacity, and he was sure the demonstration would draw a crowd. But it was already ten minutes past the time the presentation should have begun, and the room was barely half full. Walt asked his people to spread out some-what, to give the impression of a larger crowd. Tom sat near the back with Stu. The presenters sat patiently together in the front row. Finally Walt stood and addressed the audience.

"I think some people must be having a hard time finding the room, but we're going to get started, anyway." He laughed nervously. "This is a demonstration of cross-age tutoring—*C.A.T.*, we call it. We've been in this tutoring pro-ject in our district for over a month now, and we're excited about the results so far. As all of you know, the LENA pro-gram is very demanding. And as we look toward expansion next year, we want to be sure we have skilled teachers to carry the goals forward.

"We realized we had a wonderful resource at our disposal. Most of our seniors have been in the program for six years, and they have a wealth of knowledge and understanding that should be put to use. So about twenty of our best students this semester have participated in a pilot project. We rescheduled their classes into the seventh and eighth periods, to allow them to leave campus during the middle of the day and work with youngsters in our elementary schools. This has required a great deal of commitment on the part of these young people, but they tell us they've gained as much from the experience as have the young students they're tutoring. We've found that they bring a new vision to the subjects they are imparting. Our teachers are creative, but the *students*... Well, they present concepts we wouldn't have thought of in a hundred years. And do the elementary kids ever respond! So..." Walt stepped back and then walked over in front of the row of presenters. "Here's what we're going to do. We have three high school students with us today who will demonstrate their tutoring methods." He motioned for each one to rise as he called the names. "Beth Crawford...Frank Ziderly...and Mark Banazech."

The audience applauded politely.

Walt smiled and continued, "We decided to use three staff members as our elementary kids." He repeated the introduction process with the three women. "I'd like you to meet our little third-graders. Nita Masters...Brenda Calloway...and Marla Vedder."

Light applause again sounded in the room.

"I'll let them proceed. I'm going to sit back with you and enjoy the show!"

The raised platform at the front of the room was set up with two small chairs, and the students and staff members paired off for the presentations. Beth and Nita were the first to perform. Nita had a pad and a set of crayons and pretended to be a third grader who was reluctant in art, because she had not experienced success. Beth coaxed her into closing her eyes and feeling her anger at her lack of skill. Then she asked her to draw lines and shapes, with her eyes still closed, that expressed this anger. The result was a chaotic jumble of color, but Beth praised her for her artistic effort, and Nita pretended to be happy about her newly found skill.

Frank Ziderly and Brenda performed next, and their beginning was met with laughter as Brenda nearly fell off the tiny chair that disappeared beneath her. Frank had done a great deal of reading in the area of occult science, and had developed a unit on space communication. He excitedly explained to Brenda how, one day, she could communicate with beings from other planets through cosmic powers derived from harnessing what he termed the astronomical Yin and Yang. Brenda feigned rapture at his promise of her future capabilities.

Finally, Mark Banazech and Marla took the stage. Mark shifted his muscular frame on the chair and addressed the audience. "A lot of the little kids I work with have a hard time letting their minds expand. So I work with them on body awareness, and that really seems to help." He faced Marla, took her hands in his, and held them as he spoke to her. "All right, Marla. Now we're just going to sit quietly with our eyes closed for a couple of minutes."

Tom heard the door to the room open and he looked back. Dr. Banazech walked in quietly and sat across the aisle. He sat back and slowly stroked his goatee as he watched Marla and his son interact.

Mark held Marla's hands without speaking for a full minute. Then he spoke softly. "How old are you, Marla?"

"Nine," Marla spoke in a little girl's voice.

"You know, as you get older your body is going to grow and grow and grow."

"Yes."

"Did you know your mind can grow, too? Do you want me to show you how?"

"Okay."

"We'd better make your body grow first, so there'll be room for it," Mark said.

Marla giggled.

"I can feel your hands now. They're just little girl hands. But they're going to get bigger and have long, pretty fingers."

"Can I paint my nails?" Marla asked.

"Sure. Your feet are growing, too, aren't they? Can you feel them?"

"Mmm-hmm."

"Wiggle your toes. I think I can feel them all the way over to mine."

Marla giggled again.

"I think your head's starting to grow," Mark said. "Your mind should have a little more room, now."

"I can feel it."

"And look at that! Your arms are getting longer. And your legs, too. They're so slender and soft. You're turning into quite a young lady!"

Tom shifted uncomfortably in his seat. He wondered how Mark's father was reacting to the performance. He looked across the aisle. Dr. Banazech was gone.

24

Victor Hernandez had asked all of the district people to meet in the Bacchus Lounge at 5:00 that afternoon for a light dinner before leaving for the airport. Victor hadn't arrived by a quarter after, so the rest of them went ahead and ordered from the one-page travelers' special menu. Brenda complained good-naturedly about the light fare, but Walt reminded her that they would probably be fed on the plane as well. The gathering was a relaxing conclusion to the hectic three-day convention, and most of those about the table talked quietly about the things they had seen. The three students sat across from Tom and chatted enthusiastically about the reception their presentation had received.

"I hope Dr. Hernandez gets here soon," Walt said. "We have to leave for the airport by 7:00, and most of you still have to check out."

"He probably went somewhere for dinner before joining us for this snack." Brenda laughed raucously.

Stu leaned over to Tom and whispered, "Or maybe he took in another show and it hasn't let out yet."

Tom chuckled softly.

"Stu, there's a project staff meeting after school tomorrow, isn't there? Walt asked.

"Yes," Stu said, looking up.

"Good." Walt raised his voice to capture the attention of the others. "I want you all to collect your thoughts on the way home, and be ready to share at least one significant thing you've learned from the convention. It's important we keep the momentum going when we get back."

Tom started to pick up his iced tea, and then glanced over the table to find the sugar. "Excuse me. Does anyone have..." He stopped when he saw two individual packs by his silver. "Never mind." He picked up the packs, shook them lightly, and tore off the tops. He poured the contents into his glass and stirred slowly as he listened to the growing level of the conversation about him. He felt a hand on his arm and turned to see Marla's questioning eyes.

"Do you suppose Walt would mind if I sat in on that meeting?"

"I don't know," Tom said. "Why don't you..."

A loud series of discordant notes suddenly split the air. Everyone at the table jumped in alarm. Ed Staley stood suddenly, pushed a button on his tape player, and the noise stopped.

"Sorry, guys," Ed said. "I thought I had the earphones plugged in."

"What was that, Ed?" Susan asked.

"Spherical music."

"What?" Susan's lips crinkled about her large teeth.

"Spherical music," Ed repeated. "I think I told you guys about it before. It's based on the fifty-three tone scale, instead of the traditional twelve tones. We're able to produce these now with all the electronic instruments. They even allow playing notes in the physically inaudible ranges of sound. Most people don't even think about those, but they're still there—hammering away on our psychic receptors. But now we can control them and work toward releasing some underlying subliminal responses."

"I just got an outrageous idea!" Susan said. "That would

make a great companion to the dancing lights art process I looked at."

"Yeah. You guys wouldn't believe me before, would you?" Ed said petulantly. "That's why I think we need to force Underwood to bring his department into line. Kids need the related mathematical skills to allow them to grasp the full..."

"Ed..." Stu scolded.

"Let me hear the music again, Ed," Susan said.

A sudden explosion of negative responses resounded from the others at the table. Ed frowned as he walked over behind Susan and motioned for those beside her to change places. They grumbled quietly but shifted to allow him to sit next to Susan. Ed unclipped the small phones from the head piece and handed one to Susan. She smiled and placed it to her ear. He then turned on the player again, and the two of them sat side by side, listening to the music through the earphones.

Tom sat back and slowly drank his tea. He chuckled softly at the sight of Ed and Susan sitting together. They had previously shown nothing but mutual animosity. The others, too, as they sat about the table, seemed to have discovered a new sense of camaraderie. He remembered what Stu had told him—these are good people, just very individualistic and very dedicated to the program. Tom realized how true that statement was; he had realized a closer relationship with all of them during these three days than he had in his entire time at the school. They were so excited about what they had learned and so eager to get back and impart their knowledge to the kids. And as Tom visualized them standing before their classes, leading their students through highly motivating experiences, he felt a strange twinge of guilt for harboring such negative feelings about the goals of the program. The students would be guided through stimulating experiences which would result in greater creativity and an expanded awareness of the phenomena of the world and their place in it. What could possibly be wrong with that? Chris Donnelly had told him he was thinking too traditionally. Was that the problem? Was he simply reluctant to change?

In the LENA program the curricular distinctions become less important, Chris had said. The subjects were merely convenient vehicles through which the insights were transmitted. What was the other word he used? Merging. Yes, that was the description that gave Tom the greatest concern. There *was* a merging. Regardless of the subject matter of the course, all of the activities seemed directed toward the goal of creative self-fulfillment. The presenters seemed united in their rejection of dichotomous standards. But how could the accumulated knowledge of the centuries be effectively imparted to tomorrow's leaders, if the primary objective was the realization of each student's personal inner truth?

As the waiter began placing plates on the table everyone was distracted from their conversations. Tom's plate was placed before him, while another waiter held out a pitcher.

"More tea, sir?"

"Hmm? Oh, yes, please."

"Nice appetizer!" Brenda said, laughing.

Tom looked for the sugar again, and as he unwrapped his silver, he found two more packs under his napkin. He absently picked them up, tore off the tops, and stirred the contents into his tea.

"Well, look who's here!" Brenda said.

Victor walked into the lounge and waved at them. Then he motioned behind him and Dr. Banazech joined him. Together they walked over and stood behind Walt.

"Sorry I'm late," Victor said. "I've convinced Dr. Banazech to come and chat with us for a few minutes."

Everyone responded enthusiastically and scooted their

chairs to allow room for the two of them to sit next to Walt. Tom glanced across the table, noticing Mark seemed somewhat uncomfortable with his father's unexpected appearance.

"We really feel privileged that someone from our area...and, well, the father of one of the project students...is one of the major presenters," Victor said. "I hope you all had the opportunity to listen to Dr. Banazech at least once."

"I certainly did," Nita said. "And I've received a lot of help from your books, too."

"Thank you," Dr. Banazech said.

"I'd really be interested to hear your reaction to our cross-age tutoring project," Nita said.

"I'll bet you were proud of Mark, weren't you, Doctor?" Brenda said.

"Actually, I was somewhat disappointed," Dr. Banazech answered.

A tense silence fell across the table. Tom looked at Mark who sat in his chair without moving, his head raised slightly. His expression, strangely, had not changed. But there was something perceptibly different about his demeanor. It was almost as though Mark was smiling through a frown.

"Well, I'm sorry to hear that," Nita said. "Will you tell us why?"

"The concept of using advanced students to teach beginning students has some merit," Dr. Banazech answered curtly. "But it must be handled in a controlled environment, particularly when it involves psychologically volatile experiences. The assignment requires a level of maturity that many students have not yet achieved."

Lee Wong sat forward and folded his hands on the table. "I think you'd be pleased to know that, from what I have observed, your son *has* achieved that level of maturity."

"Physical maturity, perhaps," Dr. Banazech said. "Not psychological maturity."

"Well, that's something we'll have to be especially alert to." Walt laughed nervously. "Maybe someone else has a question for Dr. Banazech."

Tom felt a flash of heat which emanated from his spine and rose slowly to his forehead. It seemed an unusually strong reaction to the tension at the table. His face was suddenly covered with perspiration, and he wiped it with his napkin. He took another drink of his tea, and the cool liquid pushed aside the radiating warmth. He shook his head slightly to stop the low buzzing in his ears and attended to the voice of Chris.

"...particularly well related to my field." Chris was apparently addressing Dr. Banazech, but his voice seemed to float vaguely, without direction. "What insights have you discovered in the relationship of biological characteristics and intelligence?"

The perspiration again rose from Tom's forehead, and he reached for his iced tea, but the glass was empty. He forced his head toward Dr. Banazech, who appeared to be responding to Chris's question.

"Of course. You should read some papers by my son, Vernon." Banazech's mouth seemed to remain closed as he spoke, but his goatee bobbed up and down rhythmically as the words issued forth. "He has a successful practice in Switzerland and has documented a number of controlled studies. In fact, I'll be joining him in a week or two for a seminar in Prague."

Tom looked up at a light, and it seemed to take the shape of Switzerland. And then a dot appeared in its center, and grew until it took on the appearance of Mark with a goatee...smiling. He let his head fall. He looked across the table to the other Mark, without the goatee...frowning. He heard a loud clicking and turned to see Stu, holding his pipe casually, bumping the stem lightly against his teeth. But the clicking sound pierced Tom's ear and he sat back. He felt a hand on his arm...Marla...too close. "Sorry..." he mumbled. But the hand...tighter. A smell...what? Tobacco? No. Stu's pipe...not lighted. And he wasn't puffing, just clicking. But a stream of smoke rose in a purple line from the bowl of his pipe. And the smell...incense...strong, pungent. Tom shook his head, but the smell increased, and now the stream of smoke spread out and covered those at the table. They seemed to be in a boat, because it rocked from side to side, and the cold froth of water lapped over the sides. Someone's voice... "Make choices... Make good choices." Yes... Nita and Lee, sitting on either side of Brenda... Yes. She's the one...throw her over-board. Tom laughed giddily at the thought and then it became so, and the boat lurched, and everyone laughed.

Tom leaned on the table. Past Marla. Ed and Susan, still listening silently to the music. But Tom could hear it now...its subsonic tones. His body twitched inwardly to the subliminal rhythm. Their heads...so close together, with the tiny phones in their ears...no they are their ears. And they came closer until they were joined at the ears, and their forms stood, and with their heads still joined they began to dance to the rhythm of the inaudible tones, and the smoke from Stu's incense pot encircled them, and their feet searched about for stability, and they stepped cautiously onto a three-legged pedestal. And the pedestal spoke, "Ask me a question, and see what happens..." No, just the word..."question." Lee's voice. "Question...concentrate...meditate..." Yes. Lee was there still. His soft voice...sure...stable. But he sat cross-legged atop a large felt-covered table. A tattered, mismatched bow tie bobbed up and down on his larynx as he spoke. The others at the table hung on the tie and tried to stop it, but Lee swung his head. His hairs flew out and fell in clumps on the table. Tom leaned forward and squinted as the clump diminished to a bright point of light. It grew into a pulsating cell, and then a tiny ape jumped from the cell and scurried across the table on all fours.

"...scientific basis for the reality of life..." Chris again. Yes. Tom pushed his head around with his hand and saw him. Chris was speaking, but his head was that of an ape, with a grossly receding forehead. But his voice was clear. "...which began, of course eons ago with the non-rational interruption of psychic recognition." Yes, better. The forehead grew forward, and the facial hair disappeared, and he didn't stop. "Promise. Promise of life. Promise of change. Factual basis for irrational thought, here in the spherical music of the mind." Didn't stop...not the words, not the head... Chris's forehead throbbed as he spoke. His frontal lobe bulged and the slick white skin moved outward from his hair line, his head dropping forward from the weight. "Weighty matter...future of our society depends on..."

Tom's head fell heavily to the side, and he felt a stream of hot breath on his neck, and he followed the hand on his arm. It was Marla's, and she was smiling. "Hello..." Why? We've already met... And Stu's voice was behind him. "Tom...Tom..." And he chuckled as he remembered his mother, reading to him. "Tom, Tom the piper's son. Stole a—" Stole a what? And when is stealing sociologically acceptable? And maybe the piper told a big lie, or a little lie. And what does it really matter? No, it doesn't matter, because Marla's hot breath was still on his neck, and he forced his body around in his chair and he took both her hands, and her feet reached out, and she wiggled her toes, and he felt his numb lips tumble over his slurred words. *"You're slender, and soft...turning into quite a young lady..."* Marla laughed giddily, her hot breath drifting gently across the table. But then her voice grew light, and young, her face grew smaller, and her little-girl eyes twinkled with delight—she became Jennifer. A brightly colored rainbow throbbed from her Shakti and climbed the rocky cakras to the waiting Shiva... And her hot breath pierced into his mind, and her toes reached out and wiggled against his fingers.

"No!" Tom felt a sudden surge of energy and he pushed himself away from the table and stood. The chair shot back from him and tumbled onto the floor.

"Tom...Tom..." Not the piper's son. It was Stu, standing too... But his incense burner...he still held it in his mouth, and the others rocked helplessly in the doomed lifeboat. Had to go...had to get out. Can't be the one chosen...

Tom clutched his legs with his hands and forced them to move. He felt his body floating away from the lifeboat. A gateway...light streaming through. He passed through, and then looked back, just for a moment...remember Lot's wife. A sign above the gateway—Bacchus Lounge. Can't lounge. Have to run! He pushed his clutching hands rhythmically to the sound of the unheard tones, and his body shot forward. He heard laughter and the tinkling of glasses. Where? So many people at the tables. And the machines with the skinny legs and the wide, spinning mouths... Ching! Ching! Ching! And the crying feeders still stood and pushed their thumbs against the slot. No...non-rational machine. No pre-frontal lobe...have to continue...have to evolve. But beyond the ringing machines a pair of doors opened and a line of girls ran out. They jumped up on the felt-covered tables and cooed with their red lips, then they swung down and ran back to their caves.

The cold smooth surface of the glass door thrust itself upon his back and he felt a surge of clarity. The interior of the hotel stood before him for just a moment. But then it collapsed into a spinning spiral of colors which fell heavily into silence from the wide spinning mouths... Ching! Ching! Ching! He pushed back hard to escape the shaft of hot breath, and the door opened, and he followed it out, and then closed it behind him and held it fast. Yes. The cool air. My mind...think...I can. He breathed deeply and the lights again ceased from their circling and fell into reality. He stepped away from the door and walked clumsily down the stairs into the entryway. Breathe deeply...breathe deeply... Don't take it for granted. The *Prana*—the vital breath, the soul energy emanates from the life force, and circles up the spine...

No! Don't breathe deeply...the cool, circling air...the circling lights. In the drive...people, circling. Bald heads and white robes. And they danced about and banged on tambourines and chanted, "Hare Krishna...Hare Krishna..." Yes. They are real. They can stop the spiraling lights... His legs wobbled, but he stumbled toward them, and three of them reached out with gnarled hands and spoke with protruding teeth, "Brother... You are seeing the truth... Be with us... Dance with us!" Their hands fell on his arms and their hot breath spilled out across his face. They spun and circled and the lights followed them and tumbled into a spinning rainbow.

Tom stood in exhilaration for a moment in the stability of his dizziness, but then Stu's voice whispered behind him, "Tom...Tom..." The piper's son. It was a pig! He stole a pig. Yes. And away he run. But Stu was still there, and now his face stretched out and a long white goatee hung beneath it... And he split in two, and they pulled him away from the circling dancers...and back through the smooth cold doors. And the hot air drifted across his face again, and the hard hands on his arms pulled him further in. And a brown square mouth opened its gaping darkness, and they tumbled in, and the mouth closed and they lurched upward. The light...so dim. But above the mouth, from the inside...smaller lights shone brightly, telling tales...one, two, three. And they blurred into a rainbow, and for each color there was a tale...four, five, six...so close. But the mouth opened again, and the creature belched them forth. And the mouth closed behind them. "Six..." He heard the word from Stu and the face with the goatee. "Six..." again. No. A veil remains. Shakti still struggles... Still captured by the rainbow.

He lifted his bobbing head and screamed through mumbled words, "No! Don't stop. Have to go to seven! Joni stopped at six. Have to go to seven!" The clutching hands grasped harder as he struggled to return to the closed brown mouth, and another gateway swung open, and he was drawn in, and thrust roughly on a soft, felt-covered table, but it bounced as he struggled, and the boat rocked back and forth, and the frothy water spilled out on those remaining. But he was alone in the boat, and Stu stood outside on the water with the man with the goatee, and their faces fell down in sadness.

Tom turned on the softness and grasped at the puff of reality beneath his head and his gaze fell on the face of a clock. His eyes narrowed as he concentrated on the long slender hand which passed so rhythmically about the circle of dots...ching...ching...ching. He heard words tumbling from the goatee, "Controlled environment..." Control. He could control. Breathe deeply... No! Think. Concentrate! He squinted harder and the long slender hand shone and pulsated at his command. It slowed and the voice from the goatee became longer and slower, tumbling into subsonic sound. But Stu's voice was still there. "Tom are you all right?" And Tom squinted and laughed giddily and commanded the long slender hand, and it stopped and spiraled backward. Stu's voice followed it: "...thgir lla ouy era moT."

Tom crushed his eyelids softly into a blink, and the long slender hand moved forward again. "Tom...Tom..." The piper's son. Stole a pig and away he run. Away he run...away he run. Don't run backward... Evolution goes only forward. We need an explosion...a mutation. A mutation of time... Tom held his head motionless on the soft cushion of reality. He felt his frontal lobe reach out again and his eyes beneath it stretched forth from their sockets and fell on the round dotted face, and the long slender hand spun faster and faster, until it became a hot spiral of color. And the rainbow grew smaller and hotter, and it fell as a blazing dot into a deep, black, circle of darkness...

Tom forced his eyes open suddenly and clutched at the pillow which was wet with his sweat. He turned over on his back and struggled to regain focus. He was on the bed in his hotel room. Across from him, seated in the two overstuffed chairs, were Stu and Dr. Banazech.

"Well..." Stu looked up from the magazine he was reading. "I see you're back with us."

"What?" Tom shook his head and the image became clearer. "What happened?

Stu glanced at his watch. "Your estimate was remarkably accurate, Doctor."

"What happened?"

"You've been on a little trip, Mr. Kerzig," Banazech said. "And since I've been assured by Mr. Welbourne that you would never do such a thing on your own volition, I can only assume that one of your colleagues gave you the LSD."

"LSD?"

Banazech stood up and walked slowly over to Tom. He held out a pair of empty sugar packages. "I picked these up from your place at the table. I'd have to do a test to be sure, but I'm quite confident that these were the vehicle."

Tom abruptly sat up on the edge of the bed. A sudden shot of pain pierced his head, and he clutched it with his hands.

"Slowly, Mr. Kerzig," Dr. Banazech said.

Tom reached out to the table beside the bed and grabbed the clock. The long slender second hand clicked rhythmically about the face of the dial. It was ten after eleven. He set the clock down and looked at Stu.

"Don't worry about that," Stu said. "We've arranged for a later flight. We'll have to leave in a few minutes, though, if we expect to make it. Otherwise, we'll just stay over."

"He'll be fine now," Dr. Banazech said.

Tom stood slowly and stretched his body. He held his hands out before him and then passed them slowly over his arms. His skin tingled slightly, but he felt alert. The pain in his head was now gone completely. He looked at Stu and shook his head slowly. "Who would have done this?"

Stu shrugged. "Your guess is as good as mine, Tom."

"I mean, it must have been someone who brought it along for..."

"Oh, Mr. Kerzig," Dr. Banazech interrupted. "As I said in my first lecture, the idiotic legislation has made this gutter fodder. Las Vegas is teeming with illegal derivatives. You're fortunate that you weren't given any that was contaminated."

"Fortunate?"

"Yes, and perhaps that's not such an ill-chosen term," Dr. Banazech said. "It was, of course, a juvenile trick to play on you. But now, at least, you have had the benefit of the experience."

"Dr. Banazech, let me tell you something," Tom said. "I have just enough recollection of what happened to be able to assure you that there was nothing mind-expanding or exhilarating about my experience."

"That's because you had no prior expectation, Mr. Kerzig," Dr. Banazech said.

"What?"

"As I told you the other day, in all cases, the effects of the drug are related to the *expectation* of the user. If you had been aware of the impending experience, and had laced your consciousness with positive expectations, they would have materialized. But with this...shoddy game-playing...your experience was related to whatever combination of thoughts was passing through your mind at the time the drug took effect."

"The point is, Tom, it was a childish trick," Stu said. "But it's over with now, and you're none the worse for it. Isn't that right, Doctor?"

"Absolutely," Banazech said. "There are no harmful after-effects. You won't even have a hang-over tomorrow morning."

"Do you feel good enough to leave?" Stu asked.

Tom took a deep breath. A slight feeling of dizziness swept over him. But his mind was clear. "Sure. I'm fine."

The three of them headed toward the door.

"Doctor Banazech, I'd like to have those sugar packages," Tom said.

"If you're anticipating some sort of investigation, Mr. Kerzig, I'd recommend against it," Dr. Banazech said. "These things are best left alone."

Tom held his hand out and looked directly at Dr. Banazech. The doctor sighed, reached into his pocket, and withdrew the packages. Then he held them out and dropped them into Tom's hand. Tom felt the few remaining grains in the paper envelopes. He glanced at the clock as he recalled the events of just a few hours ago. He rapidly reconstructed the dinner in his mind. Who? Stu was to his left. And to his right...Marla.

Stu opened the door, and they walked toward the waiting elevator.

25

Tom was quite fatigued the next morning, since he had only gotten about three hours of sleep. Dr. Banazech was right, though; he apparently had no bad after-effects from the LSD. He did feel a bit uncomfortable during first period, however. Mark, Frank, and Beth had clearly shared the incident with the other students, because they whispered and giggled during the entire class period. He considered discussing with the class what had happened, but he decided that, for now, at least, the matter was best left alone.

The project team meeting was held in Stu's room again that afternoon. Tom had met briefly with some students after school, so by the time he arrived at Stu's room, the others were already seated. Marla had apparently received permission to attend, as she had requested, and she sat between Walt and Nita. As Tom entered the room, he was met by several whistles and hoots which he waved off as he sat down.

"We're glad you made it back from your trip safely," Chris joked.

"You really should have dressed more warmly, though." Marilyn laughed. "I mean, at that altitude..."

"I took notes," Susan said. "I got some great ideas for a new surrealistic art work!"

"All right, people," Stu chided. "You all know Tom was the brunt of a silly practical joke. And if any of you were involved in it, I suggest you make your peace with him."

Tom looked around the table at the smiling faces. Dr. Banazech was right, of course. Anyone could have obtained the laced sugar packages. But who could have slipped them under his napkin? Stu and Marla sat on either side of him, and the three students were across the table. But of course someone could have paid the waiter to set them at his place, too. Any of them might have arranged this. But why?

"Let's get started." Stu glanced at a printed agenda which rested on the table before him. "You remember that Walt asked us last night to be thinking of a significant thing we learned at the convention, so that we could share our thoughts today." He looked around the table. "Lee, why don't you start us off?"

"That's a good idea," Ed said. "We didn't see much of you during the three days, Lee."

"He was probably practicing his Karate chops with the slot machines," Marilyn kidded.

Lee smiled and leaned forward. "Actually, the reason you didn't see me is that I was busy attending all the sessions that related to my field, rather than speaker-hopping like the rest of you."

The group responded with sarcastic boos and hisses.

"I found the presentations very helpful," Wong continued. "But I'd have to say that the most rewarding experience took place yesterday. I was invited to lunch with a small group of state physical education coordinators. We were joined by Vishnadi Kalundi."

"Oh, really?" Walt raised his eyebrows.

Lee nodded. "You know I've had considerable success with my seniors that elected the combative course. But with those who remain in the advanced conditioning course, I've always felt a lack of purpose. It has become nothing more than an exercise program. But Vishnadi gave us a concept at lunch that I think I can use. It's a metaphor I think they can relate to."

"What is it?" Marla asked.

"It is the relationship between a drop of water and all the seas on earth," Lee explained. "I will ask them to imagine themselves as the tiny drop—apparently insignificant, and yet containing the same basic elements as the totality of the waters surrounding the globe. And as they merge with the whole, their essence becomes one with its power. I'm sure I can develop some movement patterns which will aid their concentration. And I believe the activity will give them a great deal more inner fulfillment."

"That sounds wonderful!" Walt said. "A drop of water and the ocean. Yes."

"Susan, how about you?" Stu said.

"Well, I think Ed and I found our most significant experience by accident last night."

The room was again filled with hoots and whistles.

"No!" Susan sat back, her face beet red. "You know what I mean! The combining of light forms and spherical music. The presentation I went to that used the laser technology made me see that kids can really experience a kind of transcendence through that medium. And then, when I heard Ed's music demo, it really clicked!"

"That's right," Ed said. "I had always been able to find a deeper meaning for the twelve-tone scale for the kids by tying it in with the twelve signs of the zodiac. And that still applies...as a beginning. But the shift to the fifty-three tones becomes a sort of...well, cultural evolution. And if we can get kids to imagine their own intellect moving out from the rational, but overly structured pattern of the twelve to the probing openness of the prime number fifty-three... Wow! And Susan's lights can really accelerate this movement."

"I never thought of it that way," Walt said. "That's good!"

"My turn?" Marilyn asked.

"Go ahead," Stu said.

"Well, you know I was going to share the results of my survey with you at this meeting. I'm really glad I waited until after the convention, because I got some absolutely dynamite state-wide results to compare with mine. One of these days you guys will realize that the health and personal values curriculum is just too important to limit to a single year."

Ed and Chris jeered and waved their hands downward in denial.

"Let's not get into that, now," Stu said. "Just tell us about what you learned."

"Well, all right." Marilyn laid a sheet filled with figures before her and pointed with her pencil. "Listen to this. On a state-wide average, kids know about 3.3 types of contraceptive devices."

"How can anyone know about 3.3 types of anything?" Susan asked.

"It's statistics, Susan. It's just for comparison." She shook her head in disgust and continued. "Now, our kids only knew about 2.9 types of contraceptives."

"Hmm!" Walt shook his head in feigned disbelief. "What does that tell you?"

"I have to do a more complete job of teaching our kids about safe sex." Marilyn looked at another item on her paper. "Let's see... Our kids have sex about as much as the average," she said without looking up. "Oh, but here's an important one. Of the kids who've had sex five times or less, on a state-wide average, 43 percent of them have felt guilty about it. But *61* percent of our kids have had guilt feelings. So that tells me I'm not doing a good enough job at making the kids feel positive about their sexuality."

"Or that someone else is doing a better job at something else," Tom suggested.

"Hmm?" Marilyn looked at Tom momentarily and then quickly returned to her sheet. "I'm going to give you all a copy of this, so I won't need to take a lot of time today. But here's one we should be aware of. There's been a big increase in our district in drug use this year over last year. But our kids still aren't using drugs as much as the state-wide average."

"We just have to try harder," Ed joked.

Everyone at the table laughed.

Marilyn rolled her eyes. "No, listen. What I mean is, we know the kids are going to continue to use drugs. The state figures are a clear sign that drugs are here to stay, whether we like it or not. I think it's time we decided to take some kind of positive approach, so our kids won't get caught up in the terrible side issues like dealing and getting hooked on the really hard stuff."

A cold swell suddenly crossed Tom's spine as he recalled his meeting with Bonnie and her somewhat flippant suggestion that kids should be provided some acceptable, safe way to achieve their desired sensations. "Excuse me, Marilyn," he said. "Are you suggesting we should get into some kind of *safe drug distribution* program?"

"Oh, I didn't say that." Marilyn glanced tentatively at Walt and continued. "All I'm saying is that drugs aren't going to go away. And we need to make sure our kids don't get into the stuff that can take them down the tubes." She took a stack of the sheets and passed it to her left. "Why don't you just take one of these, and maybe we can talk about it more at one of our next meetings?"

"That's a great report, Marilyn," Walt said as the sheets were passed around. "I look forward to studying the other results."

Stu sat quietly at his place, moving the stem of his pipe slowly across his bottom lip. Then he set the pipe down and sat forward, folding his hands on the table. "I'd like to share some things that I learned next," he said. "I did do a little *speaker-hopping*, as Lee called it, because I was anxious to get an overall picture of where we're going. Sometimes we become cloistered in our narrow subjects and we can't see the forest for the trees, so to speak."

"That's a good point," Walt said

"In this year's presentations I noticed a quantum jump in...well...experimentation," Stu continued. "And, if I may carry the forest metaphor a bit further, it seems a number of individual trees were aflame with exploration into uncharted territory."

"Yes, I noticed that too," Walt agreed.

"My point is..." Stu paused for a moment, then continued slowly. "Perhaps we should proceed cautiously, lest we start a forest fire."

"Oh, no...no..." Walt frowned and shook his head.

"I agree with Stu," Tom said. "If all of the suggested practices were put in place, I hate to think what might happen to the curriculum...and the kids."

"You're both overreacting," Walt said. "This isn't the time to start getting cautious. Why, look at all the wonderful results we're having already with the cross-age tutoring, for example."

"Maybe that's a good example to consider," Stu said. "We all remember what Dr. Banazech said about the inadequate maturity level of the kids doing the tutoring."

"I didn't understand his concern on that issue," Lee said. "He certainly doesn't have anything to worry about with regard to his own son's maturity level. Why, as an example, Mark is leading my combatives class right now in my absence."

"Yes, but that's not the same as transmitting delicate psychological concepts to younger students, Lee," Stu said.

"Yes, it is," Walt said. "And we can't take the doctor's statements at face value. He has a conflict of interest. He'd like to have a psychiatrist on every campus. That's why we have Nita. And she's doing a magnificent job!"

"I'm not arguing that, Walt," Stu said. "It's just that..."

"We don't have time to carry on with this argument," Walt interrupted. "We have some other items, I'm sure." He reached over impulsively and grabbed the agenda from in front of Stu. "Let's see... Yes, that's next. The board meeting is only eleven days away, people. I don't have to tell you how important it is that we get a favorable decision. We may have a few individual concerns here and there, but we all want the LENA program expanded into the entire school. I'll be talking with each of you individually between now and then to see which of you might be asked to speak. But you should be thinking about this right now. And you'd better be prepared to say something good about the program...or nothing at all!"

Stu sat back slowly, placed the stem of his pipe against his lip again, and gave Walt a half-hearted salute.

"Tom, before I forget, I don't think I told you about supervising a club meeting next Tuesday night for Bonnie," Walt said.

"No, I hadn't heard. What club is that?"

"The Futures Club."

"Futures? Do you mean stocks and bonds?"

Several people around the table laughed spontaneously.

"No, it's not stocks and bonds," Walt said.

"Then what? I need to have some idea..."

"Don't worry about it," Walt said. "Bonnie said that Mark Banazech runs the meeting. All you have to do is be there. It's at seven o'clock in Bonnie's room."

"Well..."

"I think that takes care of everything today," Walt said. "Thanks for your great reports. Keep up the good work!" He stood, tossed the agenda back to Stu, and walked quickly out the door.

The others stood and began to leave. Stu walked to the front of the room and sat behind his desk. Marla smiled as she passed Tom, and he held up his hand to capture her attention.

"Did you want something, Tom?" Marla asked, smiling.

"Ah..." What would he say? *Do you know who slipped me the LSD? Did you slip me the LSD? Would you ever think about...* No. His suspicions were sending him into fanciful assumptions. On the other hand...his behavior toward her...

"Nothing," Tom said finally. "I...ah...I just hope I didn't do anything last night to embarrass you."

"No." Marla lowered her eyes slightly and shook her head. "Not at all." She turned away from him then.

Tom followed her to the door, where he was met by Nita. She glanced around the room as if to see that everyone had left and finally rested her eyes on Stu sitting at his desk.

"You were unusually quiet today," Tom said. "Is everything all right?"

"Well, I came back to two disturbing phone calls."

"Oh?"

"The first one was from your wife. She's decided to change her policy. And that could have a drastic effect on the way I handle things here."

"What do you mean?"

"Well, for some reason, she's decided that if a girl in her case load wants an abortion, she's going to talk to the parents about it first...no matter what the girl wants!"

Tom's heart jumped. He had gotten through to Clair! Or

someone had. It didn't matter who.

"I don't know what got into her to cause this sudden change," Nita said. "But I just thought you might speak with her. You're her husband... I mean, *were*. I mean, well, I just thought you could find out what's going on."

"Actually, you wouldn't want me to talk to Clair about that," Tom said, "because I agree with the change completely."

"What?" Nita looked at Tom and frowned. Then she lowered her head and spoke in low tones. "I suppose I shouldn't be surprised. You don't have any experience in these things. You don't have to deal with the parents." She looked up again. "That was my other phone call."

"Who?"

"The Graingers. You know, the parents of the girl who had the abortion. They want to come in and talk with me again. It seems they went to some meeting last Sunday night and..."

"I know," Tom interrupted. "I saw them there."

"You were there?"

He nodded.

"Boy, I'm really batting zero, huh?" she said with exasperation. "Well maybe you can tell me what they want to talk to me about."

"I don't know. I do know they are very, very upset. They wish they had been told about their daughter's pregnancy. And I would want that, too, Nita, as a parent."

"Ahh..." She motioned in disgust. "You can't judge those people by your values, Tom."

"Why not?"

"And besides, what's the purpose?" she asked, releasing a long sigh. "It's too late, anyway. The baby is dead!'"

Nita dropped her head, placed her hand gently on Tom's chest, turned, and walked away.

Tom leaned back against the doorjamb and looked into the room. Stu still sat behind his desk, reading a book. Tom walked slowly to Stu's desk. "Walt basically appointed himself chairman at the end, didn't he?" he said.

"Hmph!" Stu nodded and continued reading.

"What are you reading?"

Stu smiled and held up the book for Tom to see: *Democracy in America* by Alexis de Tocqueville.

"Oh, yes," Tom said. "Any new insights?"

"I seldom harbor illusions that I can *change* things that are happening in the world," Stu said. "But I'm still constantly prodded by the desire to *understand* them. And Tocqueville helps me do that."

"Walt shouldn't have done what he did," Tom said.

"Oh, no. It's not that. Walt's okay. He's just...nervous. And the others..." He shook his head slowly. "They're good people. All...good people."

"I know."

"That's why it's difficult to understand at times what's happening...in the broader picture, I mean."

"The forest," Tom said.

"Yes, the flickering forest," Stu mumbled. "So much of what's happening is good. It's warm and reassuring..."

"Yes."

"It's like American democracy, Tom," Stu went on. "Freedom, motherhood, apple pie, and all those wonderful, positive aspects no one could possibly denigrate. And yet, if Tocqueville was correct in saying that our very freedom can be the catalyst for our loss of purpose..." Stu held his place with one finger and flipped back several pages. "I keep coming back to this corollary—equality and freedom and material gain. These combine to give us an overpowering sense of self. But are these always the consequences?" He placed his finger

about halfway down the page and read from the text:
" 'It throws him back for ever upon himself alone, and threatens in the end to confine him entirely within the solitude of his own heart.' "

"That can certainly happen," Tom said. "Without the presence of some external purpose."

"That's why so many intellectuals became revolutionaries in the early twentieth century."

Tom recalled the study of Malreaux he was pursuing with Bonnie's seniors. *Man's Fate*...the struggle to escape the absurdity of life through some purpose...dignity...freedom. "Without the presence of some external purpose," he mumbled again.

"Isn't that what we're about, though?" Stu asked "I mean the whole purpose of the *LENA* program is to help the students identify their strengths, beliefs, and values in order to build a life-structure toward success that will..."

"*Internal,*" Tom interrupted. "That's an internal purpose. There are no standards, no accepted goal by which to measure...anything. Nothing is forbidden, everything is accepted. And everyone is running helter-skelter toward some undefined circle of pleasure."

"Ah, yes!" Stu raised his finger and turned the pages back to the place he had saved. "Listen to Tocqueville's reproach of equality. 'Not that it leads men away in pursuit of forbidden enjoyments, but that it absorbs them wholly in quest of those which are allowed. By these means, a kind of virtuous materialism may ultimately be established in the world, which would not corrupt, but enervate the soul, and noiselessly unbend its springs of action.' "

"Perhaps," Tom said. "But I believe the program is pushing kids beyond the state of enervation."

"Toward...?" Stu raised an eyebrow and waited for Tom to complete the sentence.

Tom could easily complete it. Toward corruption. That was the nagging feeling that picked away at his consciousness each time he considered the activities of the program. But Stu had reminded him and he agreed—these were good people. He was perhaps unnecessarily tainted by his involvement with Bonnie's part in the program. If she were at the head of every class... He shuddered to think about it. But, at least, the issues would be absolutely clear and he could complete the sentence without a second thought. He became suddenly irritated with himself that issues of principle could be assuaged by the concept of degree. Was there a conceptual difference? Big lie or little lie. Was it just too difficult to attack a diminutive departure from the truth? Or were such departures, in fact, a rational, necessary aspect in the building of a forest?

"Towaaarrrddd...?" Stu repeated, stringing the word out coaxingly.

Tom shook his head.

"Not ready to complete the picture just yet, are you?" Stu asked.

"No, not yet," Tom mumbled. "Not yet."

26

Clair was waiting at the entrance to the school office when Tom arrived. They had made an appointment to speak with Jennifer's third-grade teacher, and Tom wanted to be there at a time that class was in session. So he had arranged for a substitute for his fifth period class, and now here they were. They went inside and stood before the cluttered counter. A young woman looked up from her desk and smiled at them.

"We have an appointment to meet with Miss Stinneman," Tom said.

The woman glanced at a large calendar on her desk. "Oh, yes, you're Mr. and Mrs. Kerzig." She stood and motioned for them to follow her. They walked to the back of the office and passed through a wide archway. A lush yard lay before them, and around it were low classroom buildings in a pentagonal arrangement.

"She's in room seven," the woman said, pointing. "It's almost directly across from us."

Tom saw the room. All of the inward-facing doors had large numerals on them. "Thanks." They stepped onto the soft grass and began walking across the enclosed yard.

"I spoke with Nita yesterday," Tom said. "She told me about your call. I'm really pleased that you did that. It was a good decision."

"It wasn't really a decision," Clair said. "It was an anxiety response. The Graingers made me feel guilty. I just knew I couldn't withhold that kind of information from a parent again...even if I should."

"If you felt guilty, there was a reason. It was because you did something contrary to what you knew was right."

"Maybe I used the wrong word, then. They made me feel...*uncomfortable.*"

"Give yourself more credit than that, Clair," Tom said. "You wouldn't have called Nita about a major policy change just because of a feeling of discomfort."

"Mmm..."

"Face it. All your training in situational decision-making couldn't lead you completely away from what you know to be true."

Clair shook her head. "It was an anxiety response."

They arrived at the door to the classroom. They walked in quietly and stood in the back of the classroom. Miss Stinneman stood at the front, and the students were gathered together there, seated on the floor in a large open space, their eyes intently on her. Jennifer was at the front of the group and did not see them come in. The minor tones of slow, soft music issued from a tape player on Miss Stinneman's desk. She looked at Tom and Clair, smiled, and pointed to a low, round table in the back corner of the room. Tom led Clair to the table, and they sat on the small chairs.

"All right, class," Miss Stinneman said to the students. "Take another deep breath and hold it for a while this time. Feel the energy spreading out from your tummies to your back and all the way down your legs."

Tom glanced at the nearby wall and was reminded of Bonnie's room. A large rainbow covered an eight-foot display board and white doves flew about in a circle at one corner. Tom passed his hand aimlessly over some items on the table, turning them toward him so that he could identify them.

There was a large picture book entitled *Fun with Astrology*, and a set of small books, each of which bore the general heading: *The Adventures of Psychic Susie*. In the center of the table, a heart-shaped disk with three legs rested atop a Ouija board.

"In and out, in and out," continued the soft, coaxing tones of Miss Stinneman. "You're doing such a fine job today. I have to go to the back of the room for a minute. Do you suppose you could do our mantra all on your own today?"

"Yes, Miss Stinneman," the class chanted in unison.

"Good. Now, remember," she stepped to the wall behind her and pointed to a large picture of a pyramid with a piercing eye near its apex, "concentrate on this picture. With your eyes open first. Good. And now closed. Bring all your energy out and see all the beautiful things you imagine. Ready? Begin."

The students all closed their eyes and their bodies raised in unison as they breathed deeply. Then the sound of the mantra issued from their mouths: "Ommm..."

Tom looked at Clair and frowned. She just raised her eyebrows and shrugged.

Miss Stinneman's dress rustled as she walked quickly to the table and stood across from them. She extended her hand. "Hello, Mr. and Mrs. Kerzig," she said softly.

"Hello, Miss Stinneman," Tom said, shaking her hand.

"Colleen, please," she corrected. "I'm just going to finish this exercise with the students and then they're going to have a special visitor. That will give us a few minutes to talk."

The teacher smiled, turned, and rustled back to the front of the room, where she moved among the chanting students, adjusting the postures of those whose faces were not directed motionlessly toward the pyramid.

The door at the rear of the classroom opened. Tom looked up and was shocked to see Beth Crawford come in.

She was dressed in a white nurse's uniform. Beth closed the door quietly behind her, and stepped back, startled, as she saw Tom and Clair. She walked over and sat beside them.

"Mr. Kerzig, what are you doing here?" Beth asked.

"Hi, Beth. I don't think you've met my wife."

Clair smiled.

"We're here to talk to our daughter's teacher," Tom said.

"Oh, your daughter's in this class? Neat!"

"Why are *you* here?" Tom asked. "And what's with the uniform?"

"Oh..." Beth self-consciously straightened her stiff white hat. "I'm doing a cross-age tutoring activity and this is my costume. I'm working with the whole class together today. I'm really excited!"

"Beth is one of the seniors who tutors the younger children," Tom explained to Clair. "She even took part in a presentation at the LENA convention this week."

Beth nodded. Then her eyes met Tom's and she suddenly lowered her head and giggled. She tried to look at him again, but she was unable to stop laughing. She turned her face toward the front of the room. Then she nodded and stood. Tom glanced toward the front and saw Miss Stinneman motioning for Beth to come. Beth gave them a quick wave and walked forward.

"What was she so tickled about?" Clair asked.

"Well, I was..." Tom paused and shook his head. "It's a long story. I'll tell you later."

The students had all risen from the floor and were taking their places at their desks. Jennifer looked at her parents now for the first time, and sheepishly raised her hand beside her face and waved her fingers. When the children were all seated, Miss Stinneman took Beth by the arm and presented her to them.

"We have a special visitor today, class. This is Nurse Beth. She has come from the hospital to tell us some very important things. So I want you to give her your very best attention."

The teacher patted Beth on the arm and left her standing alone before the class. Beth beamed and began talking to the students.

Miss Stinneman walked briskly to the back of the room and sat across from Tom and Clair. "Now, then, we'll have time to talk. I'm so pleased you allowed Jennifer to come into the program this semester, Mrs. Kerzig. She's a bright addition to the class." She turned to Tom. "I don't know how much you know about the LENA program, Mr. Kerzig—"

"I teach English to a class of seniors in the program," Tom said. "In fact, your presenter is one of my students."

"Oh?" She sat back and smiled broadly. "Well, then, I certainly don't have to tell you about its goals, do I?"

"Well, actually I've just taken another teacher's place temporarily. I've worked with the class for only a few weeks. And I'm afraid my involvement has raised some concerns in my mind, Miss Stinneman...ah...Colleen."

"Tom mentioned a couple of those things to me, Colleen," Clair added. "Jennifer described an exercise to Tom that put forth a situational justification for telling a lie."

"Oh, that must have been the Santa Claus exercise," Miss Stinneman said.

"That was part of it," Tom said.

"Of course," Miss Stinneman continued. "That was part of a values clarification unit. I wouldn't be concerned about that at all. Jennifer handled the complexity of the issues extremely well. The exercise is designed, of course, to help children become more responsible in what they say and do. It's very effective."

"There's another thing that really surprised me," Tom said. "Jennifer seems to know a lot about Hindu meditation, and I wondered about that. But then I saw what you had them doing just a few minutes ago."

"Oh... That?"

"Jennifer even knows about the cakras," Tom continued. "They're the psychic centers in the body, according to some mystical religions."

"Oh, well, Mr. Kerzig, we don't use the word *Hindu*, of course." Miss Stinneman chuckled. "And this certainly isn't a mystical or religious exercise. This is a *public* school, you know. No, we're just using some of the helpful concepts. Notice how quiet and attentive the children are. And their concentration powers have increased dramatically. You may even have noticed it at home."

"Well, I haven't noticed that so much," Clair said. "I have noticed that Jennifer has become, perhaps..." Clair paused momentarily and glanced toward Tom. "Well, perhaps more distant."

"Ah! That's the initial outward manifestation, Mrs. Kerzig. She's becoming more *contemplative*. That's the word. That's a wonderful sign!"

"And these..." Tom motioned toward the astrological and psychic books and the Ouija board. "What's the reason for these?"

"Motivation," Miss Stinneman said. "You'd be amazed at how excited the children get as they read of the adventures of Psychic Susie. And then, during our meditation time, they project themselves into the adventures. They share them and help each other find the special meaning behind their journeys. It's a wonderful motivational tool!"

The children in the classroom giggled suddenly and Tom looked up to see what had happened. Beth was nodding and had a big smile on her face.

"Oh, they're just—"

Tom motioned for the teacher to be silent. He leaned forward slightly as he listened to what Beth was saying.

"No, really, boys and girls. I know you're only in the third grade now, but in just six years you'll be in high school. You have to start thinking about your bodies, because as you grow they'll become more and more beautiful. And when that happens, the boys will be looking at the girls and the girls will be looking at the boys. And there's nothing wrong with that. You'll experience a lot of wonderful feelings because of your bodies."

"Well..." Miss Stinneman laughed nervously. "I wonder what..."

"I want you to think about that for me," Beth continued, "because next week you'll have another special visitor. And he'll help you draw some neat pictures of each other, so that you'll understand more about your bodies. Won't that be fun?"

"I believe she's finished," Miss Stinneman whispered. "Excuse me." She stood and walked quickly to the front of the room. "Well, boys and girls, wasn't it wonderful for Nurse Beth to visit us today? What do you think?" She clapped her hands, and the children joined her in applauding Beth.

Beth waved to the students and walked to the rear of the room. She giggled lightly as she passed Tom and Clair, waved, and stepped quickly out the back door.

"Now, boys and girls, we're about to go into our quiet time. I want you all to think for a minute about what you want to share and then come forward and form a circle."

The students sat forward quietly and placed their heads down on their arms. One by one, they stood from their desks, walked to the front of the room, and sat on the floor. Miss Stinneman tapped Jennifer lightly on the shoulder and motioned for her to follow. Jennifer rose, and the two of them came back to where Tom and Clair sat.

"I thought you'd want to say hello to Jennifer," Miss Stinneman said.

"Hi, Jennifer," Clair and Tom said in unison. Tom reached out to embrace her, but she pulled back.

"A little embarrassed in class, you know," Miss Stinneman said.

"We just came to see what you're doing in school," Clair said.

"I know." Jennifer glanced back toward the front of the room, where most of the students were now sitting. "I need to go now." She started to leave, but then she turned back and spoke haltingly. "You can't stay now. We're having our secret circle." She looked at them tentatively for a moment. Then she turned, ran quickly to the front of the room, and sat on the floor in the circle which had now formed.

"She's right," Miss Stinneman said. "This is our private time."

"Secret circle?" Clair repeated.

"Yes." Miss Stinneman looked at Tom. "Mr. Kerzig, you certainly know what that is."

"I don't think I've..."

"It's an important exercise in building the child's self-confidence," she explained. "Children must know there is some place they can go and bring their most private thoughts and fears, share them with others who will never tell. It creates a wonderful sense of security and an awareness that their feelings are all right...that *they* are all right." She glanced toward the front of the room, where all of the children now sat quietly in a circle on the floor. She turned back and patted Clair on the hand. "Thank you so much for coming. Visit us again, sometime, won't you?"

Tom stood up and waited for Clair to join him. Then

the two of them walked quietly out of the classroom.

"What do you think, Clair?"

"I don't know. Her activities seem a little strange. But the students seem so responsive. And they're so well-behaved. Jennifer seems happy."

"And what about Beth's little presentation?"

"She's *your* student," Clair scolded.

"The cross-age tutoring is not my project."

"Well, Colleen seemed to realize she'd gone a little too far. She'll probably talk to her."

Tom glanced back at the closed door, his eyes scanning aimlessly across the form of the seven. "If it was just what we saw today. But I've had my head filled with these things. Over and over and over again."

Clair looked at the closed door and stood silently for a moment, as though looking through it. "I didn't particularly like the idea of the secret circle." She shook her head. "No. I didn't like it at all! The idea of Jennifer holding any kind of secrets from me really sets me off!"

Tom nodded slowly.

"But, look, Tom, in your business and in mine, certainly, there are times when kids ought to be able to tell private things to someone besides their parents. I mean, look at the cases of sexual abuse and—"

"In a secret circle with their other classmates?"

"No...no, of course not." She glanced at her watch. "I've got to get back to work."

They began walking back toward the office, across the lush grass. It felt good to Tom to be with Clair today. It was as though...as though nothing had happened between them.

"Clair...Jennifer needs us," he said. "She needs us to be together."

Clair stopped walking and looked up at him. The word "no" appeared to form on her lips. It was what he expected. Instead, her eyes met his in silence for a brief moment. She looked plaintively back toward the classroom.

"Jennifer and I are going to spend next weekend with my parents," she said without looking back. "I haven't seen them since the separation. I thought..." She looked back toward him. "I want to try to sort things out."

"That's good. I'm glad." But Tom's heart was racing. "And after... Maybe we could talk."

Clair nodded slowly. "Jennifer's been asking..."

"What?"

"Maybe you could come to dinner sometime."

"Yes."

"When would you—"

"Whenever you say," he replied quickly to the incomplete question.

"Well...maybe Wednesday."

"Yes. I'd like that."

"All right. Wednesday," she concluded with a sigh. Then she looked back toward the classroom and rubbed her hands slowly together. "I wonder what secrets she has."

Tom was ecstatic about the possibility that Clair might finally be coming around. But his concern over Jennifer clouded his joy. He let his eyes follow the pentagonal row of buildings, and he imagined children in every classroom, huddled in circles, sharing their private thoughts and fears. Things for no one else to know...just the teachers and the other students. A slight breeze rose and brushed through the branches of a pine tree in the center of the yard. It sounded like the silent whispers of a thousand children.

27

Tom was accustomed to seeing the church parking lot full and the area surrounding the large auditorium teeming with people. But this was Saturday morning and the grounds were barren. Pastor Bentley had called Tom the night before to tell him he had read Joni's paper. He had seemed excited and asked Tom to meet with him this morning.

No one was in the small waiting room, but the door to Pastor Bentley's office was open. Tom could hear voices inside. He stepped up to the doorway and tapped lightly on the frame. The voices halted, and in a moment Pastor Bentley appeared in the doorway.

"Good morning, Tommy! Come in. Come in."

Pastor Bentley ushered Tom into the small office. Another person was there, seated before the desk—a short muscular man with a crew cut. It was Mike Underwood.

"I didn't tell you last night that Mike would be here," Pastor Bentley said. "But you two know each other, of course."

Both men nodded, and Tom sat down beside Mike while Pastor Bentley dropped into the chair behind his desk.

"I've been talking to Mike about Joni's participation in the school club that he sponsors," Pastor Bentley said. "I'm sure you know about that, too."

"Club?" Tom shook his head.

"Christian Perspectives Club," Mike said.

"Oh, yes. Charlie Shaeffer mentioned that to me," Tom said. "Does it meet on campus?"

"Are you kidding?" Mike laughed. "When we first started the club, I asked Walt if I could meet with the kids in my room after school or some evening. He pulled out a big legal book and started quoting passages about the separation of church and state."

"A complete misinterpretation of the law," Pastor Bentley said.

"Well, Walt is always a bit gun-shy on that issue," Tom said.

"Yeah," Mike agreed. "So, we just meet at members' houses on a rotating basis."

"And Joni was a member of the club?" Tom asked.

"Yeah."

"That's why I called Mike," Pastor Bentley said. "When Lloyd and Sally told me he sponsored the club, well, I wanted to talk to him to see what he thought."

"I've been searching my mind for an explanation for the last two weeks myself," Mike said. "So when Pastor Bentley called, I was relieved to find out I wasn't the only one who wasn't taking her death for granted."

"They'd had a club meeting just the night before, Tommy. Mike says there's no way, no *way* Joni was suicidal, or even depressed about..." He stopped abruptly and turned to Mike. "I'm sorry, Mike. I should let you tell this."

"That's fine, Pastor. I couldn't have said it better."

"How often do you meet?" Tom asked.

"Once a month."

Once a month. And Mike had formed that definite an impression. But what of that? Tom had worked with her for only two days. Still, the club atmosphere, and those around her... "Club?" he mumbled absently. He remembered the group he was to meet with next Tuesday. "Was Joni a member of any other club on campus?"

"Like..."

"The Futures Club."

"Oh, *that* one? Absolutely not! Why do you ask?"

"I'm taking over the supervision of that for Bonnie," Tom said. "I'm meeting with the members Tuesday night, and I just wondered... I don't even know anything about it. When I first heard about it, I thought it had to do with stocks and bonds."

"Stocks and bonds?" Mike laughed loudly.

"That's the reaction I got when I mentioned it before."

"No, that's a club that's...well..." Mike leaned forward and placed his right hand on one corner of Pastor Bentley's desk. "If the Christian Perspectives Club is here..." he stretched his arms wide and placed his left hand near the other corner, "...the Futures Club is here."

"In terms of..."

"In terms of their views of life," Mike said. "The Futures Club gave Bonnie the opportunity to take the concepts of the LENA program a few steps further. They do things that are... Well, whenever I talked to Bonnie about it, she told me the kids in that club were on the *cutting edge* of the new breed of man. I don't want to prejudice you too much. Let me know what you think after you've had a chance to see for yourself on Tuesday night."

"Okay."

"Incidentally... *They do* meet on campus, don't they?"

"Yes. In Bonnie's room. Why?"

Mike looked at Pastor Bentley, and the two of them chuckled.

"Mike and I were just talking about the restrictions on religious affiliations," Pastor Bentley said. "A lot of things are going on in our schools, even in the classrooms, that convey a religious message of some sort—New Age, Eastern religions, even occult beliefs. But if Christianity ever pokes its head out, it gets chopped off."

Tom recalled his meeting with Jennifer's teacher the day before and the question he raised about the meditation activity. "They'll say, of course, that they're not promoting any religious notions," he said. "Just using some of the helpful concepts."

"A rose by any other name..." Pastor Bentley quoted.

"...still has thorns," Mike concluded.

"And that brings us to the reason I asked you to come in this morning, Tommy." Pastor Bentley opened his center drawer, pulled out the copy of Joni's composition, and set it on the desk.

Tom and Mike scooted their chairs closer to the desk. Tom looked at the paper. Sections of it were highlighted in bright yellow and notes were scribbled in the margin.

"I hope this was mine to keep," Pastor Bentley said. "I'm afraid I've marked it up quite a bit."

"Sure."

"You know, when you first mentioned the paper to me, you said that it was very dark," Pastor Bentley said. "Perhaps even satanic."

"Well, some of the images..."

"In one respect you were right," Pastor Bentley went on. "Satan plays a big part in this paper. He's the caller...the tempter...the dark master." Pastor Bentley turned the paper around so Tom and Mike could read it, and he pointed to sections of it with his pen as he read upside down. "But Joni sure knew her Bible. Look at this—'great swelling words, flattering.' That's from the book of Jude. And here—'warring against the law of my mind.' That's the flesh and the spirit reference from Romans 7:23."

"But she does return to the out-of-body assignment here," Tom pointed to a highlighted section, "when she mentions flying away in a dream."

"But that's right out of Job," Pastor Bentley said. "It refers to the short-lived triumph of the wicked. And, remember, Paul warned the Ephesians not to walk the way of the rest of the Gentiles."

Tom glanced sheepishly between Mike and Pastor Bentley. He had no knowledge of the Bible passage. "I...ah..."

"They were alienated from God because their understanding was darkened," Pastor Bentley explained. "And here," he pointed, "the shadow places a veil over her window. And then," he turned the page and pointed to another highlighted section, "creates his own false light."

"What about the reference to wiping the scum from the trees and making a carpet of it?" Tom questioned.

"Ezekiel," Pastor Bentley said. " 'Woe to the bloody city, to the pot whose scum is in it, and whose scum is not gone from it!' "

"Babylon," Mike muttered.

Pastor Bentley turned to the next page. "Look at the tempting, the urging. The book of 2 Peter warns about the swelling words of emptiness—the promise of a corrupt liberty."

"Look at this," Mike said, pointing. "The dark master says her star is greater than..."

"Isaiah 14:13," Pastor Bentley said. " 'I will exalt my throne above the stars of God.' "

"That's the story of our generation," Mike murmured.

"Isaiah also warns about the excitement from hell and the stirring of the dead."

"But here..." Tom turned to the next page and nodded as he saw that the reference he had questioned was highlighted.

"Yes. That strange grisly reference to the vomit."

"Job, Proverbs, and 2 Peter," Pastor Bentley said. "The attempt to gain eternal sustenance from our own worldly creations. And once we take that fatal step, our only recourse is to go back again and again and again."

" 'And replenish ourselves from the filth of ourselves,' " Tom quoted from Joni's paper.

"The lie of the self-made man," Mike said. "Finding God within yourself."

Tom flipped to the front page, glanced at the title, and then turned to the last page. "But the assignment was to write about an out-of-body experience."

"Exactly," Pastor Bentley said. "Joni knew the promise of Romans 12:5. We are one body in Christ. But she was also aware of the terrible temptations of the world."

" 'It's easy to have an out-of-body experience,' " Mike quoted.

" 'Deceptively easy,' " Tom concluded.

Pastor Bentley nodded excitedly. "And I only touched on a few references. The paper is loaded with biblical references. I'll tell you, that girl was bright! She would have been quite a Bible scholar—" Pastor Bentley stopped abruptly, sat back, and placed his hand over his face as the tears began to fall. "No one's death has ever given me this much trauma. It's the inconclusiveness, or..." He wiped his face with his hand, picked up the paper, and set it to the side of his desk. "I'm all right. I'm just so glad you're both here. I think you know how I feel."

"Yes." Tom took the paper again and opened it to the last page. "But even with the window open to the light, the dark master beckons."

"The call of the world is powerful," Pastor Bentley said.

"And the star is distant, beyond her grasp?" Tom questioned.

"Perhaps," Pastor Bentley mumbled. "But what..."

"I don't know..." The other reference still hung there, unresolved. The note: "Death—The Penultimate Cakra." Perhaps the veil was still drawn and the final recognition just out of reach. But how more final—the capsules, the needle.

"Suppose..." Tom mumbled. "Suppose she followed the beckoning."

"No." Pastor Bentley shook his head rapidly.

"The biblical references are clear, I know," Tom said. "But suppose this paper is a description of the terrible forces pushing *her* to...to follow."

"Not Joni," Mike said.

"What about a sudden change in her personality?"

"That's a story-book explanation," Mike answered.

Tom shook his head slowly. "I experienced it."

"What are you talking about?" Pastor Bentley asked.

Mike smiled. "Oh, I'll bet you're referring to your little LSD trip, aren't you?"

"You heard about it?"

"Things like that get around," Mike said.

"LSD?" Pastor Bentley's eyes were wide.

"It was an accident, a trick," Tom reassured Pastor Bentley. "Someone gave it to me without my knowing."

"That's terrible!"

"Yeah, but at least now I can relate," Tom said. "The distortion of reality was so acute, that..." Tom shook his head.

"But do you think you could have done anything so drastic as to give yourself a lethal shot of heroin?" Mike asked.

"I don't know." Tom recalled briefly the rush of feelings and images he experienced while under the influence of the drug. Things he would never have thought of doing, consciously, at least. But placing an injection in his arm... And where would he have gotten it? Where would Joni have gotten it? "I don't know, Mike. I just don't know."

"Well, I think you're making it too complicated, Tommy," Pastor Bentley said. "Joni knew what was right and what was wrong. She was strong in the Word. She would have followed the right course, regardless of any chemical influence."

"When I'm sitting here, talking with you, I can easily agree," Tom said. "The dichotomy is so clear—light and dark, good and evil, life and...death. I believe that, and I want to follow that belief. But the world is a lot less clear-cut."

"Especially in the LENA program," Mike said.

"Yes, that's true," Tom agreed. "And I just had a three-day immersion of that. No right or wrong. No absolutes."

"You can see why we didn't want any part of it," Mike said. "The math teachers, I mean."

"Yeah. Ed Staley would sure like you to get into it, though."

"Oh, yes. His fifty-three-tone scale," Mike said. "He told me about it. Hey, we could handle that and give him all the mathematical backing he wants...for any tonal arrangement. But that's not the issue. The issue is the source of knowledge—the source of truth."

Pastor Bentley sat forward, suddenly interested. "Explain what you mean by that, Mike."

"Well Ed would like to... And it's not just Ed, it's the whole thrust of the program," Mike explained. "But I'll use Ed as an example. He would like to have the students use some complex tool—like the fifty-three-tone scale—to project creative arrangements with no rules, no direction, no guidance. Then he would like our people to construct mathematical principles to explain their creations. He believes each person should be able to create rules to match his own view of reality."

"Yes!" Pastor Bentley clenched his fists and pounded them on the desk. "That's exactly where the world's headed! The only truth is the truth from within. Why can't they see how false that premise is?"

"Because it comes from me, and what comes from me must be good," Tom mumbled.

"What's that from?" Mike asked.

"Oh, just the overall tenor of the convention. But maybe one good thing came out of that three days. I think Stu is beginning to realize that the activities need to be screened very carefully."

"Stu..." Pastor Bentley looked first at Tom and then at Mike.

"Stu Welbourne," Mike said. "He's the chairman of the social science department at school."

"And also the LENA project chair," Tom added.

"Stu is the most stable member of the group," Mike said. "But he's always been supportive of the program."

"And he still is," Tom said. "He's just spending a lot more time studying his Tocqueville."

"Tocqueville?" Mike squinted and frowned.

"Of course," Pastor Bentley said. "That's very appropriate."

Tom smiled and looked at Pastor Bentley. "And most recently, his prediction about virtuous materialism."

"Yes. People becoming so absorbed in the pursuit of pleasures that are allowed," Pastor Bentley said.

"So you've read him, too, then?" Tom asked.

"Oh, yes. He had some brilliant perceptions," Pastor Bentley said. "And he also predicted one element that allowed us to get to that point." Pastor Bentley raised his finger, smiled, and rose from his chair. He stepped over to a low book shelf, squatted, and began searching through the titles. "He predicted that we would allow it, and he was right."

"We..."

"The people...society...and, most particularly, the church." Pastor Bentley pulled a single volume from the shelf. Then he moved back to the desk, sat, and placed the book before him. It was a larger edition of the book Stu had referred to. Several small yellow tabs projected from sections throughout the book. Pastor Bentley squinted at tiny notations on the tabs. "Ah, here it is." He placed his finger at the point of one of the tabs and pulled the book open.

"Why..." Tom began.

"Why am I studying the works of a nineteenth-century historian?" Pastor Bentley interrupted. "Probably for the same reason as your friend Stu. I want to try to get a better understanding of why our society is so embroiled in the self-serving mode. And, more particularly, why our churches haven't done more to combat it. And Tocqueville had some very interesting notions. Listen..." Pastor Bentley placed his finger on the page and read several phrases haltingly. " 'The more conditions of men are equalized...the more important it is for religions...not needlessly to run counter to the ideas which generally prevail.' " Pastor Bentley looked up and shook his head. "But the ideas which generally prevail lately are those which we must run counter to, if we are to be true to the Word of God."

"But there are many successful religions that *don't* run counter to them," Mike said.

"Ah!" Pastor Bentley turned the page and pointed to another section. "You said a mouthful, Mike!" He read from the section. " 'By respecting all democratic tendencies not absolutely contrary to herself, and by making use of several of them for her own purposes, religion sustains an advantageous struggle with that spirit of individual independence which is her most dangerous antagonist.' "

"And without absolutes..." Mike began.

"There can be nothing absolutely contrary," Pastor Bentley concluded. "Too many of my colleagues find themselves in that position today. They have given way on so many of what they term insignificant aspects of the truth, that they are in a spiral of acceptance leading straight to apostasy."

"How do we stop the spiral?" Mike asked.

"The spirit of individual independence doesn't have to be antagonistic to religious truth," Pastor Bentley said. "There is a greater freedom—a freedom that's based on absolutes."

"Yes," Mike agreed.

"But..." Pastor Bentley snapped the book shut. "This could lead into a lengthy philosophical discussion, couldn't it? And, Mike, I know you have another appointment."

Mike glanced at the clock on the wall and then stood. "That's right. I appreciate your inviting me today."

Tom and Pastor Bentley both stood and the three men exchanged handshakes.

"My pleasure." Pastor Bentley stepped quickly to the door and opened it.

Mike waved and left the room.

"Thanks, this has really been helpful—" Tom began.

Pastor Bentley halted him at the doorway. "How's everything else going, Tommy?" he asked with a smile.

"Everything else?" A brief recollection of yesterday's meeting with Clair crossed Tom's mind, and he beamed as he grasped Pastor Bentley's arm. "Everything else is going much better! I think Clair may finally be coming to her senses."

Pastor Bentley smiled and nodded.

"I'm having dinner with her Wednesday night."

"That's great! When she called to talk to me on Thursday, I prayed that things would work out."

Tom let his hand drop slowly. "She called you?"

Pastor Bentley looked surprised. "Yes, well, I assumed she'd told you."

"No."

"I told her I'd be available at any time to help you work out your differences."

Pastor Bentley's statement cast Tom into a momentary state of confusion. He couldn't imagine Clair calling Pastor Bentley to talk about their problems. He thought their discussion Sunday had caused the change in her attitude. "Well, sure," he said absently. "Whatever it takes to make her happy."

Pastor Bentley frowned and leaned against the door jamb. "You know, it's probably a two-way street."

Tom placed his hand on the opposite doorjamb and gave Pastor Bentley a suspicious look. "I have a feeling Clair told you about our conversation after the meeting at church last Sunday night."

"Yes."

"Did she tell you she accused me of being *self-righteous?*"

Pastor Bentley chuckled lightly. "Yes. Yes, she did."

Tom shook his head. "Where did she get an idea like that?"

Pastor Bentley looked at Tom for a long moment. Then he held both hands out, palms up. One hand then closed into a fist. "I think she sees you two this way," he said slowly.

"Which one am I?" Tom asked.

Pastor Bentley raised the fist slightly.

"Closed?"

Pastor Bentley continued speaking without moving his hands. "I have to admit that I wasn't paying enough attention five years ago to notice. But this..." He jerked the fist slightly. "...is an easy posture to fall into—especially for us men. We want to be strong, dependable."

"Is there anything wrong with that?"

"Clair told me she was searching for answers then."

"Yeah, she told me all that."

Pastor Bentley raised the open palm. "So she was like this—an open vessel."

Tom laughed lightly. "That's a term one of the presenters at the LENA convention used. It was on the last day, and she really made it sound dramatic. Something about awakening and renewal. Oh, yes. Now I remember: 'And now you stand as empty vessels, waiting to be filled with the truth of your potential.' "

"An empty vessel can be filled with anything that's available," Pastor Bentley said.

Perspiration began to form on Tom's forehead, and he dropped his hand to his side. "What am I supposed to do?"

"The hardest thing." Pastor Bentley raised the fist toward Tom. "And that is to realize that even a closed fist is an empty vessel." He pried the fingers of the fist open and pointed to the interior. "Being closed doesn't make it full."

Tom forced his eyes away from Pastor Bentley's hands. "There are just so many harmful influences. I blame Clair's college courses for a lot of her problems. And now, some of the things Jennifer is being exposed to..."

"Do you remember what you told me a little while ago when I asked why the New Age proponents can't see how false their premise is?" Pastor Bentley continued.

"I...ah...I don't ..."

"You said, 'Because it comes from me, and what comes from me must be good,' " Pastor Bentley reminded him.

"Well, I wasn't talking about..."

Pastor Bentley patted him on the arm. "Think about it, Tommy." He ushered him slowly out the door. "You two come in whenever you want!"

"Sure. Thanks." Tom waved weakly and turned as Pastor Bentley closed the door behind him. A faint nausea crept over him and he began walking briskly toward the parking lot to counteract its effects. He couldn't imagine what Clair told Pastor Bentley to make him say the things he did. He had felt so exhilarated and optimistic yesterday. But now, he felt suddenly as though things were slipping from his grasp again.

Tom breathed deeply and let the cool air fill his lungs. There was too much to do to worry about that now. The convention had put him behind in his preparation. But then, tomorrow was Sunday. He could spend all day getting ready for next week.

28

On Tuesday night dark clouds covered the sky and the fresh smell of an early spring rain filled the air. Tom hurried through the light sprinkles and ran into the classroom building. In the dimly lit corridor ahead he could barely make out the form of an object moving toward him. As the distance between them diminished, he recognized the custodian, Larry, pushing his cleaning cart. Larry squinted and then smiled as he recognized him.

"Some of the kids are already here for the meeting, so I let them in," Larry said.

"Oh?" Tom was surprised that Larry would open the classroom without a teacher present.

"Yeah." The smile disappeared from Larry's face. "Miss Teague always had me do that if the kids got here before she did. I...I hope that's okay."

"Well...yeah. That's all right for tonight, Larry."

Larry raised his eyebrows and let a quick breath pass through his lips. "That's good! Have a nice evening, Mr. Kerzig."

The custodian pushed his cart on down the corridor. Tom continued toward the bright light emanating from the open door to Bonnie's room. When he entered the room, he saw that the desks were pushed back to provide a large open space. Several people sat in a roughly defined circle on the floor, talking softly to one another. They were all students from his first-period class: Mary Ann, Jim, Ed, Megan, Tina, Jason, and Mike. They acknowledged him silently as he entered and then continued with their conversations.

Tom noticed that the door to the adjacent department office was open. He glanced into the room and saw Mark Banazech take some items out of the large bottom drawer, close the drawer, and then lock it. Tom stepped inside.

Mark looked up abruptly and shoved the key into his pocket. "Oh, hi, Mr. Kerzig. This is where we keep all our club stuff. Bonnie let me have the key, since I'm always the one that gets everything set up."

Tom pointed to the items Mark was holding. "Have those been in here since last month's meeting?"

"Sure. Like I said, this is where we keep all our club stuff." Mark brushed past Tom and left the office.

Tom knew that wasn't the case. The drawer was empty and unlocked when he, Joe, and Inspector Gruber were last in here. Did Mark lie intentionally? And why did he have a key? Tom followed Mark out and closed the door behind him. He watched as Mark placed the items on a table at the front of the classroom; two large, satiny fabric items—one purple and one white, a stack of small booklets, two long candles in brass holders, a matching small brass vessel, several colorful crystals, and some kind of electronic device shaped like a pyramid. After placing the items, he glanced briefly at Tom and chuckled.

Tom heard a noise at the door and looked up to see Frank Ziderly and Beth Crawford walk quickly in. Beth waved at him and directed Frank over to where he stood.

"Mr. Kerzig, I didn't expect to see you here." She laughed nervously. "I guess I did, I just didn't think about it." Beth tugged lightly on Frank's shirt sleeve. "Frank, guess what. In one of my cross-age assignments I'm working with Mr. Kerzig's daughter's class."

"Oh, yeah?" Frank said absently.

"Are these all the club members?" Tom asked, pointing to the group.

"This is my first night," Beth said, "so I don't—"

"Yeah," Frank said. "This is it."

"I'm just joining tonight." Beth smiled broadly and placed both hands on Frank's arm. "Frank's been after me to do it since the first of the year, but I just kept putting it off."

"Let's go." Frank, motioned with his head.

Frank and Beth joined the others on the floor. The group was now nearly circular, except for a gap toward the front of the classroom. Mark approached the group, holding the pyramidal object, which now trailed a long extension cord. He placed the object in the center of the circle. Then he got the stack of books and the pile of crystals from the table, returned with them, and sat in the gap. He raised his arms, with his palms out, and the others followed suit. Then they placed their palms together.

"We are the power in our lives," Mark said.

"We are the power in our lives," the group responded in unison.

"We are the leaders of the new age," Mark said loudly.

"We are the leaders of the new age," chanted the others.

They let their fingers fall into tight handclasps. They held the clasp for a moment. Then they emitted a loud shout, separated their hands, and lowered their arms. Mark picked up the crystals and passed them to his left. Each person took a crystal and passed the remaining ones to the left. One remaining crystal found its way back to Mark. He placed it in the palm of his hand, stared at it for a moment, and then closed his fingers over it. He looked across the circle to where Beth sat.

"Beth, welcome to the group," Mark said. "Frank tells

me you've decided to join our elite club."

Beth smiled and nodded.

"You'll never be sorry. Did Frank tell you about the installation ceremony?"

Beth shrugged and looked at Frank. "Well, a little."

"We'll have that a little later in the meeting." Mark looked back at Tom who still stood near the door. "Mr. Kerzig, do you want to join our circle? Bonnie always does."

"No, thanks. I'll just watch from here." Tom stepped over to the desk and sat quietly in a chair next to it.

Mark watched him for a few moments and then turned back to the group. "Now, even though Bonnie isn't here, we'll follow the same order of business. Remember, the first thing we do is recite from the Manifesto."

"What?" Tom sat forward suddenly in his chair at the sound of this word.

"Not the Communist Manifesto, Mr. Kerzig. The Humanist Manifesto."

The members of the group laughed spontaneously.

"You know what that is, don't you?" Mark asked.

"Oh, yeah, sure." Tom knew what it was, but he didn't know that much about it. Actually there were two. The first Humanist Manifesto was a philosophical statement of beliefs put forth by a group of intellectuals in 1933. It was an influential force in the development of educational theory in the mid-twentieth century. The second Humanist Manifesto was proposed and adopted by another group of philosophers and academic leaders in 1973. Tom knew that it, too, was a heavily utilized document in the development of current educational theory. His college professors had made frequent reference to it, but he had never actually seen the document.

"Here, Mr. Kerzig." Mark held up one of the small booklets and tossed it.

Tom reached out with one hand and caught it.

"Nice reflexes." Mark took a booklet himself and passed the stack to the others in the circle. "Now, we've already studied the first five tenets," Mark said to the group. "We'll recite those first and then go on to the sixth. Let's see..." His eyes moved slowly around the circle. "Jim, why don't you take number one? Mary Ann—two, Megan—three, Ed—four, and Tina—five."

The seated students shuffled to a more erect position and opened the booklets. Then Jim looked up and waited for Mark's nod.

"Tenet number one—religion," Jim began. " 'We believe that traditional dogmatic or authoritarian religions that place revelation, God, ritual, or creed above human needs and experience do a disservice to the human species. We find insufficient evidence for belief in the existence of a supernatural: it is either meaningless or irrelevant to the question of the survival and fulfillment of the human race. We can discover no divine purpose or providence for the human species. No deity will save us; we must save ourselves.' "

The rest of the group looked up with closed eyes and chanted in unison: "No deity will save us—we must save ourselves."

"Wait minute," Tom said. "Where are you finding that?"

"Number one," Mark said pointedly, his head cocked critically over his shoulder.

Tom flipped the pages rapidly to the first tenet. Surely that kind of language wouldn't have found itself into an educationally influential document like this. But there it was. Jim had read excerpts, but they were direct quotes from tenet number one. Tom felt suddenly guilty that he had not paid more careful attention to this document before. But it had always been alluded to in terms of general concepts, never by specific reference. Tom glanced briefly at the front cover. The booklet was distributed by the State Department of Education.

"People in the future will be a lot more humanistic," Mark went on. "I mean, we'll have to learn to get along with each other. That's all this means. Bonnie tells us that sometimes people do get upset with some of the language. I guess that's what you're thinking about, huh?"

"Yes, partly," Tom said.

"Bonnie talked about that when we learned this first tenet. She said we should just always say that religion isn't necessarily *bad*...it's just *irrevalent*."

"Irrelevant," Tom corrected under his breath. He had just corrected Mark on that mispronunciation yesterday. Oh, well, not now.

"Did you find it, Mr. Kerzig?" Mark asked with a thin smile on his face.

"Yes, I did."

Mark turned back to the group. "Okay, Mary Ann."

Mary Ann looked down at her book and quoted, "Tenet number two has to do with religion, also. 'Promises of immortal salvation or fear of eternal damnation are both illusory and harmful. They distract humans from present concerns, from self-actualization, and from rectifying social injustices.' "

The group chanted with closed eyes, "Promises of salvation and damnation are harmful."

"Tenet number three—ethics," Megan began. " 'Moral values derive their source from human experience. Ethics is autonomous and situational, needing no theological or ideological sanction. Ethics stems from human need and interest. To deny this distorts the whole basis of life. Human life has meaning because we create and develop our futures. Happiness and the creative realization of human needs and desires, individually and in shared enjoyment, are continuous themes of humanism. We strive for the good life, here and now.' "

The group responded in unison, "Moral values derive their source from human experience—we strive for the good life, here and now."

Ed sat forward slightly as he read. "Tenet number four has to do with ethics, too. 'Reason and intelligence are the most effective instruments that humankind possesses. There is no substitute: neither faith nor passion suffices in itself.' "

The group chanted with closed eyes, "Reason and intelligence are the most effective instruments."

"Tenet number five has to do with the individual," Tina said. She began reading dramatically, " 'The preciousness and dignity of the individual person is a central humanist value. Individuals should be encouraged to realize their own creative talents and desires. We reject all religious, ideological, or moral codes that denigrate the individual, suppress freedom, dull intellect, dehumanize personality.' "

The group responded, "The preciousness of dignity of the individual is the central value."

"Okay, that's good," Mark said. "Now, I know that Bonnie wants us to memorize those, so let's be working on that." He glanced at his book. "Let's go on to tenet number six. It's on the individual, too. Here's what it says." He read from the book, stumbling occasionally on certain words, " 'In the area of sexuality, we believe that intolerant attitudes, often cultivated by orthodox religions and puritanical cultures, unduly repress sexual conduct. While we do not approve exploitive, denigrating forms of sexual expression, neither do we wish to prohibit, by law or social sanction, sexual behavior between consenting adults. The many varieties of sexual exploration should not in themselves be considered evil. Individuals should be permitted to express their sexual proclivities and pursue their life styles as they desire.' " Mark paused for a moment and then looked at the others. "Who'd like to tell us what that means to you?"

Tom shifted uncomfortably in his chair. He wasn't sure where Mark would lead this discussion.

The members of the group glanced at one another. Then Beth raised her hand.

"Go ahead, Beth," Mark said. "I'm glad you're jumping right in."

"Well, this fits in with what I started with my cross-age activity last week," Beth said. "I'll have to change a lot of the big words, of course, but it can help me show the kids how their sexuality is probably their most important gift, and how they shouldn't ever be ashamed of it."

Most important gift? Where was Beth going with that activity?

"Mike and I talk about this a lot," Jason said in a high raspy voice. "And you guys are really fabulous, but a lot of kids in school think we're weird. I think we should distribute copies of this to *everyone*. Don't you, Mike?"

Mike nodded. He was the smaller of the two boys, and his thin brown hair fell loosely over his gaunt face. It seemed to Tom that, just in the last three weeks, Mike had lost a great deal of weight. His complexion seemed pale and ashen. He smiled now, however, nodded again, and spoke with a firm voice. "Everyone," he agreed.

"Well..." Mark dropped his eyes to the book. "Bonnie usually does this, but since she's not here, let's go ahead and pick out a section for highlighting." He took a pen from his pocket and marked in his book as he spoke. "Why don't we mark this, 'Many varieties of sexual exploration...should be permitted'?"

"Couldn't we say, *encouraged*?" Jason suggested.

Mark glanced at his book briefly, then looked up at Jason. "That word isn't in here. I don't think we could get away with that."

Jason shrugged. "Have them rewrite the Manifesto."

The members of the group laughed. Mark nodded and closed his book. The other students closed their books and set them aside.

"It's time for our centering." Mark looked at Tom and pointed toward the light switch by the door. "Mr. Kerzig, would you turn off the lights?"

"The lights...yeah, I guess."

Tom stood slowly, walked to the door, and turned off the lights. The room was enveloped suddenly in total darkness. Then, from the space in the center of the group of students, shafts of colored light shot out randomly in a circular motion. The students' faces were obscured in the general absence of luminescence, but periodically, a colored shaft would strike them, and their features would appear momentarily as bizarre masks. The smell of incense, faint at first, then pungent, permeated the closed room and thrust its way into Tom's nostrils. Toward the top of the pyramidal object, a single light glowed, appearing to throb and circle as it changed from white to blue. Mark's large body was no more visible than those of the other students, but he spoke in a low and commanding voice.

"Let's have some good breathing first," he said. "In...and out. In...and out."

Tom sensed that the others were responding to Mark's direction, but it was difficult to tell. Soon, though, the regular, sustained sound of breathing filled the room.

"Let's do three mantras," Mark said.

Without further direction, the students took one additional breath and expelled it in the low, unison sound, "Ommm..."

Tom heard a slight shuffling, and thought he could detect Mark's figure standing, leaving briefly, and then returning as the group executed the second and third mantra. Mark's voice resounded again.

"I am the center of pure self-consciousness," he said.

"I am the center of pure self-consciousness," responded the group in unison.

"I am the center of my will to be and to act," he continued.

"I am the center of my will to be and to act," they responded.

"I can direct and harmonize all the processes of my body."

"I can direct and harmonize all the processes of my body."

"I have the power over laughter and tears."

"I have the power over laughter and tears."

"I have the power over love and hate."

"I have the power over love and hate."

"All of my feelings are good and pure," Mark said with growing emphasis.

"All of my feelings are good and pure," echoed the others.

"Only I can judge."

"Only I can judge."

"Only I can determine my destiny."

"Only I can determine my destiny."

"All things must work toward my self-fulfillment."

"All things must work toward my self-fulfillment."

After a moment of silence, another figure seemed to stand and move about silently. The group began emitting a low, continuously sounded mantra. It was almost impossible to detect where any members caught fresh breaths of air. Tom recalled what Mike Underwood had said the day before about the Futures Club. The kids in the club were on the "cutting edge" of the new breed of man, Bonnie had told him. But Pastor Bentley hadn't been surprised by the things going on in the schools, even in the classrooms—religious messages of some sort: New Age, Eastern religions, occult beliefs. Or all of the above. And now Mark was playing the part of the high priest.

The smell of sulfur momentarily overshadowed the incense, and two bright lights flickered above the colored laser shafts. The light was emanating from the two candles. Mark was clearly visible at one side of the circle. He was wearing the purple satin robe. Sitting, facing him was Beth, covered with the white robe. The two candles burned brightly, one to either side of them, and the rest of the students continued in their uninterrupted chant.

Mark reached forward and took Beth's hands in his and held them as he spoke to her. "All right, Beth. Now we're just going to sit real quietly for a couple of minutes."

Something about this scene seemed vaguely familiar. Then Tom remembered. This was like the routine he had demonstrated with Marla at the convention.

Mark stared unblinkingly into Beth's eyes for what seemed a full minute, as the soft humming continued. Finally, he spoke firmly, "If you want to be a member of the Futures Club, you have to show that you have the ability to pass through the levels of thinking and feeling that hamper most people. Can you do that, Beth?"

"I...I don't know," she mumbled.

"I'll help you," Mark said. "Keep hold of my hands. Can you feel them?"

"Yes."

"Now, you're growing in your awareness," he continued. "Reach out...reach out with your body. Feel your knees, nearly touching mine, but not quite. Can you feel it?"

"Yes, I think so."

"Now we begin," Mark said slowly. "Your being, your consciousness, your power...it's all centered in you, struggling to be free. You can feel it from where you sit. It's there, growing. It begins at the base of your spine. That is Shakti. She is restless energy. She is you, and she awaits within you to rise and be united with Shiva. I will be your Shiva tonight. Let me help you rise. Feel yourself stepping through the levels...through the cakras—your psychic centers. Can you feel your consciousness rising?"

"Yes...I think...I don't know..." Beth's voice was hesitant, wavering.

"Think of me, waiting at the top," Mark continued passionately. "Once there we will be joined in sensual union!"

Tom had heard enough. Club or no club, he wasn't about to be a part of this any longer. He rose suddenly, stepped to the door, and flipped the light switch. The room was suddenly flooded with light. Tom squinted to accommodate to the sudden change, and he saw the students doing likewise. A flurry of shouts and curses rose from the group.

"What did you do that for?" Mark demanded.

"Let's just say I think we've had enough club activity for tonight," Tom said. "I don't know where you're headed with this, Mark, but I don't approve of what I've seen so far, and I don't care to have it go any further."

The students jeered in protest.

"This is Bonnie's club," Mark spat. "This is what she has us do."

"Then I'll have to talk with Bonnie...with *Miss Teague*," he said pointedly, "and have her tell me exactly what the activities are supposed to be.

"That won't help us with tonight's meeting, will it?" Mark asked angrily.

"Mark!" Tom looked directly into Mark's eyes and spoke slowly and firmly. "Tonight's meeting is over. Let's put things away and go home."

Mark started to respond, but turned away and roughly pulled the satin robe over his head.

Frank cast a frown in Tom's direction and walked up to Mark. "Let me help you."

Mark and Frank began picking up the items from the floor. The other students walked slowly to the door. They paused briefly to grumble at Tom and then continued into the corridor. Beth slowly pulled the white satin robe over her head and handed it to Frank. Tom followed her out the door and stopped her.

"Beth?"

She turned her head toward him, but her eyes didn't seem to respond.

"Beth?" he repeated.

She blinked and a narrow smile appeared on her lips.

"Are you all right?"

"Sure, Mr. Kerzig, I'm fine."

"You don't have to do this, you know," he said.

"Do what?"

"All this installation nonsense. Think about it. Can't you see what he's trying to do?"

Beth shrugged. "There's nothing wrong here, Mr. Kerzig. Mark was just helping me find my way through my psychic centers. Bonnie used to talk about it in class all the time. I just never got into it as much...until now."

"It's deception."

Beth smiled and shook her head slowly. "You shouldn't

get so upset, Mr. Kerzig. There's nothing wrong here."

Mark and Frank stepped brusquely through the doorway and stood behind Beth.

"Everything's put away, Mr. Kerzig," Mark said petulantly. "Thank you."

"Are the others all gone?" Frank asked Beth.

"I think so."

"Well, listen," Mark began. "Let's go find some place private." He looked at Tom pointedly. "Off the school grounds." He took Beth's arm. "Just the three of us. We can still do it. We'll finish the installation ceremony."

"Didn't we finish?" Beth asked.

"No way!" Mark exclaimed. "We just began. We'll find some place...where we won't be bothered." He turned her away, and the three of them began walking down the corridor. "And we'll go up...level by level. It'll be great. You'll see. And then we'll reach the top, the greatest...the *penultimate cakra!*"

"No, Mark," Tom mumbled inaudibly. "The penultimate isn't the top. It's only the..."

A chill hit his spine like a knife.

The *penultimate cakra!* Joni's suicide message hadn't been a suicide note at all, Tom realized. Those weren't even Joni's words. Tom shuddered as a hideous image crossed his mind—Mark, standing beside Joni's lifeless body...pressing, one by one the keys on her typewriter...leaving the terse, inaccurate message.

The three students suddenly stopped in their movement away from him. Mark turned back slowly and looked at Tom. His face was expressionless, his eyes unblinking. Tom felt his own eyes drawn deeply into Mark's. There was something...a recognition, an awareness. Not just on Tom's part but on Mark's as well. Tom struggled not to reveal his thoughts, but he knew it was too late. Then, strangely, Mark's lips curved into a strange smile. It was the same frowning smile he had given his father at the convention. The boy's lips quivered slightly, then he turned and led the others down the corridor.

29

Sometimes knowledge comes as the result of a slow, deliberate accumulation of relevant information. Other times it comes as a sudden, blinding revelation. The latter was the case in Tom's encounter with Mark. One carelessly used phrase, and the recognition of Mark's involvement had flashed suddenly and incontestably into Tom's consciousness. He had no doubt that Mark had written the note found in Joni's typewriter. No other explanation made sense now. And if he had done that, he had also been involved somehow in her death—either as a witness...or as the perpetrator. But why? There had to be a reason. And Tom believed that, somehow, Bonnie held the key to the explanation.

Thick, dark clouds still filled the sky, but the light rain had stopped temporarily as Tom turned onto Bonnie's street. The crowded condominium complex loomed conspicuously above the adjacent dwellings. Tom drove slowly and squinted in an attempt to distinguish Bonnie's pink gates in the darkness. Then the rays of a nearby street lamp fell on the distinctively painted iron, and Tom pulled the car to a stop. He glanced at his watch. It was just after 8:00, so she should still be up.

Tom left the car, passed through the gate to the narrow porch, and rang the bell. He thought he heard the sound of rock music inside. He waited for a moment and then pressed the bell again. The music stopped. A bright light came on above him and the door opened, clinking to a stop against a heavy security chain. Bonnie's face appeared in the narrow opening. Her cheeks looked drawn and wrinkled, and there were dark circles under her eyes. She wasn't wearing her wig, and her three-week growth of hair lay haphazardly across her head. She was holding a glass in her hand, and the ice in it tinkled as she stepped back slightly, in recognition of him.

"Tom! This is a surprise." Bonnie brushed her hair back carelessly and smiled at him. "Scuse me. I'm not..." She pushed the door closed slightly, released the security chain, and then opened it just wide enough to expose her body. She wore a pink satin robe and heavy black slippers. The smell of alcohol was heavy on her breath. "As you can see, I'm not ready for guests. What are you up to, Tom?"

"I need to talk to you."

"Well, sure, but..." She glanced behind her. "Things are such a mess in here. I'm really embarrassed."

Tom looked over her shoulder into the dimly lit interior. "Are you alone?"

"Looking like this?" she blurted, pointing toward her face. "Are you kidding? Of course I'm alone!"

"Well, then come with me."

"I don't look good enough to go anywhere yet."

"Okay. We'll just take a drive."

Bonnie took a long drink from her glass. Her haggard cheeks rose in a coy smile. "My, aren't you being spontaneous tonight!"

"It's important, Bonnie."

Bonnie smiled and tapped her long fingernail against her glass. "Okay, okay. Just give me a minute to slip something on." She pointed to the porch as she began closing the door. "Do you mind? It's such a mess in here."

"No. That's fine."

"Be right out." She closed the door.

Tom folded his arms and leaned against the wall. It was better this way, after all. Too many things in Bonnie's condominium could distract her from responding to his questions. In the car she would have nothing to do but sit and talk to him. And another link might be made, as well. So many of the unresolved questions seemed to originate from the night of the accident. The recollections of the Valentine's Day dance were still vivid in Tom's mind. The loud, discordant music, the slowly circling spots of reflected white light against the darkness of the gymnasium. And Bonnie—her white dangling heart bobbing wildly above a tight-fitting red dress, her body moving sensuously to the beat of the music, and her short dark hair shifting with the motion of her head. And then she left. And if Joni was right, she wasn't alone.

Tom shivered slightly as a gust of wind rose up. A few sprinkles of rain began to fall and he pressed closer to the wall so that he was protected by the shallow, overhanging roof. Bonnie was just going to slip something on. He couldn't imagine what was taking so long. But then, the door finally opened and she stepped onto the porch. Tom saw she was wearing a wig again. But this was a different one. It was bright blonde and hung to the middle of her back. She removed her key from the door and turned to face him.

"Ta-da!" she sang, holding her arms out in a *how-do-I-look* gesture. Her face was covered with heavy makeup which concealed the wrinkles and the dark circles, and her lips were painted with bright red lipstick. She wore a long coat, but underneath it was a short, low-cut red dress. The smell of alcohol was still strong, mingling nauseatingly with the heavy aroma of perfume.

"Is that a new one?" Tom pointed to her wig.

"Yep, I've decided this is the new me. What do you think?"

Tom shrugged. "It's different."

Bonnie giggled and slapped him on the shoulder.

"It's starting to rain," Tom said. "Let's go."

They hurried to the car and got in. Tom started the engine and drove away from the curb, setting the windshield wipers for an intermittent swipe to clear the periodically falling drops.

"This is kind of exciting," Bonnie said. "I haven't gotten out much."

"I guess not."

"Oh! Tell me about the convention. Did you get to the two presentations I told you about?"

"Yeah."

"Well, what'd you think?"

"Helene Farris seems like a harmless little grandmother," Tom said. "Until she starts to speak."

Bonnie giggled. "I know what you mean. What did she talk about?"

"The continuing evolution of human intelligence."

"Oh, yes. She's brilliant on that topic."

"Well, she really wasn't, Bonnie. She has a very poor understanding of scientific theories. And everything was just...thrown out."

"Oh?"

"Her major claim to a physiological tie was her prediction that we'll all soon develop huge foreheads to accommodate our greatly expanded intelligence."

Bonnie brushed her fingers through the bangs of her wig. "Not right away, I hope." She laughed. "I know that some people criticize her for that, but Helene is getting at a greater truth. And she uses science as a vehicle to bring it out. What did you think her main concept was?"

"Probably that the free exercise of our instincts will lead

us to the full realization of our evolving intellectual skills," Tom said.

"Yes, yes, yes, yes!" Bonnie gushed. "Oh, I wish I could have heard her."

"I don't think she would have told you anything you don't already know or believe."

"But it helps to hear it repeated. Gets the juices going! How about Kurt?"

"Yeah, Quinlan gave a presentation on teaching students to deal with dilemmas," Tom said.

"Did he do the simulation with members of the audience?"

"Yes."

"Wasn't that great?" she asked.

"He put on quite a show, but..." He shook his head.

"Not your cup of tea?"

"His activities force people into risk-filled behavior. He compels you to construct a new value response, even when an existing value may be completely adequate. And his techniques were manipulative."

"Sometimes it takes a little manipulation to get people to recognize their own true values."

"What are the *true values?*" *Tom* asked.

"Whatever completely explains and supports your own inner sense of being. And risk is often the vehicle by which this is discovered. We feel a little glow inside and we externalize it as a wish, a desire. And acting on that desire may be risky. But we know we must act, because it comes from within us, and it can only be a manifestation of the truth of our existence."

Bonnie's response sounded just like the rhetoric used by the presenters at the convention. As she spoke the words seemed to float somehow past her thought process directly to her mouth. There was such a dichotomy between her words and the discussion he had Saturday with Pastor Bentley and Mike.

"Doesn't that make sense to you?" Bonnie asked. "Can't you see that the only way to find your true values is to discover your own personal truth?"

Tom was silent for a moment. Then he remembered a remark Pastor Bentley had made on Saturday. "That sounds like a religion, Bonnie."

She smiled faintly and shrugged. "Well, that's a point of terminology, and we don't get into that directly in the classroom, of course. But *inwardly*, and in activities outside the school, we *can* talk about the god-values."

"The god-values?" he mumbled.

"We *are* a part of the universal will. And naturally our inner truth is a part of the universal truth. And in that sense, our values become god-values. What we decide is good for us is also good for the total flow of humanity. Christians can think of it as a *Christ-Consciousness*. That symbol has a certain power and beauty..." Bonnie let her voice trail off as she gazed quietly out the window. Then she shifted in her seat and spoke excitedly. "What was the high point of the convention?"

"Well, for everyone else, it was probably my little trip," Tom said. "Someone slipped me some LSD during our last get-together on Wednesday."

"Oh!" Bonnie laughed impulsively and then placed her hand over her mouth. "That's radical! That's probably the only way you'd ever get to experience it. Do you see what I mean now about mind expansion?"

"It was bizarre, all right."

"But I mean, I'm sure you were okay, weren't you?"

"Eventually. Stu waited with me until I came out of it.

And so did Dr. Banazech."

Bonnie suddenly became quiet and a puzzled look fell on her face. "Frederick?"

"Yes. He was a presenter."

"I know."

"I heard him the first day. His ideas about hallucinogenic drugs are very much like yours, you know."

"Yes, well, I attended his presentation last year," Bonnie said.

"Just one presentation?" Then Tom remembered something Stu had told him. "Wasn't it more than that? Wasn't he the presenter at the seminar you attended five years ago?"

"What of it?" She gave him a quizzical look. "How did you know about that?"

Tom didn't answer but slowed the car and looked through the speckles of rain on the windshield at the sign on the road: LOOKOUT POINT. An arrow below the words pointed to the right. He turned the car up the narrow road.

"Where are you going?" Bonnie asked.

"I thought we'd go up to Lookout Point."

"What for?" Bonnie seemed suddenly tense.

"It'll be a good place to talk. Overlooking the city."

Bonnie curled back into the corner of the seat and ran her hand up and down the lapel of her coat.

Lookout Point was on a relatively small hill, near the center of town. But access to it was gained by means of a narrow, winding one-mile road. The rain was falling harder now, and Tom turned the windshield wipers to a more frequent interval. When they had driven about halfway, they approached a blinking warning light on the left side of the road. Tom slowed the car as they passed it. The light was on a temporary barricade which stretched between two sections of permanent guard rail at the edge of a small turnout. Heavy shrubbery commenced on either side of the barricade, leaving a gaping space beneath the blinking light.

"That's where you went over, isn't it?" Tom asked.

"Yes," Bonnie said softly.

"You're lucky that tree was just a few yards down. Otherwise, you might have gone all the way." Tom glanced at Bonnie who sat clutching her coat, her eyes closed. "Dangerous road."

"Yes."

Tom pressed down on the accelerator and the car lurched ahead. "I sat in for you at the Futures Club meeting tonight, Bonnie."

"You did?" Bonnie sat forward, suddenly more relaxed. She looked at the clock on the instrument panel. "It was only eight o'clock when you got to my place, wasn't it?"

"Yeah."

"The club meeting usually lasts for two hours. Did you leave early?"

"No. I called the meeting to a halt."

"What?" Bonnie sat up stiffly and frowned. "Why did you do that?"

"Some things were going on that I didn't approve of. That's one of the things I need to talk to you about."

"Well, what... I mean, we're a little more laid back there than in a regular classroom setting," Bonnie stammered. "But maybe the kids pushed it a little, since I wasn't there. What, ah...what did they do?"

"Well, the very first exercise gave me a start. But I guess I'd have a hard time quarreling with you about it, since it's from a state-approved supplement."

"Oh, you mean the Manifesto."

"Yes."

"Did they work on a new tenet?" she asked.

"The sixth. The one that talks about the approval of a wide variety of sexual expression."

"Ah, yes," she said with a coy smile. "What else?"

"And then the Yoga routine. The heavy breathing...the humming of the mantra..."

"That's a relaxation exercise, Tom," Bonnie said peevishly. "It just clears the mind so that the inner energy can flow freely."

"And the chanting, 'All of my feelings are good and pure'...'I have the power over laughter and tears'...'I have the power over love and hate.' What's the purpose for that?"

"You're such a stickler for absolutes, Tom, you should recognize the value in that," Bonnie said. "There is a duality of forces in each of us—those that are supportive of our inner meaning and those that would tear it down. And those forces can take the form of positive and negative energy flows. They can raise us to laughter or tears. They can bring us to love or to hate. And they exist within us simultaneously. They are part of us and we are part of them. We have to recognize that all the forces are good, since they are a part of us. And then we can take control of them, use them. The good and evil, light and dark. They are the Yin and Yang of our inner beings—the all-inclusive, cohesive force. The god-presence in each of us."

"And all actions are justifiable?"

"All actions that are consistent with the truth of our self-recognition. That shouldn't be hard for you to understand."

He gave her a puzzled look. "Why?"

"All your sanctimonious demands for *standards*," she said snidely. "Aren't they based on your own privately developed state of self-righteousness?"

The term stung him like a whip, and he clutched his

fingers about the steering wheel. "That's ridiculous."

Bonnie curled back against the door and laughed derisively.

Tom wanted to respond, but all he could think of was Clair's accusing statement at the restaurant and Bentley's nagging reminder: 'Because it comes from me...and what comes from me must be good.' They had reached the summit. Tom pulled out on the broad paved observation area and pulled the car to a stop just short of the guard rail. He turned off the engine and listened to the pelting rain beat in steady rhythm on the car. Within seconds, the windshield was blurred with the streams of water, but the lights of the city a few hundred feet below shone brightly—the shimmering dots refracted as they passed through the rivulets and cast out slender arms of color.

"Not much of a view in the rain," Bonnie said.

"At least there's no one else here." Tom glanced quickly to either side. "Is this where you came that night?"

"Yes, I...it helps me meditate."

"Strange," Tom muttered. "Usually people come up here in pairs. It's a favorite spot for lovers, I'm told." Tom paused for a moment as he watched for a reaction. Then he continued, "The other club activity was actually the one that convinced me to call the meeting to a halt."

"What was that?"

"The new-member installation."

"Oh, did they have a new member?"

"Beth Crawford," Tom said.

"Oh, yes. I knew she was thinking about it."

"But the ceremony, Bonnie..." Tom proceeded slowly, emphasizing each aspect, watching Bonnie's reactions. "Mark performed the ceremony...by candlelight. He held Beth's hands and guided her gently, seductively through the cakras.

He told her she was Shakti and he would be her Shiva."

"I don't know, Tom," Bonnie blurted out suddenly. "I'd had to have been there. You can't possibly explain... You don't know the meaning of..." She stopped abruptly and leaned her head against the door window.

"I want you to tell me the truth, Bonnie," Tom said. "I want you to tell me who was with you that night...the night of the accident."

"I told you. No one!"

"That just doesn't make sense. Not here, not with the way the accident happened. Someone was with you here. Someone else was driving your car that night!"

"If I thought you were going to start this third degree again, I never would have come with you," Bonnie screamed. "Take me home, Tom. Take me home right now or I'll get out and walk!"

Tom raised his hand and nodded slowly. "All right," he said quietly. He started the car and turned the windshield wipers higher to clear the now heavily falling rain. He turned around and headed back down the narrow road. "You know, there was one thing I gained from my LSD experience. I realized that there are some things a person can just never do while under the influence of it. And one of those things is to drive a car."

"Tom..."

"No question. My recollection is too distinct. This road is no challenge for me now at all." Tom pressed down on the accelerator and the car's speed increased. "But now that I've had the experience, I would never take a hallucinogenic drug and get behind the wheel of a car." He pressed harder and the car accelerated more. "I have more sense than that."

"What are you doing, Tom?"

"And you have more sense than that, too." He increased

the speed again and the tires squealed as the car sped around the sharp corners. "No matter how much I disagree with your philosophy and your teaching methods, I'll give you credit for not being stupid! You would never have driven your car while you had that dose of LSD in your system."

"Slow down..."

"Who was with you, Bonnie?"

The car lurched around another curve, and there, before them, was the blinking light. Tom headed directly for it and pressed down on the accelerator.

"Who was with you?"

Bonnie screamed, clutching at his leg, "Mark, look out!"

Tom pulled the car to a sudden halt at the edge of the barricade. Bonnie's scream still rang in his ears. "*Mark,* look out..." "*Mark,* look out..."

Bonnie slowly released her grip on his leg and moved back. Tom placed the car in park, engaged the brake, and turned toward her. She was huddled in the corner. Her eyes were filled with fear and her body was heaving with sobs.

"Tell me, Bonnie. Tell me!"

Bonnie stared at him for a moment. Then she sighed deeply and spoke softly and haltingly. "His whole future, Tom... It could be ruined. He has his scholarship. And Frederick, his father...he wouldn't understand. I mean, he knew it would be all right, in a controlled situation... But Mark is so strong. He thought he could handle it...and he might have, if..." Bonnie breathed deeply, and her body relaxed. "The world isn't ready yet, Tom. The world would punish him. His whole future..."

"Mark was driving then, wasn't he?"

"Yes. He wasn't hurt. He pulled me into the driver's seat and said he'd go for help. And he did. The ambulance came right away..."

"It wasn't just the drugs, though, Bonnie," Tom said. "It was Mark's being here with you."

She looked at him for a moment. Then she shook her head and mumbled, "The world isn't ready."

"Ready for what? The fact that you were having an affair with Mark?"

"Oh..." She grimaced and shook her head. "That's such a common, contemptible word. Everyone uses it with such sanctimonious whispers."

"What then?"

"You wouldn't understand."

"I don't understand *now,*" he said.

Bonnie shifted her body in Tom's direction. She lowered her head and picked nervously at her thumbnail. Then she looked up and began speaking softly but firmly. "We had reached the pinnacle, Tom. It was a complete merging of our super-conscious levels. We had achieved transpersonal reality!" Her voice grew louder and she leaned forward and gestured as she spoke. "We had found the moment—the explosive moment of transcendence. The timing was perfect...the meditation...the hallucinogenic enhancement...and the sexual conquest."

"You can't dress it up with fancy words," Tom said. "You were having a sexual relationship with one of your students."

"Mark is eighteen..."

"Are you trying to justify it on the basis of the *consenting adult* theory? That doesn't wash. He was your student and you are responsible!"

"Of course I'm responsible," Bonnie said. "I'm responsible to provide the greatest avenue for intellectual expansion."

"Bonnie..."

"The world isn't ready. *You're* not ready. You don't understand." She moved closer to him. "Listen... The mind! The mind has the power to control the experiences of the body. The totality...the physical, the mental, the spiritual..." She placed one arm behind him and grasped his hand as she spoke with growing intensity. "There's no way for you to understand until you've experienced it...the dazzling moment of consciousness expansion through the unity of the spiritual and the physical. And the religious expression and the sexual expression will join in a magnificent orgiastic union." She leaned closer, her body pressing against his. "The moment of truth, Tom...and the sexual union becomes a beautiful spiritual moment—a form of prayer."

Tom clutched the steering wheel and pressed his head against the cold window. Bonnie's face was inches from his, and her heavy makeup was lost in the blur of her nearness. But her lips were there...large, red, and sensuous. Tom felt a hot pulsing within his body, and he struggled against the urge to ignore the grotesqueness of the moment and to surrender to the sudden rush of hidden excitement. He breathed deeply, and the aroma of alcohol and perfume thrust itself upon his senses and burned like a powerful incense. Bonnie was there, but her body was so close and pressing against him, and she became a vague pattern of lustful desire...Shakti, awaiting the moment of union with Shiva... He clenched his teeth and closed his eyes. Then he grasped Bonnie firmly by the arms and pushed her back to the other side of the car. The aroma diminished, and as he opened his eyes again, he could see her clearly—the heavily caked face, the brightly painted lips, the wig resting crazily atop her head.

"No, Bonnie," he said firmly. "No! Listen to me. There is so much more involved here than your fanciful notions of spiritual union."

Bonnie sat quietly in the corner, but her body heaved with the movement of her breathing.

"Are you listening?"

She nodded slowly.

"Do you remember why I initially thought someone was with you?" he asked.

"I...I don't..."

"Joni told me, remember," he reminded her. "She saw you that night, you and Mark. And after I mentioned that to you in the hospital...you told Mark, didn't you?"

Bonnie breathed deeply and looked at him without responding.

"Didn't you?" he repeated heatedly.

"Yes," she mumbled. "I thought he should be aware..."

"Joni didn't commit suicide, Bonnie. Mark killed her."

"No!"

"Mark killed her to keep her from revealing that you two were together that night!"

"No, Tom, that's absurd!"

"Joni didn't use drugs," he continued. "You must have known that. And Mark had access. It's clear now that he also had what he considered to be the justification."

"Circumstances, Tom," she mumbled. "Just circumstances."

"Not after what happened tonight."

"What do you mean?"

"Mark slipped. He blurted out the very phrase he had written on Joni's typewriter—her suicide note. *Death is the penultimate cakra! All else is illusion.*" Tom recited the message without hesitation. It was burned into his memory. "The penultimate cakra, Bonnie. I thought at first it had some hidden meaning. But it didn't. It was just Mark's inaccurate expression!"

"Penultimate cakra...penultimate cakra..." Bonnie

clenched her hands together and held them to her chin. "Yes, that was Mark's phrase. I corrected him on it several times, but he persisted." She collapsed in the corner and dropped her head into her hands.

So it was done. Inner truth, universal truth, moment of truth. All those were irrelevant notions and paled before the absolute truth: Mark had killed Joni. There was no doubt about that now. Tom looked at Bonnie's huddled figure. Light and dark, Yin and Yang, good and evil—all were combined in that clump of flesh, but there was no power now...no power over laughter and tears, no power over love and hate. All had merged senselessly in one violent, hideous act, designed and justified by the inner recognition of a sick human being.

Tom turned slowly and grasped the steering wheel with both hands. The engine was still running and the windshield wipers crossed rhythmically back and forth, but they could never quite clear everything. Clear, blurred...clear, blurred... The blinking red warning light cast in one moment a distinct message of danger, and in the next, a hazy invitation to follow it. And beyond and below...the dotted white marks from the city...clear, blurred...clear, blurred... The world will understand, the world will not understand. Stand back, come forth...run, follow. And then, in the distance, a flash of lightning crossed the sky, and Tom counted with the beating of the wipers—one, two, three, four, five, six, and the thunder rumbled across the city before he reached the seventh...the penultimate cakra...the recognition of life at the instant of death...run, follow...run, follow. All else is illusion.

30

The next morning, Tom stood near the door and watched as the students entered the classroom. Things had been going well with this class, but since he had returned from the convention, he had felt them slipping away from the direction he had established. He knew his action at the meeting last night would not help the situation. As the club members entered the room, they either avoided his glance or scowled at him. Except Beth. As she came in, she stepped up to him and paused for a moment. There was something different about her appearance today. She seemed to want to say something, but her expression was distant, confused. Frank stepped up beside her and guided her away from Tom. Everyone was seated quietly as the tardy bell rang, but Tom saw immediately that it was not the typical seating arrangement; all of the club members sat at the back corner of the classroom, surrounding the single, empty desk that was Mark's.

Tom quickly scanned the room and verified that there were no other absences. Since Mark was not there, he assumed Gruber had arrested him. Tom had called Gruber the night before, after he had taken Bonnie home. Gruber had been grateful but strangely, not surprised.

"Good morning, class," Tom began tentatively.

The few remaining talkers turned and watched him silently. Even the club members were attentive, but their expressions were more of silent disdain than anticipation.

"We're going to try to conclude our study of *Man's Fate* this week," Tom said. "An important part of the unit is your compositions, in which you analyze the flaws in your selected characters. I'd like to give you most of the period to work on those, but first I want to answer any questions you might have. Have any of you had any difficulty identifying the flaws or their implications on the characters' lives?"

There was no response at first. Then the club members looked at one another and chuckled softly, and finally Andrew raised his hand.

Tom wasn't sure whether Andrew had a legitimate question or this was some scheme to irritate him, so he recognized the boy cautiously. "Yes, Andrew. Who is your character?"

"It's Gisors."

"All right. What's your question?"

"Well, Gisors found his meaning in life through the use of opium."

"Yes."

"I want to see if you think I'm on the right track." Andrew smiled and glanced at those about him. "Since we heard about your experience, I've decided Gisors' only flaw was...he used the wrong drug!"

The class exploded in laughter—except for the club members. They just sat back smiling smugly. It was a set-up. He would just have to deal with it. He was disappointed, however, that Andrew had instigated it. He thought he was beginning to turn this boy around.

"What of Gisors' statement in defense of himself, Andrew?" Tom asked, ignoring the jibe. "That every man is a madman. How are you dealing with that?"

The laughter ceased and Andrew looked up confused, as though he hadn't anticipated that his statement would elicit further discussion. He laughed nervously, then opened his book and flipped quickly through the pages.

"That's a key phrase, Andrew," Tom continued. "We highlighted it in our discussion on Monday. Remember?"

"Yeah." Andrew smiled and placed his finger on the page. "See, *madman* was just his terminology. Other than that he's headed in the right direction. He says here, 'But what is human destiny if not a life of effort to unite this madman with the universe?' " Andrew sat up, his smile broadening. "Gisors is in the flow. He'll find the universal truth."

The same phraseology, Tom thought. *Everything is positive. There are no consequences.* "As you do your paper, Andrew, I want you to look a little deeper. Find out what happens to him, and describe how that relates to his pattern of escapism."

Andrew frowned, closed the book, and slumped in his desk.

Beth was sitting next to Andrew. Her face still carried that plaintive, questioning look. But her eyes seemed focused on the rainbow hanging on the side wall.

"Beth, you look as though you have a question," Tom said.

Beth turned toward him, almost startled. "Ah, no. No, I don't think so."

"Who is your character?"

"Ch'en."

"Oohh, terrorism!" Andrew rubbed his hands together.

"Murder," Mary Ann chirped.

"An ecstasy toward *downward.*" Frank emphasized the words crisply.

"What about Ch'en, Beth?" Tom asked. "What word sums up his character for you?"

Beth thought for a moment. And then she mumbled, "Moth."

Several members of the class giggled, and Tom silenced them.

"That's good, Beth. Go on."

"It was what Kyo said about him," Beth continued. "He said Ch'en was like a moth who secretes his own light—in which he will destroy himself."

"Yes, what about that symbol?" Tom asked. "How does it relate to Ch'en's ultimate outcome?"

"I don't like the symbol, Mr. Kerzig," Beth said. "It's so negative. I mean, we're all learning how important it is for us to find our own light and use it for the direction in our lives. There's nothing destructive about that, is there? I mean, how could Ch'en destroy himself in his own light?"

Tom remembered Joni's paper, the dark master scraping the vomit from the gnarled branches. Before he could respond to Beth's question, the door opened and Joe Carter stepped inside the room. He waved toward the class and beckoned to Tom.

Tom acknowledged Joe and addressed the class. "Why don't you go ahead and start writing? Beth, I'll get to your question in a few minutes."

Tom followed Joe through the door and saw Gruber standing in the corridor. The inspector waited for the door to swing shut, and then approached them.

"Morning." Gruber had a heavy scowl on his face.

"Mark isn't in class this morning, is he, Tom?" Joe asked.

"No." He looked at Gruber. "Didn't you—"

"I tried. He wasn't there when I checked his home at 10:00. His father expected him, so I waited outside all night. He never showed up."

"He knows..." Tom mumbled.

"Mmm-hmm." Gruber nodded.

"Did you check Bonnie's place?" Tom asked.

"I had a man posted there all night, too," Gruber answered. "No luck. Listen, it's important that the other students don't know what's going on. But somebody may know where he is. Keep your ears open."

"I'm going to a scholarship dinner tonight," Joe said. "Mark is supposed to be there. If he's not, maybe someone can give me a lead."

Gruber took his wallet out of his pocket and removed two business cards. He handed one to each of them. "The first number's the station, the second one's my home. Give me a call the minute you find out anything." Gruber started to leave. Then he turned back with his hands on his hips and lowered his eyebrows. "Is this kid some kind of kook, or what?"

Joe shook his head. "He's a leader."

"Hmph!" Gruber stood without moving for a moment. Then he turned and walked heavily down the corridor.

"I'll let you get back to class," Joe said. "But first, when you took Bonnie home last night, what was she like?"

"Non-communicative."

"Do you think she might have tipped him off?"

"I don't know. I don't think it would have mattered, anyway. Mark realized last night that I knew...the moment he let that phrase slip."

Joe took Tom by the arm. "If either one of us learns anything today, let's get together."

"Good idea."

"See ya." Joe dropped his hand and walked away.

Tom opened the door and stepped back into the classroom. The sound of low whispers ceased, and most of the students had their heads bent low over their desks. Beth sat upright, though, her unblinking eyes staring toward the circle of doves above the rainbow, held captive by a narrow stream of light which issued in from the window.

Tom stayed at school late that afternoon, grading papers. He was having dinner with Clair at 7:30. He should have been excited about this, but he was filled now with a strange sense of reluctance. Clair had violated their relationship by confiding in Pastor Bentley before he'd had a chance to meet with her and set things right between them.

Tom found Larry and asked him to open the door to the office. All of the staff members had left, and none of the office lights were on. A dim security light barely illuminated the area surrounding the teachers' mail boxes. Tom let his eyes adjust to the darkness, then walked quickly to his box. The box contained a single note. He took it out, walked over to a more brightly lit area, and read what appeared to be a hurriedly-scribbled message:

Tom,

Meet me at the new court at 9:00.

Important information!

Joe

Tom wondered if Joe was perhaps still here. He hurried over to his office and tried the door. It was locked, and the office was completely dark. He read the note again. Joe must have learned something. Why didn't he just come up? "Nine o'clock," he muttered angrily under his breath. He would have to leave Clair by 8:30...come back to school. But then...perhaps that would be better.

He thrust the note into his shirt pocket, walked out the front door, and latched it securely behind him.

He had just about reached his car when he heard someone calling his name. He turned to see Marla, running across the lot, waving to him. She continued running until she reached him. Then she rested her arm on his shoulder, lowered her head, and caught her breath.

"That was a pretty good sprint," Tom said. "They should put you on the track team."

"Yeah." Marla was still breathing heavily, but gradually she regained control. "I didn't know you were working late today."

"I was grading some papers. I didn't notice your room was open."

"I was over with Marilyn and Susan, talking about the cross-age tutoring program."

"Oh. How are your classes going?"

"Great! I've gotten so many new ideas since I got back from the convention. And then today, when I met with Marilyn and Susan, I got some good ideas about health and art. They were really helpful. But I didn't want you to think I was neglecting you. So that's why I chased you down tonight."

"Oh?"

"It's so late that I thought..." Marla tilted her head coyly. "Well, I thought maybe you'd let me take you to dinner tonight."

"Well..."

"That's another thing I learned in just that one day," she continued. "I need to follow my feelings, let this little inner glow inside me burst out and express itself." She laughed giddily.

"I can't tonight, Marla."

"I thought maybe you'd learned to follow *your* feelings a little more, too, Tom. That night at dinner you were really...I don't know...warm and exciting."

That night at dinner... Did she mean after he'd started having a reaction to the LSD? He definitely remembered the magnified sensations of that time...her hand on his arm and his slurred words, "*You're slender, and soft...turning into quite a young lady...*" And Marla's giddy laughter and hot breath upon his neck. But what did that have to do with now? Marla didn't stop talking. She stepped closer and kept chattering excitedly about the inner glow, and the need to help her students to self-realization through her own self-realization.

For a blinding moment Tom heard his mind whisper, *Why not?* Marla wouldn't accuse him of being self-righteous... Bad night, anyway...have to leave early. Just call Clair and reschedule...easy to justify. He lowered his eyes, and tried to focus on the hazy image before him. But then, the image distorted, and the smooth young face suddenly took on the appearance of Bonnie's, and her perfume drifted heavily over him with the oppressive aroma of death.

"No, Marla, no!" he shouted.

"What?" She stepped back further now, bewildered.

"Look, I'm sorry. I can't accept your invitation. I'm having dinner with Clair tonight."

Marla gave him a quizzical look. "Your ex-wife?"

"We're just separated," he muttered with vague resolve.

She shrugged and smiled faintly. "That's all right. I'll catch you when you're feeling more responsive."

Tom sighed. "There are things beyond our feelings. Important things...absolute things." He touched her arm and continued toward his car.

Tom stopped by his apartment to clean up before going to meet Clair. A whirlwind of crazy images kept circling through his head. It seemed as though all the weird notions held by Bonnie and the presenters at the convention were converging on him. Before, he had harbored a negative, though somewhat moderate view of the experiences. But now everything he'd seen and heard over the last few weeks had converged into the overpowering feeling that Joni's death was the direct and thoroughly expected result of a program of self-serving practices. He remembered Marla in his eleventh-grade English class—how she was so like Joni in her appearance and actions. And now she was following directly in the model Bonnie had cast forth. The shallow words that guided their thoughts: "Let the glow bubble," "Follow my feelings," and, yes, "Find myself." He had accused Clair of blindly following that same destructive line. And she had, but...hadn't he done the same thing? An open vessel, or a closed fist? What difference did it make, really? Self-righteous? Or was Bonnie right? Was it just a matter of terminology?

Tom hurriedly parked the car at the curb and jumped out. He ran up the stairs to the front porch, swung out the screen, and knocked on the front door. After a moment, the porch light came on and the door opened. Clair greeted him with a warm smile. She was wearing his favorite dress.

"Hi, Tom." She opened the door wider. "Come in."

"Thanks." He stepped inside and closed the door behind him.

She gestured self-consciously toward the dining room. "I thought we'd eat in there."

Tom stepped past her into the dining room. It was dimly lit and the table was set for an intimate meal. The smell of roast beef emanated from the kitchen.

"This is...this is great, Clair!" He looked at her, and all the warmth from a previous time surged within him as though it were never interrupted. But then he glanced at the table again. Something was missing. There were only two place settings.

"Where's Jennifer?" he asked.

"Oh, I forgot to tell you. She's at a special program and

social Colleen's having for some of her students at the Parlor.
I didn't think you'd mind if dinner was just for the two of us.
She'll be back after—"

"What kind of program?" A strange feeling of dread
crept into Tom's mind.

"I'm not sure. Actually, it was organized by that cross-age
tutoring group."

"Didn't you take her?" he asked.

"No. One of your student's picked her up."

"Who?"

"He's a nice young man."

"Clair..."

"His name is Mark Banazech."

Tom grabbed Clair by both arms and held her in front of
him. He couldn't speak.

"Tom...what's the matter? You're hurting me!"

"Clair! Mark...Mark killed Joni!"

Clair jerked back suddenly, shaking her head from side
to side. "No, Tom. No... No..."

"When did they leave?"

"Ah...thirty minutes ago."

Tom still held tightly to both Clair's arms while he frantically mapped out the quickest route to the Parlor. He
dropped one arm and dragged her with him. "Come on!
Maybe we can... Come on!"

The Parlor was the favorite Saturday afternoon spot for
kids when Tom was growing up. Ice cream, games, and good
clean fellowship. But as the world changed, so did the Parlor.
The interior lighting was dimmed and the loud sound of
video games blended together in a deafening roar. An entire
section was devoted to pre-teens that featured dancing to

"soft-rock." A separate room was made available for special programs. That's where Colleen Stinneman's class would be.

Tom led Clair quickly through the crowd of young players and burst through the door to the special room. Twelve or fifteen children sat around a long table which was bedecked with party toys and balloons. Jennifer was not among them. The students wore crazy paper hats, painted to resemble signs of the zodiac. Each one had a half-finished bowl of ice cream. But they were intent on watching the front of the table. A middle-aged woman, wearing the costume of a fortune teller, sat there with a young boy before her. She was holding the child's hand and tracing her finger along the lines in his palm. Colleen Stinneman stood at the side of the room, smiling. Three others stood around the table—Frank, Beth, and Mary Ann.

Colleen Stinneman looked up as they came in and waved. Tom motioned for her to join them. Frank frowned at him, as Mary Ann and Beth turned away and whispered to one another.

"Well, Mr. Kerzig...and Clair. I didn't expect to see you here."

"Where's Jennifer?" Tom asked.

"What?"

"Where's Jennifer, Colleen?" Clair pressed.

"Well, I thought..." Colleen glanced nervously toward the group of children. "Mark stopped by over a half hour ago. He said Jennifer had a cold and couldn't make it. And since he had a lot of studying to do, he left.

"Oh...oh, no..." Clair moaned.

"What is it?" Colleen asked. "I don't understand."

Tom motioned for Colleen to back off. Then he pulled Clair into the corner of the room. "I have to think..."

"What should we do?" Clair was nearing hysteria.

"Just a minute." Tom reached into his shirt and pulled out Gruber's card. The note came out with it. Tom had totally forgotten about the meeting with Joe. "That's right." He glanced at his watch. It was nearly 8:30. "Listen, Joe may have some information," Tom stammered. "He asked me to meet him at 9:00 at the courts. I don't know why...said it was important." He handed Gruber's card to Clair. "This is the inspector's card. Call him right away...from here. Tell him what happened. I'll meet you both at the house later. If he comes by here, you can ride back with him. Otherwise..."

"I'll work that out," Clair said.

"Okay." He took her hand and looked deeply but momentarily into her eyes. "It's going to be all right."

Clair nodded, tears streaming down her cheeks.

Tom gave her hand a final squeeze, then left the relative silence of the special room. He ran quickly through the gaudy montage of children and video games and trays filled with heaping mounds of ice cream.

31

Tom ran across the dark campus to the gymnasium. His mind still reeled with the knowledge that Mark had taken Jennifer. If only Joe had some clue as to where Mark might be. He began to wonder if he should have had Clair tell Gruber to meet him here. But if he did, Gruber couldn't have questioned the other students and Colleen Stinneman. No, it was better this way. Tom would get whatever information he could from Joe and then meet Clair and Gruber at the house and try to put things together—form a plan. His body was perspiring from the exertion of the run, but periodically a cold flash shot up his spine as he pictured Joni's lifeless form and the image of Mark, hulking over her typewriter. Why did he take Jennifer? What could he possibly be planning to do?

The exterior light above the entry to the racquetball courts was out, and Tom searched the dark wall for the door as he hurried toward the building. When he was just a few feet away, the faint image of the doorknob appeared to him. He ran to it and turned it. The door was unlocked. As he stepped inside the dark corridor he heard the sound of a ball rhythmically hitting a racquet and then the wall of the court. He ran his hand quickly across the wall just inside the doorway, and as it fell across the switch, the corridor lights flashed on. He walked rapidly to the door to the new court and rapped on it.

"Joe! Are you in there?"

There was no answer. The sound of the ball continued.

Tom pushed the door open and stepped inside the court. "Joe?"

The door slammed suddenly behind him, and he turned around to see not Joe, but Mark standing behind him.

"What?" He jumped back startled. He glanced quickly from side to side. "Where...where's Joe?"

Mark's large frame stood directly in front of the door. He tossed the racquet and ball carelessly to the floor and stared at Tom with one eyebrow raised. A thin smile appeared on his face.

"I'm glad to see you got my note, Mr. Kerzig," he said slowly.

"*Your* note?"

"I knew you'd check your box before you left school. You're such a conscientious teacher." Mark's smile broadened. "Conscientious...just not very bright!"

"Where's Jennifer?"

"Who?"

"Where's Jennifer?" Tom shouted.

"Oh, that's right. Jennifer is your daughter, isn't she, Mr. Kerzig?" Mark said with a calculating expression. "Well, you see, Jennifer and I had to do a little studying. I love working with her. She's a beautiful child."

"What have you done with her?"

Mark crossed his arms and walked closer to Tom. Then he leaned down and whispered coarsely, "She's right behind you."

Tom spun around and found he was facing the glass wall next to the adjacent court. "What are you talking about?"

Mark emitted a low cackle. Jennifer was in the other court. He stepped closer to the wall and cupped his hands beside his eyes. Inside the other court he saw faint images of colored laser beams crossing the floor and bouncing off the window. Every few seconds one of the beams would rebound from the small figure sitting cross-legged on the floor.

"She can't be disturbed right now, of course," Mark taunted. "She's meditating." He stepped to the recessed control panel in the corner of the court. "Do you want to listen?"

Mark pressed a switch on the panel, and the sound of Jennifer's voice suddenly issued from the small speaker. She was chanting the low, monotonous *ommm* of the mantra.

"Jennifer!" Tom called loudly, banging his knuckles against the glass.

"Did you forget, Mr. Kerzig? That room's completely sound-proof. And that's a two-way glass, so all she sees is a mirror."

Tom spun around and glared at him. "Why are you doing this?"

Mark closed his eyes and pressed his finger to his lips. "We've put together a little program...with lights and a tape recording. I know you'll enjoy it!"

Tom turned toward the glass again as the lights in the other court came on. But they weren't the court lights. Two small flood lamps on stands cast a bright glow on Jennifer and the front part of the court where the pyramidal laser device sat on a low platform. The colored beams were no longer visible because of the increased surrounding light, but the throbbing blue and white circle toward the top shone brightly. Jennifer was staring at it intently. A pile of crystals lay before the laser device and a candle sat on each side. At the back of the platform stood a large tape player, and on the wall directly above hung the huge rainbow from Bonnie's room. Tom heard a faint click, and a red light appeared on the tape player. The faint sound of weird, discordant music played in the background as Mark's voice emerged from the speaker—firm, yet low, and flattering.

"Very good, Jennifer. You did an excellent job on the

mantra. Now we'll do our self-realization exercise. Are you ready?"

Jennifer nodded.

"All right...repeat after me," said Mark's taped voice. "I am the center of pure self-consciousness."

"I am the center of pure self-consciousness," Jennifer responded with a high, firm voice.

"I am the center of my will to be and to act," Mark's voice continued.

"I am the center of my will to be and to act," she repeated.

"I can direct and harmonize all the processes of my body."

"I can direct and harmonize all the processes of my body."

"I have the power over laughter and tears."

"I have the power over laughter and tears."

"I have the power over love and hate."

"I have the power over love and hate."

"All of my feelings are good and pure."

"All of my feelings are good and pure."

"Only I can judge."

"Only I can judge."

"Only I can determine my destiny."

"Only I can determine my destiny."

"All things must work toward my self-fulfillment."

"All things must work toward my self-fulfillment."

There was a slight pause in the dialogue, and Tom turned toward Mark, the anger welling up inside him. But Mark only smiled, placed his fingers over his lips, and pointed toward Jennifer.

"Very good, Jennifer," Mark's taped voice continued. "Now we're going to do something exciting. I'm not really sitting in front of you this time, but I want you to close your eyes and pretend that I am. All right?"

Jennifer nodded and closed her eyes.

"Now, Jennifer, if you want to be a good LENA student, you have to show that you have the ability to pass through levels of thinking and feeling that other people haven't even considered. Can you do that?"

"Mmm-hmm," Jennifer mumbled.

"I want you to reach out and pretend to hold on to my hands," the voice coaxed.

Jennifer reached out her small arms and pretended to grasp the nonexistent hands before her.

"Can you feel them?"

"Yes."

"Now, you're growing in your awareness," the voice continued. "Reach out...reach out with your body. Feel your knees, nearly touching mine, but not quite. Can you feel them?"

"Yes."

"Now let's begin," issued the voice slowly. "Your being, your consciousness, your power...it's all centered in you, struggling to be free. You can feel it from where you sit. It's there, growing. It begins at the base of your spine. That is Shakti. She is restless energy. She is you, and she awaits within you to rise and be united with Shiva. I will be your Shiva! Let me help you rise. Feel yourself stepping through the levels...through the cakras—your psychic centers. Can you feel your consciousness rising?"

"Yes."

"Think of me, waiting at the top," Mark continued passionately. "Once there we will be joined in sensual union!"

The anger inside Tom suddenly exploded and he rushed toward Mark. But his movements felt strangely sluggish, and as he approached Mark, he saw the boy's muscular body shift and tilt, then a massive shoe headed directly toward him. A pain pierced his chest—sharp and overpowering. He felt himself crumpling to the floor and his hands grasped at his chest in a futile attempt to stop the throbbing pain in his ribs. He forced his head back against the glass, and saw Mark standing above him, laughing.

"That should be your third rib from the top on the right side, Mr. Kerzig," Mark said derisively. "If you think that's painful, think how it would feel with two, or three."

Tom tried to slide to a sitting position, but the pain was almost unbearable. He slumped back again and shook his head slowly. "Why, Mark? Why did you kill Joni? Were you really that afraid people would find out you were with Bonnie that night?"

"Afraid?" The smile abruptly left Mark's face. "No, I wasn't afraid. If Bonnie and I want to do the things we do, that's our business. I don't care what people think. No, it was Joni. She was a threat."

"How?"

"Her attitude and her beliefs. They were a threat to the program. I worked on her for two years to get her to reject her outdated Christian philosophy, but she wouldn't drop it. And she was beginning to contaminate others with her views."

Tom shook his head. "*You're* the contamination, Mark."

Mark scowled and thrust his foot toward Tom. The shoe caught him on the left side of his chest, and a second pain merged excruciatingly with the first.

"That one was only a bruise, Mr. Kerzig, trust me," Mark sneered. "But don't talk to me like that!"

Tom raised his head and cold shocks rose through his

neck. "How...how did you do it? How did you even get into her house?"

This question seemed to please Mark. He stepped back and smiled broadly. "That was easy. I knew her parents were going to be gone that night, so I just knocked on her door." He pretended to knock, and then he spoke in a high, sarcastic voice, " *'Excuse me, Joni,'* I said *'But I'd like to hear more about Jesus!'* " He laughed loudly. "Well, that was the magic word! She let me right in. And then..." He reached into his shirt pocket. "We went into the kitchen and had some coffee." He pulled two sugar packets from his pocket and waved them in front of Tom. They were the same as those he'd used at the convention.

"You were the one."

"I hope you enjoyed your trip," Mark scoffed. "Joni sure did! She went swooping around the kitchen. Of course, I had to help her. I picked her up in my arms, just like Prince Galahad."

Even through the pain and the recognition of the horror of the act, Mark's inaccurate terminology shot forth like a grisly calling card, and Tom found himself involuntarily muttering an inaudible correction. "*Sir* Galahad."

"I carried her into her room and laid her on her bed. She wasn't even aware of my injecting the heroin into her arm."

"And then you typed the suicide message."

"Sure, the final touch," he said proudly.

"Except that was your downfall."

"Huh?" Mark frowned.

"You used the wrong term," Tom explained. "*Penultimate* doesn't mean the best. It means *next to the best.* But then, you're only second-best, anyway, aren't you, Mark?"

Mark snarled and brought his foot back to kick again. Then he relaxed and smiled. "What does it matter? I make my own rules."

"So, what are you going to do now?"

"Well, you're going to have a terrible automobile accident, Mr. Kerzig. Unfortunate, really. Since you tried that LSD in Las Vegas, you just had to have some more." He reached into his pocket again and pulled out a small vial filled with clear liquid. "And, foolishly, you drove your car afterward. Killed you of course. Even broke a rib or two in the process." He laughed.

"Suppose I refuse to drink that?" Tom asked.

Mark pointed toward the adjacent court. "I can just tie you up here and make you watch me finish the ceremony with Jennifer in person."

"Don't you... Ah!" He reached out to strike Mark, but a sudden shock of pain from his ribs thrust him back.

"So?" Mark taunted.

Tom turned his body slowly around and looked inside the next court. He pressed his face against the glass and listened. Jennifer lay on her back on the floor, and Mark's voice flowed from the speaker, softly, invitingly. It spoke of the warmth of the sun, and the rays penetrating all the parts of her beautiful body, preparing her for her union with Shiva. Tom could feel Mark's repulsive presence behind him and hear his low chuckle.

"All right, Banazech, back off!"

"Huh?"

Tom turned suddenly, ignoring the pain, and saw Mark jerk abruptly around. The door to the court was open, and Gruber stood inside, holding a gun.

"Inspector!" Tom forced himself around and felt his body heave in painful, joyful recognition. "How did you know to come here?"

"Your wife called and told me what happened," Gruber said. "She also told me about your supposed note from Joe.

Trouble is, he had called me just before your wife did. He'd just gotten home from the scholarship dinner. He didn't say anything about meeting you or having any important information. So this could be the only explanation." Gruber stepped closer. "All right, Banazech, assume the position against that wall."

Mark stood quietly, his hands clutching his thighs, and his eyes narrowed to slits.

"I told you to assume the position against..."

"That was very good, Jennifer!" Mark's recorded voice suddenly boomed into the room.

"Huh?" Gruber looked up abruptly and shifted his body toward the sound.

"Inspector...no...watch out!" Tom cried.

But it was too late. In one unbelievably rapid movement, Mark took a deep breath, spun about, and thrust his foot squarely into Gruber's face. The inspector staggered back as blood rushed from his nose. Then he fell in a heap on the floor.

Mark threw Tom a contemptuous look. Then he walked slowly over to Gruber and removed the gun from his hand. He returned to Tom and tossed the vial to him. "Drink this."

Tom stared at Gruber's motionless form across the room. Blood still trickled from his nose. Tom's hand clutched at the tiny vial, and he looked up at Mark's looming form. Had to delay him somehow. "This changes things, Mark," he said.

"Why?"

"Gruber," Tom said.

Mark smiled and shook his head. "Just a slight modification. Seems Gruber came in here and found you high on LSD. Before he could arrest you, you hit him in the face with the racquet. And then you shot him with his own gun. The rest remains the same."

"Mark, listen. It's not too late. End it. You need help..."

"Help?" Mark sneered. "What kind of help? *Psychiatric* help? From my father, I suppose, huh?" He stepped closer to Tom and continued loudly, "Or maybe my brother! That would be better, wouldn't it?" He pointed the gun toward the bottle in Tom's hand. "Drink it!"

Tom raised his hand. "Wait. First...tell me. Why...what's so important about all this?"

"Why? You really are stupid, aren't you? Don't you know anything about the goals of the *LENA* program by this time? We make our own world. We make our own rules. We make our own god." He paused for a moment and stood erect. "We *are* god! And anything that interferes with our divine plan has to be destroyed!"

"But, why Jennifer?"

Mark looked into the next court and smiled. Then he squatted down and, with one hand, grasped Tom by the hair and spun his head around until his cheek was pressed tightly against the glass.

"Look at her!" Mark said. "She's our future. She must be trained properly. And she's so willing. All of the children are so willing to follow!" He pulled harder on Tom's hair. "Watch! Listen!"

Tom raised his head slightly to relieve the pulling at his hair. He turned his eyes hard to the side so that he could view the scene through the glass.

"You can sit up, now, Jennifer," Mark's taped voice instructed.

Jennifer slowly sat up and resumed her cross-legged position.

"Now come forward," the tape continued. "And kneel in front of the pyramid."

Jennifer obediently rose, walked to the low platform, and knelt.

"I want you to concentrate on the crystals," the tape continued. "Aren't they beautiful?"

Jennifer nodded.

"But they're more than just beautiful, Jennifer...just like you are more than just beautiful. You have a special power inside you, and so do they. By merging your power with their power, you can do even greater things. Look at them closely."

Jennifer placed her hands on the platform and bent closer to the crystals.

"Look at them intently," the voice beckoned. "Let their power reach through your eyes...right into your spine. You can see Shiva in those stones. You can see me. Feel the power rise within you to meet the power of the crystals."

Tom struggled unsuccessfully to pull his head away from Mark's grasp. Then, out of the corner of his eye, he saw a form moving slowly toward them. It was Gruber, and he held the racquet over his head. Tom tried not to alert Mark, but his body twitched involuntarily in anticipation. Mark turned his head just as Gruber's arm came down hard, slamming the racquet against the base of his skull. Mark's eyes fluttered slightly, then closed, and his body fell heavily to the floor. Gruber placed his foot roughly on Mark's arm and removed the gun from his hand. Then he deftly removed a set of hand-cuffs from his belt.

"Are you all right?" Tom asked.

"I'll live," he muttered. His face was a bloody mess. He blinked hard, and then wiped the back of the hand holding his gun across his eyes. He latched a cuff on one of Mark's wrists and pulled it to his back. "You have the right to remain silent," he began automatically.

"He's unconscious, Inspector," Tom said.

"Anything you say can and will be used against you in a court of law," Gruber continued, ignoring Tom.

"Inspector..."

Gruber gruffly attached the other cuff. "You have the right to an attorney."

"Inspector, he's unconscious," Tom repeated more loudly.

Gruber rested the point of his gun on Mark's back and nodded slowly. "I thought Joe said this kid wasn't a kook."

"Now take your favorite crystal, Jennifer," Mark's voice recommenced, "and dance with it. Dance with me."

Gruber looked up abruptly and then wiped his face again.

Tom raised painfully to his hands and knees and watched through the glass. Jennifer had selected a crystal. She stood and circled slowly, gazing intently at the crystal. The low, discordant music increased in volume, and her body moved and swayed in rhythm to it. And then the sound of Mark's recorded voice issued forth and merged with the sound of the music, "We will cross into the new age together. Let your power flow. Let your divinity shine forth. Come, follow me...follow me..." Jennifer's body spun and circled and followed in rhythmic obedience to the sound of the inviting words. The glow from the crystal in her fingers ebbed, then swelled as it moved past the throbbing blue and white light near the apex of the pyramid. With her eyes closed, she moved in darkness, but she followed the sound of Mark's voice and her way was lit with the glow from within.

32

The antiseptic smell of hospital emergency rooms had always made Tom nauseous, but tonight the odor was a welcome aroma. He slowly pushed himself up until he sat on the edge of the bed, then took a shallow breath to test the effectiveness of the tape circling his chest. Mark was either very accurate in his statement, or he had just made a lucky guess: the third rib from the top on Tom's right side was cracked, and his left side was just bruised. He picked up his shirt and carefully slid his arms into the sleeves. Then he fastened the buttons and tucked the shirttail into his trousers. He glanced around the cluttered treatment area to make sure he had retrieved all of his belongings, then slid open the white privacy curtain. Doctors and nurses scurried about in the emergency room. He looked at the large clock on the wall near the entrance; it was nearly 2:00.

He heard the noise of sliding metal rings, and the curtain slid open at the treatment area directly across from him. Gruber stepped out and nodded. He had a large bandage across his nose and upper cheeks. Gruber glanced at the clock also. Then he walked across the narrow aisle and joined Tom.

"How are you doing?" Gruber asked.

"A lot better. But there's still quite a bit of pain."

"Did the doctor tell you how to alleviate that?"

"Yeah, stop breathing!" They laughed, and Tom hunched forward to escape the pain from the laughter. "How about you?"

"Okay. My nose is broken, but they told me if he'd kicked me an inch higher I'd probably be dead."

"Do you think he intended to avoid the lethal spot?"

Gruber chuckled. "Well, that's his story. He says he could have killed me if he wanted to, but that he just...how'd he put it...rendered me unconscious in self defense."

"That may not be too far-fetched. I mean, about his being able to determine. He knew which one of my ribs he cracked."

Gruber scowled and shook his head. "I'm still going for attempted murder." He glanced to either side. "How about your daughter?"

"Don't know yet," Tom said. "She's being examined. Clair's with her."

"Hmm..."

"Where is he?" Tom asked.

Gruber nodded to the left. "Down there...at the end of the aisle."

Tom looked to where Gruber indicated and saw two uniformed policemen standing outside a concealed treatment area. "Is he all right?"

"Sure. Just a slight concussion and a few stitches to patch up the cut on his head." Gruber grinned. "By the way, I read him his rights again before I got bandaged up. I thought you'd like to know that." Gruber pointed to the entrance. "Isn't that your wife?"

Tom turned and saw Clair talking with one of the nurses. The nurse pointed to where Tom stood, and Clair hurried over to him. She looked haggard, her eyes red from crying.

"How is she?" Tom asked.

Clair looked at him, closed her eyes, and heaved a deep sigh. "She's all right. Apparently there was no physical abuse."

Tom felt a massive wave of relief sweep across his body, and he took Clair's hands and squeezed them. "Where is she?"

"We can pick her up in a few minutes. Someone from the police department is talking with her."

"That's our psychologist," Gruber said. "Don't worry. He won't say anything to disturb her. It's just that, now, while things are fresh in her mind, she can give a good description of what went on."

"I understand," Clair said.

"Listen, I'm going to go over and make sure they still have him restrained," Gruber said. "Sometimes these hospital workers get overly concerned about hurting criminals' feelings." He turned to leave. "Great news about your daughter!" he said as he walked away.

"How about her attitude, Clair?" Tom asked. "I mean, did she seem frightened, or..."

"No, not at all. That's what I don't understand. She was so calm. She asked me why she had to see the doctor. She didn't even seem to know what had happened."

"Well, she doesn't yet. Not completely. When the police came I went with her in a separate car. I didn't know exactly what to say to her. We'll have to explain the incident later."

"That's probably better," Clair agreed. "How are you feeling?"

Tom took a shallow breath and smiled. "Tight!"

Clair placed her hand gently on his chest. Then she looked over his shoulder toward the entrance to the emergency room. "Who's that?"

Tom turned and saw Dr. Banazech speaking with the nurses.

"Dr. Banazech, Mark's father."

Dr. Banazech nodded at the nurses and walked slowly toward Tom and Clair.

"He's a doctor?" she asked.

"Psychiatrist."

Dr. Banazech approached them and extended his hand tentatively in Tom's direction. "Mr. Kerzig, we meet again under rather unusual circumstances."

Tom took his hand. "Dr. Banazech. This is my wife, Clair."

"Mrs. Kerzig." Dr. Banazech took her hand momentarily. "The officer told me that Mark was also responsible for the unauthorized hallucinogenic dose that you received in Las Vegas."

"Yes."

"And now this." Dr. Banazech shook his head. "You have my sincere apologies for my son's inexcusable behavior. And, of course, there's much more, isn't there? I wasn't able to get all the details, but...what...Mark is being accused of involvement in that girl's death?"

"You'll have to talk to the police about that, Dr. Banazech," Tom said.

"Of course. But you are his teacher. And to you I will express my complaint."

"Complaint?"

"I believe I sufficiently alluded to my concerns at the dinner that evening," Dr. Banazech began. "The lack of adequate supervision and control by the school in the pursuance of the LENA goals is appalling. You are dealing with extremely sensitive and volatile psychological factors."

"I agree."

"There is nothing wrong with the objectives of the program. They simply require more skilled assistance in their application. The students must be led through the self-realization process with considerably greater control."

Tom wondered if that wasn't a contradiction in terms. He was about to say something but then thought better of it.

Dr. Banazech looked at Tom analytically. "You're questioning me, Mr. Kerzig. And well you might, since you have been involved with the program for such a short time. Nevertheless, I look to you as an agent of the school system, and I ask you to deliver my reproach."

"All right," Tom mumbled. "But you should really talk to—" Tom stopped as Gruber approached them. "Oh, Inspector, this is Dr. Banazech, Mark's father."

Gruber stepped up to Dr. Banazech and shook his hand. "Tim Gruber. I spoke with you on the phone, Doctor."

"Yes, I'm pleased to meet you," Dr. Banazech said.

"And, ah...is Mrs. Banazech..." Gruber glanced to either side.

"No, my wife is in New York this week. I've notified her, however."

"All right. Well, I'm sure you have more questions."

"Actually, no," Dr. Banazech said. "I just came tonight to find out what you expect of me."

"Expect..." Gruber paused and narrowed his eyes.

"I mean, I believe you're aware that Mark is eighteen."

"I called you as a courtesy," Gruber said. "I thought you'd want to speak with your son."

"So I don't need to sign anything, or..."

"No."

"I see." Dr. Banazech's eyes darted swiftly from Gruber to Tom and then back again. "Well, I think I'll just be going, then."

"He's right back there." Gruber pointed toward the other

end of the emergency room. "I can take you back."

"No, Inspector," Banazech said with a tone of finality. "Mark is accountable."

"I see." Gruber scowled. "Well, you can come to the station tomorrow, if you wish. I'll be there in the afternoon."

"I'm flying to Europe tomorrow to participate in a seminar with my son," Banazech interrupted. "I believe my wife said she would be arriving here tomorrow. She may want to talk with you."

"Whatever."

Dr. Banazech glanced at his watch. "I'll be going now." He turned and walked abruptly out of the emergency room.

Gruber placed his hands on his hips and shook his head as he watched Dr. Banazech leave. "He isn't exactly the wailing, overprotective parent, is he?"

"He's written Mark off," Tom mumbled.

"I understand that," Gruber said. "And Mark is definitely a criminal. But still..."

Clair stepped forward and spoke softly. "Inspector, what's going to happen to Mark now?"

"I'll be taking him to the station shortly," Gruber answered. "I'll book him on one count of murder, two counts of attempted murder, and kidnapping."

"And then he'll be placed in jail?"

"Until his trial, you mean?"

"Yes."

"I understand your concern, Mrs. Kerzig. And the prosecutor may recommend that bail not be allowed. But with his age, and the fact that, I believe, he doesn't have any previous record...well, that's not likely."

"I see." Clair sighed and stepped back.

The curtain to the treatment area at the other end of the

emergency room slid aside, and the two officers emerged, one on either side of Mark. Part of a bandage was visible at the back of Mark's head, and his hands were secured behind his back.

"Well, there he is." Gruber patted Tom on the arm. "You two should probably stop in tomorrow afternoon and make sure your statements are complete."

Gruber motioned to the officers and started toward the entrance. They followed him, urging Mark forward. As they passed Tom and Clair, Mark turned his head in their direction and stared at them with the frown-smile on his face.

"He frightens me, Tom," Clair whispered as they passed.

"He should. He's an evil person."

"How...how does something like that happen?"

Tom couldn't answer her. He shook his head as he watched Gruber and the officers leave with Mark. Then he turned toward Clair who was still staring intently after them. He placed his hand on her arm. "It'll be all right. Jennifer's okay. That's the main thing."

"How does something like that happen?" she asked again as she turned toward Tom. Her eyes were filled with a mixture of fear and sadness. "Something...something he said..."

"Who?"

"Dr. Banazech. Remember? He said Mark was *accountable*. Didn't that sound vaguely familiar to you?"

"Clair..."

"That's what I told Misty Grainger. You know, that frail little fifteen-year-old girl with the short, stringy hair, and the freckles on her forehead."

"That's different," Tom said.

Clair still looked at him, but her gaze was directed vaguely past him. "What are we doing to our children?"

"We're doing what we were taught to do," Tom said

slowly. "But that...that doesn't make it right. And what does it mean to be *accountable*, anyway?"

Clair glanced toward the ceiling and sighed. "Roland used to tell us that our claim to humanity was directly proportional to the degree to which we recognized and responded to the responsibility to freely exercise and express our own wills."

"So, responsible to *whom*?" Tom repeated.

"To ourselves."

"Yes."

"And what about you, Tom?" she asked softly. "Who have you been accountable to?"

He placed his arms around her and pulled her body close to his. For a moment she stood pliably, responding silently to his strength. But then her hands were on his chest, and she pushed herself away, and it was there again...that rigid, unnatural barrier. It was like the impenetrable one-way glass at the new court.

"No, Tom! If you don't recognize this now, you never will! It's the same thing that happened five years ago."

"Clair..."

She raised her hand to silence him and shook her head. "I was searching. I loved you and respected you because you were good and strong, but I couldn't be—I never knew the source. But after I spoke with Pastor Bentley..."

"Bentley?"

"I realize now that we can't be responsible to ourselves, Tom," she continued fervently. "We have to be responsible to God!"

"God. Well, yes, of course."

"No, not *of course!* Not *parenthetically.* But *totally* and not relying on responsibility to ourselves."

Tom wanted to respond, but he didn't know how. Wasn't

that what he had said? They should start back to church again as a family. But there was so much more to what she was saying, and he knew it. He had known it five years ago, too. He realized that now. He just couldn't internalize it. But it was so hard. He could never place it in perspective until his experience with the LENA program. Self-righteousness could take on many forms, for the self could be so enticing.

Tom smiled finally and muttered softly, "Yes."

Clair's eyes glazed over with tears, and she raised her arm as though in acceptance of his acknowledgment. She turned the palm of her hand toward him and placed it on his chest. Then she laughed lightly and brushed a tear from her eye. "I just remembered... Dinner!" she said softly.

"Yeah." He smiled in recollection of the intimate setting they had rushed from earlier.

"Jennifer could join us now," she said tentatively.

"Unless it's too late to..."

"I thought..." Clair's fingers slid under his lapel. "I thought maybe...you could stay."

"Yes!" Tom's heart pounded. But all the words he wanted to say were locked inside. He merely grasped her hand and repeated, "Yes!"

33

The district board room held 250 spectators, and it was over half full the night of the board meeting. Walt and the teachers sat in the front two rows on the right, and Pastor Bentley, the Irvings, and about twenty people who had attended the gathering at the church sat in the front two rows on the left. The center aisle appeared to form a sort of imaginary battle line, Tom mused as he entered. He waved at Pastor Bentley and then sat in an aisle seat, next to Stu, and directly behind Walt. Marilyn Peters and Marla were in the row beside Walt. As he sat down, he heard a roll of raucous laughter, and he realized that Brenda Calloway was here also. She was sitting in the front row with Nita. The other project teachers were in the same row as he and Stu.

"How are the ribs?" Stu asked Tom.

"You've heard the joke, 'It only hurts when I laugh'?"

Stu chuckled. "Any word on Mark's status?"

"His mother posted bail Friday."

Tom felt a hand squeezing his shoulder, and he winced slightly as a feeling of discomfort transferred to his chest. He looked up to see Pastor Bentley standing above him, smiling.

"Hi, Tommy. I'm glad you came tonight."

"Hello, Pastor. I see you brought a few people."

"Well, not as many as I'd hoped. When push comes to shove, people become suddenly complacent, you know."

"Yeah. Oh, I don't think you've met Stu Welbourne, our

social science chair. Stu, this is Pastor Bentley. You and Stu have something in common. You're both avid Tocqueville fans."

"Really?" Stu seemed surprised. "Theology and history?"

"It's a long story. Let's meet sometime and talk about it." He turned to Tom. "I have to go talk to Lloyd and Sally. I'll see you later." He patted Tom on the shoulder and left.

"I forgot to tell him that you're also the chairman of the LENA project," Tom said.

"Former."

"What?"

Stu nodded and smiled. "Walt told me today. He's replacing me with Marilyn. He thanked me for all my organizational skills and commitment, et cetera, et cetera. But he thought Marilyn was better suited to lead the team into the expansion."

"Because of what happened at the last project team meeting?"

"Well, that, and I never have been *gung-ho* enough to suit Walt."

Tom looked up as the board members and district staff appeared in the front of the room.

"All right, people." Walt turned around, his eyes darting quickly back and forth over his half-glasses, and spoke to the teachers in a harsh whisper. "I've turned in cards for all of you who are speaking, so be ready."

"They're late getting started," Stu said.

"They've been in closed session." Walt leaned closer to Stu and cupped his hand over his mouth. "Dr. McCray told me they'd be discussing what to do about Bonnie." He turned back and sat erect in his seat.

"Are you going to speak?" Stu asked Tom.

"Walt didn't turn in a card for me."

"I know. But that wasn't my question. Are you going to speak to the board?"

"I thought about it," Tom said. "I naturally have some strong feelings. But I've never seen myself in the role of a political voice. I've always tried to keep myself in the position of supporting whatever decision the public makes."

"But you're part of the public, too. And you're a parent."

"I know." It was easier for Tom before Jennifer entered school. Since that time, his periodic concerns over school programs made everything more difficult. But he still had the feeling that the will and needs of the public would inevitably move the board toward making wise decisions.

Tom heard the loud rap of a gavel, and he looked up to see that Barbara Shannon had called the meeting to order. Dr. McCray and his secretary sat on the raised rostrum with the five board members. Victor Hernandez and other district staff were stationed below.

"The meeting is now in session," Barbara said in a crisp, authoritative voice. "Let me take a moment to discuss procedure. We have a single-item agenda tonight—the decision whether to extend the LENA program for another three years and expand it beyond the current pilot to include all students in the district. Since the formal recommendation has already been presented by staff at a previous meeting, we will begin this meeting with public testimony."

"Excuse me, Barbara." Roland Lessa was speaking. He sat directly to the right of Barbara. "It's been over a month since the meeting at which this was presented. Perhaps I could first give just a capsule summary of the advantages of the program expansion."

John Horning, who sat beside Lessa, leaned forward suddenly with a scowl on his face. "You can't give a capsule summary of anything, Roland! I have a feeling this thing's going to run all night as it is!"

"Well, Mr. Horning..." Barbara glanced at Dr. McCray's secretary. "We do have a substantial stack of cards from people who wish to speak. I believe we shall remain with our intended procedure." She turned toward the people and banged the gavel again. "Public testimony will now commence."

The procedure moved smoothly and efficiently. Dr. McCray's secretary called from the cards the name of each person wishing to speak, and also the name of the person to follow, to avoid any delays. Walt had purposely interspersed the project teachers' cards with the others so that a strong supportive argument could be heard throughout the evening. That was not necessary, however. The overwhelming tenor of the testimonies was positive. People spoke glowingly of how their children had received a tremendous sense of self-confidence, and had given them such wonderful reports of the exciting things they were doing in school. Only seven or eight people from Pastor Bentley's group spoke in opposition to the program's expansion, and their remarks were met by derisive comments from others in the audience.

Tom was shocked. He thought that surely a greater number of people would share some of the same concerns. If they were aware of the kinds of activities their children were involved in, how could they *not?* But then he remembered that whenever he asked parents to come to school so that he could describe what he was doing in the classroom, the vast majority of parents never showed up. And those who did made only a cursory review of the materials he'd prepared. He recalled the typical comment: "We trust you, Tom. The kids really like you!" That comment always made him feel good. But the parents trusted Bonnie, too; and the students really liked her.

Pastor Bentley's name was called during the course of the testimonies, but he asked to be allowed to speak last, and Barbara honored his request. And now, nearly two hours since testimony had begun, Dr. McCray's secretary wearily held up the last card and asked Pastor Bentley to step to the podium. He had been waiting in the aisle while the previous person spoke, and now he stepped forward and addressed the board.

"Dr. McCray, members of the board, I'm Pastor William Bentley. As I'm sure you're aware, I'm here tonight to speak in opposition to the proposed expansion of the program. It's clear to me, as I'm sure it is to you, that our opinion is in the minority. But the concerns that were expressed are real, and, I believe, very significant. You've heard about the values clarification exercise called the secret circle, where children are asked to divulge personal thoughts, feelings, and beliefs. And you were told about children being forced into moral dilemmas involving the rightness or wrongness of stealing. You were told about some activities involving exploration into psychic experiences such as extrasensory perception, psychokinesis, and astro-projection. You learned of a student who was required to stand in front of the class and tell how he dealt with his feelings after the death of his father.

"I'm sure you realize by now that many of our parents don't like the idea of their children being instructed how to explore *out-of-body* experiences. And, of course, we are concerned about writing assignments that encourage casual attitudes about sexual experience. You were told about the activity called transactional analysis for tots, in which children were told that parents are responsible for bad feelings they have about themselves, and then about an obscene rap selection being used as the background for a modern dance session." Pastor Bentley paused momentarily and glanced back toward the audience. His voice was filled with frustration. "I guess I'm hard pressed to understand why so many of you are supportive of such a program."

A loud round of boos and jeers rose from the audience. Barbara rapped the gavel sharply three times, and the noise slowly subsided.

Pastor Bentley looked at the audience with a somber expression on his face. Then he turned back to the podium and spoke directly to Daniel Worley. "When I first spoke with Mrs. Shannon, she told me I should feel somewhat reassured because one of the board members was a minister. So, Danny, I'm making a personal plea to you."

Pastor Worley sat up abruptly, glanced at the other board members, and shifted in his chair.

"My concerns have to do, naturally, with moral issues," Pastor Bentley continued. "I know our doctrines are miles apart, but I also know you must have concerns about some of these activities. I realize you don't refer to it much in your church services, but I know you've *read* the Bible, Danny. Some of that has to have sunk in, and I'd just like you to think about—"

Pastor Bentley's final words were drowned in a chorus of boos, and Barbara brought the audience back to order. Pastor Worley merely slouched back in his chair and clutched at his chin.

Pastor Bentley turned his attention to Barbara. "I've made my plea. I respectfully request that you give serious consideration to the concerns that were expressed here tonight and deny the expansion of the program." He slowly returned to his seat.

"Thank you, Pastor Bentley," Barbara said. "Are there more cards?" she asked Dr. McCray's secretary.

Dr. McCray's secretary smiled and shook her head.

Barbara looked out over the audience and slowly let her eyes pass from one side to the other. Tom felt a surge of nausea rising from the pit of his stomach. He had a bizarre vision of being a single unwilling rider on a roller coaster headed down a track leading to an unknown destination. The others on the ride were laughing, because they trusted that the operator surely knew what he was doing. And besides, they were having so much fun. Tom looked around at all the smiling faces in the board room, and his faith in the public will suddenly crumbled.

Barbara raised the gavel and was about to conclude the period of public testimony.

"Wait!" Tom stood and walked toward the podium. "I'd like to say something."

"I object," John cried. "It's too late. He didn't fill out a card."

"Just a moment, John," Barbara said.

"I apologize," Tom said. "I hadn't originally intended to speak."

"I'll allow it," Barbara said.

John sat back in disgust. Dr. McCray sat back with a thin smile, slowly tapping his fingertips together.

"I appreciate that," Tom began. "My name is Tom Kerzig. I'm a teacher and a parent." He glanced to the right and saw Walt scowling at him over his half-glasses. "I have been teaching one class in the LENA program for a little over a month now. I must say that everyone who's involved with the program is extremely committed and highly motivated. I've never seen such enthusiasm, such excitement. And yet there are some segments of the program that I object to—both as a teacher and as a parent.

"From an educational viewpoint, I'm concerned that the self-awareness aspects of the program are catered to overwhelmingly, to the exclusion of standards. And I believe that the test results over the last few years will bear that out. I also share many of Pastor Bentley's concerns. My daughter is being directed purposely into controversial decision-making in areas in which there should be no controversy. And she has been involved in situational ethics activities which have left her with the impression that *good* and *bad* are meaningless, relative terms. But my major concerns have to do with items which are much more subtle. It's the feeling, the direction. The overall tone of the program is...it's almost one of *mysticism*."

Laughter and jeers rose from the audience, and Barbara was required to resort to the gavel again.

"Could you be more specific, Mr. Kerzig?" Barbara asked.

"I wish I could," Tom said. "I've been involved with the program for just a short time. But, perhaps that's why I've noticed it. I haven't become immune. It seems there's an overpowering milieu, even a jargon, which ties these people together in some mystical bond. It's almost as though some power is driving them, forcing them to follow aimlessly."

More hisses and jeers rose from the audience, and Roland Lessa sat forward abruptly with a scornful look on his face.

"Are you trying to tell us there's some sort of conspiracy involved here, Mr. Kerzig?" Lessa asked.

"Conspiracy?" Tom turned slowly and looked at the project teachers. Stu was smiling, but the rest wore bewildered or angry expressions. *Conspiracy*...how could he say that? These people were all so individualistic, so driven to find and share their own creative expressions. And yet their very expressions of individualism seemed so much a part of some massive, involuntary wave. He struggled to conceptualize it, but the image kept slipping away.

"Mr. Kerzig," Barbara prodded him. "Mr. Lessa asked if you are suggesting the presence of some sort of conspiracy."

"I know." Tom looked at Stu, who sat smiling, his head moving almost indescribably in a shallow nod. And he remembered their discussion about the predictions of Tocqueville regarding the implications of unbridled freedom... People will not exist without direction. And where none is provided overtly they will fall unwittingly into the patterns of those about them...and the human mind will become fettered to the general will of the greatest number."

"Mr. Kerzig?" Barbara prompted.

"*Yes*, there *is* a conspiracy."

"What?" exclaimed Lessa.

"But it's a conspiracy without a leader," Tom said. "That's the only way I can explain it. A conspiracy which gets its leadership from the mindless merging of people's motives as they move toward some goal that they don't even understand."

Laughter rose from the crowd, and Barbara half-heartedly rapped the gavel.

"I know it sounds crazy," Tom continued. "But I want you to consider it. Because a conspiracy like this can be more threatening than one with a leader. Because it moves unnoticed, but relentlessly ahead, like a juggernaut. And the threats come from everywhere and yet nowhere. And you find yourselves frantically pushing corks under water, only to find them bobbing to the surface again, replenished."

The audience burst into laughter again, and this time Barbara did not bring the gavel down. Tom merely waited for it to subside.

"Have you concluded, Mr. Kerzig?" Barbara asked.

"Just proceed cautiously," Tom pleaded. "It's a massive leap from a small pilot to the entire student body. I guess I'd recommend, at least, that you postpone the expansion. Wait for a year. Become involved during that time. Visit the classes, and see what's going on." He turned to the audience and spoke passionately. "All of you... Your children's lives are at stake! Become involved with your school. Visit the programs. Find out what they're doing!" He turned back slowly and addressed the board. "Thank you for allowing me to speak." As he sat, Stu grasped his arm and squeezed it gently.

"Dr. McCray, perhaps you'd like to comment," Barbara said.

Dr. McCray still sat silently, his fingertips touching. But now he placed his hands down and sat forward. "Yes, Mrs. Shannon, I certainly would. Thank you. Let me just say, Mr. Kerzig is an outstanding teacher. His willingness to further extend himself during the last month and take the additional assignment of this LENA class is greatly appreciated. But I fear that he is reacting to a distorted view of the program. As you know, just last week he and his daughter were involved in a horrifying experience with one of our students. And the unfortunate matter we just dealt with in closed session earlier this evening involved a teacher whose ideas...well...influenced Mr. Kerzig toward what I believe is an unwarranted general view."

"And his concern about this...*leaderless conspiracy?*" asked Barbara.

Dr. McCray chuckled. "Well, I'm afraid I don't understand what he means by that. But I will say that I have absolutely no reservations about the goals and activities of the program. I think the obvious vocal majority tonight supports my trust."

"May I speak now, Barbara?" Lessa asked, somewhat sarcastically.

"Of course, Dr. Lessa."

"Dr. McCray is unequivocally correct," Lessa began. "The program is beyond reproach. I can't imagine anyone attacking it on the basis of some mumbo-jumbo about mysticism and conspiracies. As you know, I've been a strong advocate of this program from the beginning, because I've used the same techniques in my university classes with great success. We are moving into a new era of human existence. And it's critical that people learn how to tap the divine power within themselves to create a better world. I've seen it happen with my students over the years. They fall into it so willingly. Why, they're almost unaware of it, it's so natural, so right. The majority of our constituents agree with us. They have made that clear tonight. And our mandate as a board is to adequately represent the will of the majority!"

The audience applauded loudly. Barbara cast a puzzled look toward Lessa as she rapped the gavel and silenced the crowd.

Marion Coleman tentatively raised her hand.

"Yes, Mrs. Coleman."

"I just think we should thank all of the people for coming tonight and expressing their opinions. It's really helped me to know the public will."

John sat forward and slapped his arm down loudly. "I call for the question!"

"Second!" Lessa exclaimed.

"Very well," Barbara said. "Due to the controversial nature of this issue, however, I'm going to ask for a roll-call vote."

Lessa shook his head and sat back.

"Mr. Horning," Barbara said.

"Aye!"

"Dr. Lessa."

"Aye!"

"Mrs. Coleman."

"Oh, yes, I think... Aye."

"Mr. Worley."

Pastor Worley was still clutching at his chin, and didn't respond to Barbara's call.

"Mr. Worley," Barbara repeated.

"I believe I'll abstain."

"Oh, for..." John sat back in disgust and turned his back to Pastor Worley.

"Mr. Worley, abstentions are generally reserved for instances in which there is a conflict of interest," Barbara said. "You don't have any conflict of interest here, do you?"

"Ah, no. It's just that..."

"Then I believe you owe it to the other members of the board, and to the public to express your vote, either in favor of, or in opposition to the proposal."

"Yes, I suppose." Pastor Worley sat forward slightly and glanced quickly toward Pastor Bentley. Then he turned toward Barbara and spoke hesitantly. "Very well..."

"Very well *what*, Mr. Worley?"

"Nay," Pastor Worley said softly.

Barbara sighed and paused for a moment. Then she looked toward the audience and spoke firmly. "The chair also votes *Nay*. The measure passes by a vote of three to two." She banged the gavel decisively and the audience cheered.

John turned back and glared at Pastor Worley. "I move for adjournment!"

"Second!" Pastor Worley said quickly.

"All in favor?"

All five members quickly assented, and Barbara rapped the gavel to adjourn the meeting.

The people in the board room stood and moved noisily toward the exit. John stood and darted quickly out the side entrance. The other members talked quietly while they gathered their materials. Tom thought Dr. McCray was motioning to him, but he realized he was mistaken when he saw Walt rise and approach the superintendent. The other project teachers cast quick disparaging looks in his direction as they stood and gathered in the front of the room. Stu stayed beside him, though. He chuckled softly, removed his pipe from his coat pocket, and rested the stem on his lip.

"You've learned a great deal about the making of public policy tonight, my friend," Stu said to Tom.

"Was I too far out, Stu?"

"Not at all. But that doesn't mean your views are appreciated."

Tom stood up and placed his hand on Stu's shoulder. "Thanks, Stu."

Stu smiled. "My pleasure."

Tom turned and walked across the aisle to where Pastor Bentley stood. "I'm glad you came tonight, Pastor."

Pastor Bentley shook his hand firmly. "Well, I don't know if we made much headway. But you never know. We convinced Mrs. Shannon, anyway."

"And Worley," Tom reminded him.

Pastor Bentley chuckled. "I'm not so sure he was convinced of anything. I got the feeling his vote just tumbled out inadvertently."

"You may be right."

"You made some good points tonight," Pastor Bentley said.

"You think so?"

"Absolutely. There is one thing I disagree with, though. This conspiracy *does* have a leader. And don't you ever forget it. The dark master is in charge. And he'll do everything he can to keep those corks bobbing!" He smiled broadly, patted Tom on the arm, and turned to speak with the Irvings.

Tom felt a hand on his other arm, and he turned to see Walt beside him, his eyebrows raised high above his half-glasses.

"Tom, I wanted to catch you before you took off tonight. I just told Dr. McCray how much we appreciate your taking Bonnie's class. He's appreciative, too."

"Sure."

"We just decided...well, we're really asking too much of you. I mean, of you *and* the others who are giving up a free period. So I've made other arrangements."

"What arrangements?" Tom asked.

"I don't know why I didn't think of this before. She's a natural."

"Who?"

"Marla Vedder. I'll have her take Bonnie's entire assignment, and then I'll just get a substitute for Marla's ninth graders. That makes sense, doesn't it?"

Tom looked across the room at Marla. She was watching them, and as he looked at her, she smiled and tossed him a feeble wave. "Sure, Walt. That definitely makes sense. When do you want to make the switch?"

"No need to delay these things. Walt laughed nervously. "I thought we'd just go ahead and have her start tomorrow."

"Tomorrow?"

"You can meet with her before school, go over what you've done so far."

Tom looked up at Dr. McCray. The bald man smiled broadly and waved at him.

"Thanks again, Tom." And Walt walked back toward the rostrum.

Tom started to rejoin Pastor Bentley and the Irvings, but he stopped abruptly as he saw that Clair and Jennifer were walking down the aisle toward him. He stepped quickly up the aisle to meet them.

"Quite a meeting!" Clair said.

Tom nodded. Then he squatted down and gave Jennifer a hug. "Hi, honey!"

"Hi, Dad." But Jennifer seemed strangely silent—distant.

"Jennifer's awfully quiet," Tom said to Clair after he'd stood again. "She must be tired."

"I...I don't know."

Tom placed his arm around Clair's waist, and they walked to the front of the aisle, where Pastor Bentley was bidding farewell to a few remaining supporters. Pastor Bentley looked up and smiled as they approached.

"Clair...and Jennifer!" Pastor Bentley greeted them each with a pat on the arm. "It's nice that you could come and hear Tom's great speech!"

"We have something to tell you, Pastor," Tom said.

"Oh?"

"Yes. We're—"

"We're getting back together," Clair finished with assurance.

Pastor Bentley stepped forward and gave Clair a warm hug. "That's wonderful! That's the best news I've heard for...well, for a very long time."

"Pastor Bentley...Mr. Kerzig," Barbara Shannon called. "I want to thank you both for speaking. And Mr. Kerzig, I want to compliment you on your recognition of the leaderless conspiracy. I don't think anyone else understood what you were talking about. But I see it all the time in the courtroom—the mindless rush to judgment. That's the only good thing about the exceeding length of trials. It forces people to sit back and become detached from the conspiracy before making decisions."

"We appreciate your negative vote," Pastor Bentley said.

Barbara grimaced. "I think you were the one who changed Mr. Worley's mind, too. But he's so..." She held her hand up and paddled it. Then she stepped closer to Tom and spoke intensely. "You're in the school system, Mr. Kerzig. What can we do to make them realize the dangers? How can we get them to listen?"

Tom looked at her without speaking for a moment. Then he smiled and spoke deliberately. "One person at a time, Mrs. Shannon." He put his arm around Clair and drew her close. "One person at a time."

Barbara smiled, nodded, and returned to the rostrum.

Tom, Clair, and Pastor Bentley walked back up the aisle behind Jennifer. The last stragglers were heading toward the exit. Jennifer skipped lightly ahead, and then she turned and skipped back to them. A long chain around her neck bobbed from side to side as she moved.

"What's that, Jennifer?" Clair asked.

"What?"

"That necklace. Where did you get it?"

"Oh, I forgot to tell you." Jennifer grasped the fine chain toward the bottom and held it up for them to see. It was a large blue crystal, secured to the chain with a gold five-pointed star. "It was sent to school for me today. It's from Mark."

Tom's hand clamped suddenly on Clair's shoulder, and a feeling of nausea swept over him. She turned to him, her eyes filled with fear.

"How...how do you know it's from him?" Tom asked.

"There was a note with it," Jennifer said calmly. "He said he couldn't see me for a while, but that I can use our crystal, like he taught me. When I meditate, I just look in the crystal really hard. And then I can see his face. And he'll be my helper."

"No..." Tom reached out instinctively and grasped her hand. He realized Clair had taken the other.

Pastor Bentley shook his head and frowned.

"We'd better get a restraining order," Tom said softly.

"I'm afraid Mark's influence may not require his physical presence," Pastor Bentley said.

"Then..."

"Oh, you absolutely should get one," Pastor Bentley assured him. "But beyond *restraining*, there needs to be some re-*training!*"

Clair looked up fearfully. "Can we do it?"

Pastor Bentley smiled and placed his hands on their shoulders. "Together and with God's help."

"Yes," Tom said confidently.

Tom looked toward the exit where a small group of people huddled to protect themselves from the cold shaft of air. There was no moon tonight, and the light over the entrance was broken, so someone pulled out a match and struck it, and a tiny glow issued forth. The group followed the dimly effulgent leader into the darkness, toward the vaguely visible shadow of a huge, gnarled tree. And somewhere in the distance, the tiny light from the match reflected itself against a glistening smile, and a slight breeze whistled through the leafless branches, and seemed to murmur, *"Let the children come... Let the children come... Let the children come."*

But Tom smiled as he recalled the concluding words of Joni's paper. Yes, Jennifer would learn. There is a greater light! And even there, above the folds of overpowering darkness, its brilliance gleams undiminished.